D1582561

Brian Boydell composing, c. 1947.
PHOTO: D.O. MICHELSON. COURTESY OF THE BOARD OF TRINITY COLLEGE DUBLIN

LEABHARLANN
CO. CHILL DARA

REBELLIOUS FERMENT

FERMENT

A Dublin Musical Memoir and Diary

BRIAN BOYDELL

Edited by Barra Boydell

ATRIUM

First published in 2018 by Atrium
Atrium is an imprint of Cork University Press
Youngline Industrial Estate
Pouladuff Road, Togher
Cork T12 HT6V, Ireland

© Barra Boydell 2018

All rights reserved. No part of this book may be reprinted
or reproduced or utilised in any electronic, mechanical or other
means, now known or hereafter invented, including photocopying
and recording or otherwise, without either the prior written
permission of the publisher or a licence permitting restricted copying
in Ireland issued by the Irish Copyright Licensing Agency Ltd,
25 Denzille Lane, Dublin 2.

The right of the author to be identified as originator of this work
has been asserted by him in accordance with Copyright and
Related Rights Acts 2000 to 2007.

British Library Cataloguing in Publication Data
A CIP catalogue record for this book is available from the British Library.

ISBN-978-1-78205-286-9

Typeset by Studio 10 Design

Printed by Hussar Books in Poland

CONTENTS

EDITOR'S NOTE

B RIAN BOYDELL, who was born in Dublin on St Patrick's Day 1917 and died in November 2000, was a central figure in twentieth-century Irish musical life. As one of the leading Irish composers and as a performer, in particular as conductor of the Dublin Orchestral Players (DOP) from 1942 to 1967 and of the Dowland Consort from 1958 to 1969, he played a central role in musical composition and practice. As a broadcaster on national radio and television and as a public lecturer, an adjudicator at music festivals, a founding member of the Music Association of Ireland (MAI) and for many years a member of the Arts Council of Ireland, and as Professor of Music at Trinity College Dublin (TCD) from 1962 to 1982, he had a profound influence on the development of music and music education in Ireland. As a musicologist, his contribution was also highly significant: his pioneering and wide-ranging research into music in eighteenth-century Dublin resulted in publications, including his seminal book *A Dublin Musical Calendar, 1700–1760* (1988). But he was also a man of wider interests and accomplishments: most notably, before making the decision in the mid-1940s to devote himself wholly to music, he was already establishing a reputation as an artist.

Following the publication in 1992 of *Rotunda Music in Eighteenth-Century Dublin*, Brian Boydell turned his attention to the writing of his memoir. His particular focus was on the period in the 1940s when, returning to his native Dublin following his education and travels in Britain and continental Europe, he was closely involved in what he describes in his preface as 'that remarkable period in the history of artistic development in Ireland during the Second World War and shortly afterwards'. *Rebellious Ferment*, the title for this edition of his memoir and his diary of 1950, adopts a phrase used by Brian in his Preface (below) to describe the artistic environment of 'that remarkable period' in 1940s' Dublin in which he played such an active part; it also reflects the fact that his life and musical career were characterised throughout by a rebellious spirit. (His original title for this memoir, 'The Roaring Forties', alluded both to the decade it particularly documents, and to the strong winds of change that were occurring in Irish cultural life at the time. He later expanded this title in his typescript to the somewhat ungainly 'The Roaring Forties and Thereabouts' to take account of its also including events both from before the 1940s and up to the early 1970s.)

During the early 1940s a number of artists and intellectuals from overseas came to Ireland to escape the war, stimulating and invigorating artistic life in a country that was then narrowly conservative and inward-looking. In his later years Brian became keenly aware of the particular perspective which he, as an active participant, could cast on this period of 'rebellious ferment' in Irish cultural life. This was due in large part to his being considered by many of his Irish contemporaries as something of an outsider in his own country: having been educated in England – including graduating with a first-class degree in natural sciences from Cambridge and spending a year at the Royal College of Music (RCM) in London – and exposed to international musical and artistic standards in London and pre-war Germany, he returned home with a broader and richer experience than that of many of his Irish contemporaries; furthermore, coming as he did from a well-to-do, urban Protestant background, he belonged to a social class regarded by many as outsiders within an overwhelmingly Catholic Ireland which was barely two decades old as an independent state. His perspective thus enabled him to observe and contribute both as an Irishman increasingly committed to invigorating and developing Irish artistic and musical life, and as someone who could bring to that contribution the wider experiences and sometimes the more objective perspective of an outsider.

A more extended autobiography also covering his later and central involvement in Irish musical life – including his work as one of Ireland's foremost composers, his years as Professor of Music at TCD, his membership of the Arts Council, his musicological research and the recognition he received from various bodies for his contributions to Irish cultural life – would have constituted an absorbing volume and provided further insights into the workings and politics of Irish music and the arts in the later twentieth century. But notwithstanding the sometimes outspoken nature of his life and work, and the public recognition he enjoyed in his later years as one of Ireland's foremost composers and musicians, he inherited his father's belief that the writing of a more extended autobiography would constitute an inappropriate display of self-importance. Indeed, he describes the first chapter of this memoir as a 'reluctant slice of autobiography'. However, in the company of family and friends – and in later life also in broadcasts and other more public contexts – he was an enthusiastic raconteur of anecdotes and stories, especially from his earlier life.[1] It was the often well-practised retelling of such anecdotes (as he himself refers to them in his

---

1. He participated, for example, with particular relish in the making of a biographical documentary entitled *All My Enthusiasms* by Anne Makower (who had been a former singing pupil of his) for RTÉ television in 1997.

Preface) that lies at the heart of this memoir: indeed, he refers here to his 'role of raconteur'. He set to the writing of this memoir with the same wholehearted commitment that marked all his undertakings, and with the intention of publication. For one reason or another this did not come about during his lifetime, but the typescript in its draft form circulated privately and was made available to scholars.[2] The recent occasion of the centenary of Brian Boydell's birth has provided the ideal context for this memoir to be brought to a wider public, not just for its autobiographical interest and belatedly to fulfil its author's intentions, but above all for its value both as a first-hand account of a fascinating period in Irish cultural history, and for the particular perspective it casts on Irish cultural life and society during the war years and the decades of growth and development that followed.

The international renown of W.B. Yeats, James Joyce and Samuel Beckett has ensured that Irish Modernism is well established as a field of literary study. However, the period of artistic development in Ireland during the 1940s, and in particular the introduction of Modernism into the visual arts and music which this memoir highlights, have received less attention. Brian Kennedy's *Irish Art and Modernism* (which Brian Boydell cites in this memoir) and Bruce Arnold's *Mainie Jellett and the Modern Movement in Ireland* (both published in 1991) were the first major studies to begin to look at this period in the visual arts. In 2005 these two art historians co-curated an exhibition of paintings by members of the White Stag Group at the Irish Museum of Modern Art, an exhibition that included paintings by Brian Boydell. A concert featuring some of his music from the 1940s was organised by the Contemporary Music Centre (CMC) in association with the exhibition.[3] From October 2015 to February 2016 the Crawford Gallery in Cork mounted an exhibition, 'The Language of Dreams', which prominently featured paintings from the 1940s by Brian Boydell, Thurloe Conolly and others mentioned in this memoir.[4] But Irish musical Modernism in the mid-twentieth century remains a relatively unfamiliar chapter within the wider

---

2. See, in particular, Axel Klein, 'Brian Boydell: of man and music', in Gareth Cox, Axel Klein and Michael Taylor (eds), *The Life and Music of Brian Boydell* (Dublin: Irish Academic Press, 2004), pp. 1–23.
3. A CD of the chamber works by Brian Boydell performed at this concert (Oboe Quintet, op. 11 (1940); *The Feather of Death*, op. 22 (1943) and String Quartet no. 1, op. 31 (1949)) was included as an insert with the exhibition catalogue: S.B. Kennedy, *The White Stag Group* (Dublin: Irish Museum of Modern Art, 2005).
4. See catalogue of exhibition (2 October 2015–6 February 2016) by Peter Murray, *The Language of Dreams: dreams and the unconscious in 20th century Irish art* (Cork: Crawford Art Gallery, 2015).

context of Irish cultural history.[5] Drawing on the contemporary European musical avant-garde, Brian Boydell rejected the use of traditional melodies that had largely defined the language of Irish musical composition. As he notes in his Preface with reference to the cultural climate of the time, 'there was a feeling that Irish creative artists should barricade themselves against foreign influence and proudly celebrate the long-suppressed achievements of a past Golden Age.' Utterly rejecting this narrower, nationally introspective approach, Brian Boydell established himself in the 1940s at the forefront of the introduction of Modernism into Irish music. His close association with those writers and artists who generated the 'rebellious ferment' of the time and who contributed to the White Stag Group's interest in surrealism and other contemporary European artistic theories fed directly into his development as a composer. In this context, the publication of this memoir, together with extracts from Brian Boydell's diary for 1950, should prove to be of much wider than purely musical interest as a primary source for this intriguing period of Irish cultural history.

While focusing primarily on the 1940s and the early 1950s, the memoir also includes accounts of some later musical experiences extending to the early 1970s. As his narrative advanced in time, Brian Boydell was increasingly aware of the risks of treading on the possibly sensitive toes of others who might be mentioned and still be alive at the time of writing. But some episodes he felt were too important to ignore: the colourful but decisive tenure during the 1960s of Tibor Paul as conductor of the RÉSO (which became the RTÉSO during this period); his being commissioned to prepare a special arrangement of the national anthem for the launch of the Irish television service in 1961 (an arrangement that was broadcast each night at the close of transmission for some decades thereafter); the Dowland Consort, the widely acclaimed renaissance vocal ensemble which he founded and directed between 1958 and 1969, and which provided him with some of his most rewarding experiences as a performing musician; and the visit of the great Russian composer Dmitri Shostakovich to receive an honorary Doctorate of Music from TCD in July 1972. The memoir is, however, silent with regard to the latter part of his life and career when, for example as

---

5. Mark Fitzgerald's entry on 'Modernism' in *The Encyclopaedia of Music in Ireland*, ed. Harry White and Barra Boydell (Dublin: UCD Press, 2013; hereafter referred to as *EMIR*) provides a chronologically broader survey; other relevant essays include Philip Graydon, 'Modernism in Ireland and its cultural context in the music of Frederick May, Brian Boydell and Aloys Fleischmann', in G. Cox and A. Klein (eds), *Irish Music in the Twentieth Century*, IMS 7 (Dublin: Four Courts Press, 1996), pp. 56–79; and Mark Fitzgerald, 'Inventing Identities: the case of Frederick May', in M. Fitzgerald and J. O'Flynn (eds), *Music and Identity in Ireland and Beyond* (Farnham: Ashgate, 2014), pp. 83–102.

Professor of Music at TCD (except in relation to Shostakovich's visit) and long-serving member of the Arts Council, he wielded such influence as a prominent figure in Irish musical life.

Brian Boydell's memoir is complemented here by extracts from his diary for 1950. This private diary was written in a foolscap, page-per-day printed diary for 1950. He recorded details of his daily life and activities from the beginning of the year until early June, when the entries cease (except for brief, pencilled notes for some of the following days of that month). Thereafter the pages are blank. The fact that the first entry, for 1 January 1950, makes no particular reference to this being a new undertaking suggests that it could be the continuation of a similar diary kept for at least part of the previous year, but no such diary is known to have survived. The present diary came to light only when it was found in 2014, having fallen inside the back of the heavy wooden writing desk which Brian had used and which his family subsequently gave on extended loan to Fota House, Carrigtwohill, County Cork.

Each year Brian maintained a small, pocket engagement diary in which he briefly noted the dates and times of meetings and engagements. He conscientiously kept all these, and they are now held with his other papers and manuscript scores in the library of TCD.[6] These provide a substantially complete record of his appointments and scheduled activities over many decades, but without further detail or commentary. In contrast, the present diary for the first part of 1950 provides a revealing insight into his professional and private day-to-day activities at a time when, aged in his early thirties, he was beginning to establish himself as a composer, conductor and agitator for greater musical awareness and understanding. The diary reflects Brian Boydell's musical activities, interests and opinions, whether as a composer (including the first broadcast and public performances of his String Quartet no. 1, composed in the previous year, as well as the composition and first performances of the ballet suite *The Buried Moon*), as a singing teacher working both at the Royal Irish Academy of Music (RIAM) and privately, as an orchestral conductor, as a public lecturer, as a founding member of the MAI, and through the regular 'gramophone evenings' and other musical contexts in which he shared his passion for music with friends and acquaintances. At times the diary provides direct correspondences with events related in the memoir. Indeed, in some cases this allowed for editorial corrections to be made, for example where the diary provided the actual date for an event that might have been incorrectly remembered when he

---

6. TCD, MS 11128.

was writing the memoir some four decades later. The diary also reflects, often in considerable detail, his extra-musical interests, most notably fishing, gardening and his very active interest in cars and motoring. Selected passages relating to these have been included so as to provide a fuller picture of Brian Boydell the man, rather than just the musician. Private, purely family matters have for the most part been omitted.

This volume comprises much more than just a personal memoir and diary of the activities and artistic development of one of Ireland's leading twentieth-century composers and musicians. It offers a unique and individual view of Irish social and cultural life, especially during the 1940s, an insight into a very different Ireland that has since changed almost beyond recognition. The opening chapter of this memoir, in which Brian Boydell recounts his education in England and his travels and studies in Europe, likewise provides a window both into a pre-war world that was soon to change so fundamentally, and into an educational experience that included exposure, especially during his years at Cambridge, to some of the leading musicians, artists, emerging poets, thinkers and scientists of the day. But it was also an educational experience that was to shape his sense of being an outsider, first as an Irishman within the privileged world of the English educational establishment, and then when he returned to Ireland from London with the outbreak of the Second World War, as an English-educated Protestant living within a small circle of like-minded, independent thinkers who felt largely excluded from the mainstream of Catholic Ireland.

The Ireland of the 1940s and early 1950s to which he returned and in which so much of this memoir and diary are set was the Ireland of the 'Emergency' (the Second World War) and of its aftermath, a period initially of rationing and shortages, of slow economic activity, and defined politically by Éamon de Valera's inward-looking vision of Ireland as enshrined in the 1937 Constitution. Ireland was a neutral country during the war and, as Brian Boydell observes in his Preface, the authorities were 'nervously trying to steer a neutral country through the political minefield of wartime diplomacy'. His experiences as a member of the ferment of artists and intellectuals in Dublin provide a rare first-hand and often colourful narrative of this small but ultimately influential circle of artists who laid down the foundations for the later flowering of music and the arts in Ireland. Some, like Brian, would go on to become central figures in their own spheres. At the same time, he was coming into contact with representatives of the wider circle of Irish cultural life: Micheál Mac Liammóir, Hilton Edwards, Patrick

Kavanagh and Denis Donoghue, to name a few, are among those outside the more immediate musical circles whom he would come to know.

Brian's passionate interest in motoring both reflects his multi-faceted personality and provides a particular perspective on the Ireland of the 1940s. The unreliability of the first car he bought after he returned to Ireland in 1939, a much-abused 1929 Bugatti which would nevertheless ignite his lifelong interest in motoring, resulted in his often being stranded in the depths of the country where, to quote from this memoir, 'one just had to repair the fault or walk many miles home, for there were very few cars on the country roads in those days'. When petrol became unavailable during the war years, his scientific training enabled him to develop a producer gas plant which meant that he was never off the road, a rare situation for anyone other than those providing essential services such as doctors. His description of running cars on producer gas, in particular the extracts he reproduces from a logbook of journeys between Dublin and Achill between 1942 and 1943, must surely constitute a classic episode in Irish motoring history. Even by 1950, a mention in his diary (23 May) of the necessity to obtain a 'triptyque' or customs permit simply to drive across the border into Northern Ireland is a reminder of a very different time.

Today we take for granted the ready availability, through high-quality recordings and broadcasts, of an almost infinite range of music, whether through CDs, online or on radio or television. This memoir and diary underlines how different the position was in the 1940s and early 1950s, especially for an active musician and composer like Brian trying to access as much music as possible, both by contemporary composers and from the classical repertoire. He notes his excitement when the first recording appeared of a work such as Handel's *Concerti Grossi* (in Chapter 3), multiple different recordings of which are today available at the click of a mouse. In the 1950 diary he notes his attempts to make recordings for further listening of less familiar music by using his new (and, at the time, rare but unreliable) tape machine to record broadcasts on the BBC Third Programme directly from the radio (e.g. 17 March 1950).

Brian's descriptions (Chapter 3 and Diary) of some of what would eventually amount to over one thousand radio (and later television) broadcasts with RÉ/RTÉ likewise underline how different the situation was when all radio broadcasts went out live: improvising on the spot when unforeseen problems arose, commenting on the music while simultaneously having to select and turn over 78rpm records without any additional studio staff to assist (Diary, 24 May), and even having to leave in the middle of conducting an orchestral rehearsal in order to go to the RÉ studios to deliver a live broadcast, then returning to resume the rehearsal after the broadcast (Diary, 5 January).

The breadth of Brian Boydell's interests beyond music (he has more than once been characterised as having been a 'true renaissance man') and the enthusiasm not only with which he embraced all his activities, but also with which he recounts his experiences here, guarantees a wide social and historical appeal far beyond that of the purely musical with which he is most closely associated.

The chronological limits of the memoir and the individual focus of the diary for 1950 on part of one year relevant to the memoir have been commented on above. A wider perspective on Brian Boydell and his achievements is provided in particular by Gareth Cox, Axel Klein and Michael Taylor's book *The Life and Music of Brian Boydell* (2004) and by Gareth Cox's entry in *EMIR* (2013), both of which list his compositions and writings, as well as discographies. Other relevant essays, articles and published interviews are listed in the Bibliography at the end of this book, as are writings by Brian Boydell dating from the period covered by this memoir. A conference to mark his centenary was held at the RIAM and in TCD in June 2017, arising from which an edited collection of essays is in preparation.

Barra Boydell
Sydney, May 2018

EDITORIAL POLICY

T HROUGHOUT BOTH the memoir (Part I) and the diary (Part II), any obvious written and (the rare) spelling errors (including people's names) have been silently corrected, punctuation regularised, and the extensive use of initial capitalisation for nouns in the handwritten diary reduced. Minor editorial changes or insertions have been made to the texts of both memoir and diary for clarification or accuracy. All text in square brackets is editorial. Acronyms and abbreviations have been standardised (see list of 'Acronyms & Abbreviations' below) or inserted editorially where appropriate. Some few sections of the memoir have been shortened: for example, the final section of Chapter 4 originally included further examples of 'surrealoid' texts. The few original footnotes in the memoir (Part I) are marked with an asterisk and identified as 'Author's note'. All other footnotes are editorial.

All references in the memoir to the 'present' have been retained, even though these refer to the early 1990s when it was originally put to paper (and 'put to paper' it was: Brian never made the transition from typewriter to computer). Certain comments must be understood within this context. In the Preface, for example, he could still describe himself at the time as being 'one of the few survivors who shared in the excitement' of the intellectual ferment of the 1940s; or, when recounting his period as a student at the RCM in London before the war, he refers to his oboe teacher as being one of 'the rapidly dying species of orchestral player typical of the profession before the new breed of "educated" players replaced them', referencing a type of professional orchestral musician now surely consigned to history. Likewise, any views or opinions expressed in the main text are Brian Boydell's as he wrote them down at the time, however dated or anachronistic some may now appear.

In the diary (Part II), the use of an ellipsis (three points '…') indicates the editorial omission of text.

ACKNOWLEDGEMENTS

I N EDITING BRIAN BOYDELL'S MEMOIR AND DIARY I would like first and
foremost to thank my brother Cormac for his support, for reading the text
and making valuable suggestions as to the selection of extracts from the
diary, and for putting me in contact with Jonathan Williams, who agreed
to act as my literary agent. Jonathan introduced me to Cork University Press,
and his guidance smoothed the path to publication; his familiarity with so
many of the musicians, artists, writers and others mentioned in the memoir
and diary was a boon during the later editorial stages. I am particularly
indebted to Jonathan for drawing my attention to John Berryman's direct
reference to Brian in the poem 'Friendless'. Maria O'Donovan and Mike
Collins at Cork University Press have both been extremely helpful and
supportive throughout the process of bringing this book to publication, and
I also extend my thanks to their design team who responded so creatively to
my suggestions for the layout and cover of the book.

The texts of both the memoir (Part I) and the diary (Part II) remain
those of Brian Boydell's original (excepting editorial deletions and minor
corrections or changes, as noted above), but I take full responsibility for
the accuracy of information contained in the footnotes. In this regard I
owe a deep debt of gratitude to all those who so willingly answered my
queries: in particular to Axel Klein and Gareth Cox for information
relating to contemporary Irish music and musicians; to Michael Murphy
on Sir Thomas Beecham's arrangement of the national anthem; to Brenda
Alexander for information and images relating to the DOP; to Graham
Nelson for information on his father Havelock Nelson; to Ellen O'Flaherty,
assistant librarian (College Archives), who has catalogued and curates Brian
Boydell's papers in TCD Library, in particular for her help in arranging
scans for publication of photos and other images held within the archive; to
Evonne Ferguson, Jonathan Grimes and all the staff at the CMC, Dublin;
to Victoria Browne of the Irish Heritage Trust and Debbie Walsh (Fota
House), who found and returned the 1950 diary to the family; to Natasha
Sterne, Collections Librarian at the RDS; and to Christopher and Anne
FitzSimon, Richard Pine, Charles Gannon and Barbara Jillian Dignam.
My special thanks also to Irena for her patience, understanding and always
perceptive comments.

The excerpt from 'Friendless' from *Collected Poems: 1937–1971* by John

Berryman, Copyright © 1989 by Kate Donahue Berryman, is reprinted by permission of Farrar, Straus and Giroux, and of Faber and Faber Ltd. For permission to reproduce photographs and other images, I am grateful to Simon Conolly for agreeing to the inclusion of his father Thurloe Conolly's drawing 'A Surrealist Writer', to The Board of Trinity College Dublin for images sourced from the papers of Brian Boydell held in TCD Library, to Independent News and Media and the *Irish Independent*, to RTÉ Document Archives and RTÉ Archives, and to *The Irish Times*.

ACRONYMS & ABBREVIATIONS

BBC	British Broadcasting Corporation
CEMA	Committee for the Encouragement of Music and the Arts
CMC	Contemporary Music Centre, Dublin
DOP	Dublin Orchestral Players
EMIR	Harry White and Barra Boydell (eds), *The Encyclopaedia of Music in Ireland*, 2 vols (Dublin: UCD Press, 2013)
GPO	General Post Office, Dublin
IMS	Irish Musical Studies
ISCM	International Society for Contemporary Music
MAI	Music Association of Ireland
NGroveD2	Stanley Sadie (ed), *The New Grove Dictionary of Music and Musicians*, 21 vols, 2nd edn (London: Macmillan, 2001)
op.	opus
RCM	Royal College of Music, London
RDS	Royal Dublin Society
RÉ	Radio Éireann
RÉLO	Radio Éireann Light Orchestra
RÉSO	Radio Éireann Symphony Orchestra
RIAM	Royal Irish Academy of Music
RTÉ	Radio Telefís Éireann
RTÉSO	Radio Telefís Éireann Symphony Orchestra
MusB	Bachelor of Music degree (TCD)
MusD	Doctor of Music degree (TCD)
TCD	Trinity College Dublin
UCD	University College Dublin

ILLUSTRATIONS

BRIAN BOYDELL BIOGRAPHICAL DATES

1917, 17 March	Born in Dublin
1927–30	The Dragon School, Oxford
1930–5	Rugby School
1935	Studies in Heidelberg, Germany (Easter to summer)
1935–8	Clare College, Cambridge
1938, summer	Motoring holiday to Yugoslavia
1938–9	RCM, London
1939	Returns to Dublin at the outbreak of war
Early 1940s	Active as an artist, exhibiting with the White Stag Group and the Irish Exhibition of Living Art
1942	MusB from TCD
1943–66	Conductor of the DOP
1944, January	Organises concert in the Shelbourne Hotel, Dublin, featuring his compositions
1944, 6 June	Marries Mary Jones
1944–52	Teaches singing at the RIAM
Mid-1940s	Begins to present radio programmes (eventually amounting to over 1,000) on music appreciation
1948	Founding member of the MAI
1949	RÉ Chamber Music Prize for his String Quartet no. 1

1955	First adjudicating tour in Canada
1957	Second adjudicating tour in Canada
1958–69	Founder and director of the Dowland Consort
1959	MusD from TCD
1961	Commissioned to arrange the national anthem for Irish television
1961–83	Member of the Arts Council of Ireland
1962–82	Professor of Music at TCD
1965	*A Terrible Beauty is Born*, op. 59, commissioned by RTÉ to mark the 50th anniversary of the Easter Rising (1916)
1974	Honorary DMus from the National University of Ireland
1983	Commendatore della Repubblica Italiana
1984	Elected to Aosdána (the State-sponsored affiliation of creative artists honoured for their contributions to the arts in Ireland)
1990	Honorary Fellowship of the RIAM
1996	*Viking Lip Music*, op. 91, written for the Royal Danish Brass Ensemble, his final composition
1997, March	Presentation in Dublin Castle from President Mary Robinson to mark his 80th birthday
2000, 8 November	Dies in Dublin

PREFACE TO MEMOIR

THERE ARE NOT MANY of us left to tell, from personal experience, the story of that remarkable period in the history of artistic development in Ireland during the Second World War and shortly afterwards. In a country which had only recently broken free of foreign domination, there was a feeling that Irish creative artists should barricade themselves against foreign influence and proudly celebrate the long-suppressed achievements of a past Golden Age. But, there were those who had no wish to live in monastic isolation. James Joyce had left Ireland in disgust, and was largely disowned by his country. On the other hand, Mainie Jellett courageously brought back from Paris to the city of her birth the newest developments in painting. She was perhaps the first significant encouragement to those who had little desire to paddle around in the past, and wished to be part of worldwide modern trends in the arts.[1]

Debate about the different views concerning the ideal future of Irish culture continued right through the 1940s. *The Irish Times* of 10 November 1947 reported a debate on this subject which took place at the inaugural meeting of the Technical Students' Literary and Debating Society in Dublin. The speakers to the auditor Bernard Colgan's paper included P.J. Little, Minister for Posts and Telegraphs; Peadar O'Donnell; R.M. Smyllie (editor of *The Irish Times*); Lorna Reynolds and Councillor J. Phelan. My contribution was reported as follows:

> Mr Brian Boydell said that when they should be keeping their eyes and ears open to the developments around them so that they might interpret them and expand from the viewpoint of their own national vision as their contribution to the world, they were told by the loud voices of narrow-minded nationalism that they should shut their doors and develop their own culture from within.

In the 1930s, the doors that admitted winds of European change were beginning to open. Then, with the outbreak of war in 1939, a motley influx

1. Mainie Jellett (1897–1944) had studied under Walter Sickert in London before moving to Paris, where she worked with the abstract painter and teacher Albert Gleizes. There she encountered Cubism and non-representational art, which she was largely responsible for introducing to Ireland. Brian studied painting under her for a short period in the early 1940s. See further Bruce Arnold, *Mainie Jellett and the Modern Movement in Ireland* (London: Yale UP, 1991).

of artists and intellectuals, who for various reasons wished to escape to a neutral country, brought further stimulus. The barricades were down, and the doors fully open to admit a veritable gale which ignited the smouldering aspirations of those who wished to explore new fields of creative activity. Within a short time, the White Stag Group had formed around artists such as Benny Rakocsy and Kenneth Hall;[2] Seán O'Faoláin was editing *The Bell*,[3] and the Irish Exhibition of Living Art was inaugurated in 1943 with the active encouragement of Mainie Jellett, as an antidote to academic painting. The lowered voices, which before the war had whispered of modern movements such as surrealism as though communicating some indecency, now became confident. With the encouragement of such 'subversive' leaders, the apologetic squeaks became a somewhat arrogant and rebellious roar. We believed in our views, then considered so revolutionary, with burning intensity, and were completely intolerant of narrow nationalism or the academic establishment.

The rebellious ferment also infected our social behaviour. An orthodox lifestyle was considered to be unutterably boring. Beards (not at all seemly in those days – even publicly revolting); corduroy trousers and 'effeminate' suede shoes; pacifism and left-wing views; people living together in socially unacceptable circumstances …. And then, of course, we dangerous intellectuals posed a threat to those authorities nervously trying to steer a neutral country through the political minefield of wartime diplomacy. For all I know, some of the motley influx may indeed have been spies; though I don't think any of my close associates were. I do know that a few were suspected of such activity. Having spent a short time at Heidelberg University, I was of course suspected of being a German spy. But more of that later.

---

2. Basil ('Benny') Rakocsy (1908–79) was born in Chelsea and worked as a commercial artist before turning in the 1930s to psychology and painting, and coming under the influence of surrealism. He came to Dublin in 1940, returning to England in 1946 and subsequently settling in France. He met the English painter Kenneth Hall (1913–46) in 1935, and together they founded the White Stag Group in that year. Hall came to Ireland in August 1939, moving to Dublin in 1940. He returned to London in September 1945 but, suffering from depression, took his own life in 1946. On the White Stag Group, see further Chapter 4 (below). See also S.B. Kennedy, *The White Stag Group* (Dublin: IMMA, 2005); also Róisín Kennedy, 'Experimentalism or Mere Chaos? The White Stag Group and the reception of subjective art in Ireland', in E. Keown and C. Taaffe (eds), *Irish Modernism: origins, contexts, publics* (Bern: Peter Lang, 2010), pp. 179–94; and Brian Murray, *Language of Dreams, passim.*
3. Seán O'Faoláin (1900–91), whose reputation as an author rests in particular on his collections of short stories, was founder and editor of the literary periodical *The Bell* (1940–54), one of the most important and influential voices for intellectual and social commentary in mid-century Ireland. Brian contributed twice to *The Bell*, publishing articles on 'Music in Ireland' in 1947 and 'The Future of Music in Ireland' in 1951. See Bibliography, p. 204.

Being one of the few survivors who shared in the excitement, I have frequently enjoyed relating some of the more amusing and even outrageous events of the time. These anecdotes have so often led people to say: 'You simply must write these stories down!' And so, at last, I am determined to do so. If you want a well-researched and fascinating history, turn to Brian Kennedy, who has written the more serious and objective history of this period.[4*] My stories may hopefully be entertaining and add some frothy atmosphere to the remarkable history of those days. I think that I am also in the position to record for posterity some insight into personalities and events, mainly in the field of music – the art with which I was chiefly concerned.

I must however be honest enough to issue a word of warning. If one enjoys the role of raconteur, there is a great temptation to add little bits here and there when repeating the story over the years. The trouble is that these small touches of icing on the cake become absorbed into what one eventually believes to be the truth. I feel fairly sure, for instance, that the well-known actor Micheál Mac Liammóir, who was really Alfred Willmore from London, came honestly to believe that he was a pure-blooded Gael born in the cottage in County Cork which he so often described.[5] So conscious am I of this failing that I was tempted to entitle this book 'Don't Believe a Word of It', but then potential readers might take that too literally, and think the stories to be pure fiction. And so, although some of the details of the stories I have to tell may be inadvertent flights of imagination, even those that may appear to be stranger than fiction are indeed based securely on factual events.

Brian Boydell
Dublin, 1994

4.* Brian Kennedy, *Irish Art and Modernism, 1880–1950* (Belfast: The Institute of Irish Studies, 1991). [Author's note]

5. Micheál Mac Liammóir (1899–1978) was born Alfred Willmore in London to a Protestant family. As an actor he travelled extensively, becoming such an enthusiast for Irish culture in the 1920s that he settled in Ireland, learnt and spoke Irish fluently, adopted the Irish name by which he became known, and claimed descent from an Irish Catholic family in Cork. He co-founded the Gate Theatre in Dublin in 1928 with his partner Hilton Edwards.

PART I | MEMOIR

Brian Boydell, c. 1947.

CHAPTER 1
A RELUCTANT SLICE OF AUTOBIOGRAPHY

BEFORE TELLING THE STORIES, I should perhaps say something about my own role in the events I describe. After all, it is only fair that you should have some idea of what kind of impressionable reporter is relating them. This involves straying for a little time into autobiography. I am reluctant to do this, since my chief aim is to record impressions of events and the personalities (other than myself) involved in them. I also feel a bit guilty doing so, since I never quite managed to exorcise the very strict views of my father, against which I waged a rebellious war. He believed that autobiography constituted an act of indecent self-advertisement.

My father James Boydell was a well-to-do Dublin businessman, running in partnership with his brother a profitable malting concern which supplied malt mainly to Guinness and Jameson. They had inherited the business from their father, who had come over from Leigh in Lancashire shortly after 1870. As the only son, this was to be my destiny. A keen member of the Moravian church – a Protestant sect originating from well before Luther's Reformation – my father embraced a strict moral code. Even in jest he would never tell a lie, and he disapproved of ostentation and self-indulgence. As one of the Anglo-Irish community that had held the reins of influence before Irish independence, he could never really adjust to the new breed of nationalist politics. My mother Eileen, with Collins/McCarthy family background, was undoubtedly inclined towards certain aspects of nationalism, and also towards an adventuresome artistic taste which was not shared by my father. She had a great admiration, for instance, for W.B. Yeats, whom my father regarded as an outrageous poseur. But out of loyalty to her husband, she kept quiet about such notions in his presence and largely conformed to the social conventions of Anglo-Irish society. However, she welcomed many of my unconventional friends, and I could communicate with her concerning many ideas which would have given rise to an apoplectic fit if mentioned in the presence of my father.

As was usual with children of my background, we were sent to school in England with the purpose of polishing away boorish provincial manners and acquiring the civilised behaviour and accents of speech that befitted a gentleman. After all, in those days the brewers, who were the 'prefects' in Arthur Guinness & Sons, could attain such distinction only by having a public school background and a first-class degree from Oxford or Cambridge (certainly not Trinity College Dublin) – preferably in Classics. I was to begin my ascent of this ladder at Winchester College: partly, I believe, because the motto of the school is 'Manners maketh Man', and partly because its exacting academic standards appealed strongly to my mother. She had had a distinguished career as one of the early women students to be admitted to Trinity College Dublin,[1] and had a somewhat exaggerated regard for academic distinction. (I believe that the last year of her life was brightened for her by seeing the hopes for her son fulfilled when I became a professor.) In order to qualify for Winchester, I was submitted to laborious holiday 'grinds' in Greek with a schoolmaster in Blackrock who left stinking stains of tobacco-pipe juice all over my exercises. But then my father went to see my future housemaster who, in spite of the school's famous motto, was so rude to him that I was peremptorily switched to Rugby.

Prior to that, I was sent to the Dragon School in Oxford, a remarkable school, years ahead of its time. This proved a rewarding and enjoyable experience. The Dragon was co-educational (though with a very small proportion of non-boarding girls); and short trousers and open-necked shirts were worn all the year round. Everyone was expected to have a bicycle, and on Sundays we were encouraged to go off on our own in twos or threes on expeditions which could be anywhere in the attractive countryside as long as we didn't linger in the town. The masters were openly addressed by their nicknames, and 'Tortoise' encouraged my early enthusiasm for collecting fossils (which eventually led to my including geology as part of my science degree at Cambridge). Eager visits to clay pits and quarries culminated in the great excitement of finding a large portion of an icthyosaurus in the Wolvercote clay pit.

I would later perhaps have reacted against an element of brave British heartiness which was very much part of the ethos of the school; but at the time I accepted it as adventurous fun. The spirit of brave acceptance of hardship went further than open-necked shirts in the often freezing

1. See Susan M. Parkes (ed.), *A Danger to the Men? a history of women in Trinity College Dublin, 1904–2004* (Dublin: The Lilliput Press, 2004), p. 68.

Oxford winter. Everyone had to start the day with either a cold bath or a swim in the River Cherwell. One winter, when we were skating on the river, I came across a round hole in the ice, at the edge of which stood a bar of pink carbolic soap. This was where my housemaster set an example to us of Godliness and Cleanliness in the face of hardship by lowering himself through the hole in the ice each morning before breakfast, remaining in the freezing water long enough to lather himself vigorously in carbolic mortification.

And then to Rugby School ... I don't really know what made me into a rebel, constantly on my guard against the subtle brainwashing of the English public school system of the time. It seemed to me that the system was geared towards inculcating empire-building values based on the arrogant assumption that God, through the Church of England, had given to the British Establishment a superior knowledge of what was the right way for the rest of the world to behave. This idea was certainly neatly crystallised for me by my hair-shirt reverend housemaster, who wrote on my term report: 'Must not make his nationality an excuse for his behaviour'. This housemaster suspected the worst motives in everyone's actions; and he firmly believed that music was a dangerous, unmanly influence which encouraged homosexuality. He tried to prevent my friendship with the director of music, who represented for me an island of friendship and understanding in a style of life which was mainly uncongenial. Kenneth Stubbs provided the inspiration and encouragement which guided me towards music as the central theme of my life.[2] He also brought me in his car on delightful expeditions during the summertime and taught me to do watercolour sketches from nature. In the winter months the enthusiasm I already had for photography was nurtured by his giving me the use of the darkroom in his house. Kenneth became a family friend and spent several summer holidays with us back in Ireland, where we went on sketching expeditions in the West. He became indeed a father figure for me, compensating for my sad inability to communicate freely with my own father, who was so strictly conscious of the duty to guide his son in the paths of righteousness that one simply could not discuss controversial matters. When, towards the end of my time at Rugby, I developed what was a precocious and unacceptable revulsion against keeping the world in order by military means, I could discuss with Kenneth my new-found pacifist convictions.

2. Born in Canada, Kenneth Stubbs was an organ scholar at Worcester College, Oxford, before becoming Director of Music at Rugby School, where he had previously been a pupil. He was conductor of the Rugby Philharmonic Choir from 1924 to 1939.

At Rugby, we were provided with a certain degree of privacy in 'studies'. These tiny rooms, containing one or two desks with chairs and an electric fire, were shared by two younger boys, until one eventually attained the senior privilege of a study to oneself. At the end of the school year we were invited to state a preference for the companion with whom to share a study in the following year. My great friend from Edinburgh and I submitted our names together. The housemaster announced, with no reason or explanation whatsoever, that he would not permit us to share. I have always been roused to anger if faced by a restriction on my freedom of action for which no good reason is given. The unspoken reason in this case (as I realised many years later) was the housemaster's suspicion that I was potentially an evil influence leading to sins of corruption and debauchery which, in the innocence of that stage of my life, I could not conceivably have imagined. I was so angry that I went straight to the headmaster. I obtained no satisfaction, and in fact was very nearly removed from the school in disgrace for not submitting without question to superior authority. This episode left its indelible mark.

It would be a mistake to dwell too much on the grimmer aspects of life at Rugby, even if they have left their scars. In addition to the guiding inspiration of Kenneth Stubbs, there was the bonding of a couple of enduring friendships, as well as the exciting stimulus of less permanent emotional attachments (completely innocent of what suspicious minds might think such affairs could lead to). My early compositions, including two organ sonatas composed in the organ loft during a brief period of religious mania, were dedicated to the objects of my adolescent adoration.

Ever since receiving the present of a chemistry set at the age of about eight, I had devoted a great deal of energy and most of my pocket-money to establishing a laboratory at home, in which I could do experiments that revealed the magic of chemical reactions. This early interest was developed and expanded by the excellent science teaching at Rugby, and by access to the school's lavishly equipped laboratories. Enthusiasm for this absorbing study gave birth to academic success, so that during my last year at the school I was allowed to specialise in the two subjects which were the focus of my aspirations: science and music.

The facilities for music at Rugby were marvellously encouraging. To back up the inspiration radiating from the director of music, the well-equipped music building provided plenty of practice rooms, and two concert grand pianos. There were three pipe organs, including the very large four-manual instrument in the school chapel. And then there were the 'concert chorus' (or large oratorio choir), the chapel choir, and the school orchestra. With this orchestra I had the opportunity of playing movements from both the Grieg and the second of Rachmaninov's piano concertos, and an organ concerto by Rheinberger. Frequent opportunities for hearing professional performances were provided, including an annual visit by the City of Birmingham Orchestra under the conductor Leslie Heward. Voluntary classes in preparation for this visit provided us with a good knowledge of the works to be played. A lasting enthusiasm for several symphonic master-pieces owe their origin to this. We were allowed to attend rehearsals of the Rugby town oratorio society. It was at one such rehearsal of Bach's *St. Matthew Passion* that I experienced for the first time a sudden illu-minating vision of what music was really all about. The simple choral interjection 'Truly this was the Son of God' (*Wahrlich, dieser ist Gottes Sohn*) sent shivers down my spine, the like of which I had never felt before. To this day I believe this passage to be the most convincing example in music of mystical expression.

Whatever negative impressions may be retained concerning the Rugby experience, one cannot be but grateful for the excellent educational ground-ing in science and music. It enabled me to win a Choral Exhibition to Clare College, Cambridge, where I was to read for the Natural Science Tripos, and have the valuable experience of training the Chapel Choir. One more character-forming influence from Rugby days should be mentioned, for it is relevant to later years back in Ireland. The patronising attitude of the British Establishment to what they considered to be the uncouth bog-trotters from the 'Oirish cabbage-patch', so firmly embedded in the public school ethos, drove me towards rabid republican nationalism. I became an ardent admirer of de Valera, and struggled (without much success) to teach myself the Irish language from a textbook. When I returned several years later to Ireland and found very great difficulty, owing to my accent, man-ners and religion, in attempts to be accepted as a true Irishman, and saw that the Irish language was being used as a political entrance-ticket to such acceptance, I reacted in the opposite direction. The scales were by no means tipped completely: but I ended up with a distaste for all aspects of national-ist fervour and the emotional pressures of propaganda that accompany it.

A brief period at Heidelberg in 1935, between Rugby and Cambridge, when Hitler's Nazi regime was in full swing, had alerted me to the virus of nationalistic propaganda. Having embraced a creed of non-violence as a member of Dick Sheppard's Peace Pledge Union,[3] I later saw how such

---

3. Hugh Richard ['Dick'] Lawrie Sheppard (1880–1937), pacifist, Anglican priest and Dean of Canterbury, founded the Peace Pledge Union in 1936.

propaganda was to obliterate all reasoned thinking during the years of war-hysteria. In spite of all this there was no diminution in my desire to shake free of British attitudes and be identified with Irish cultural inheritance.

Having achieved my future place at Cambridge, I left Rugby before the end of the school year and spent the period between Easter and the late summer in Heidelberg, living with the family of a retired school teacher called Professor Schenck. He gave me a lesson in German each morning, and I was forbidden to speak any English even when in difficulty. Within quite a short time I achieved a useful mastery of the language. I continued my study of the piano with the leading pianist in Heidelberg (Friederich Schery) and had organ lessons at the Evangelischeskirchenmusikalischesinstitut (I had great fun writing that in my c.v. in later years!) from the well-known Bach scholar Professor Poppen.[4] The greatest musical impact of these few months, which were so crowded with exciting new experiences, was provided by the opportunity of hearing Wagner's operas at the Mannheim theatre. I attended two complete cycles of *The Ring* at the special student price of a shilling [*sic*] a time. I became quite Wagner-mad and assiduously studied the librettos (much to the disapproval of Professor Schenck, who had a very poor opinion of Wagner's literary style). My Wagner-worship culminated in an extended visit to Munich for the festival of his operas, where I heard some of the greatest Wagner singers of the time. I also attended in Munich a most impressive production of Richard Strauss's *Die Frau ohne Schatten* conducted by the aged composer. Mozart's *Die Zauberflöte* was performed in the delightful eighteenth-century Residenztheater: afflicted by Wagner-fever, and taking everything frightfully seriously, I was stupid enough to think it was all rather silly.

With the excitement of so many new musical discoveries – and the intoxication of the impressions of landscape and the way of life in a foreign country – I had little interest in politics. Moreover, in what was a first extended experience in a foreign country, so many things were alien and unexpected that the feeling of political tension was to some extent accepted by me as part of a strange new scenario. It was, however, impossible to be unaware of dark forces at work. This was brought home to me in a painfully intimate way when I observed how the Professor's children came home

---

4. Hermann Poppen was appointed first director of Das Evangelishe Kirchenmusikalishe Institut (as it would more usually be written today) on its foundation in 1931 and directed the Heidelberg Bachchor from 1919 until his death in 1956. Primarily known as a composer of church music, his publications also include editions of organ chorales by Johann Gottfried Walther (Kassel: Bärenreiter, 1935) and of Bach chorales for the Lutheran hymnbook (Heidelberg: Hochstein, 1950).

aglow with excitement, having been indoctrinated at a Hitler Youth rally. The old man had no sympathy whatever for these dangerous new ideas, but didn't dare breathe a word lest his views were reported to the SS. His chief emotional release seemed to consist of joining a few trusted old friends behind a locked door, having searched for possible hidden microphones, where they exchanged funny stories ridiculing Hitler.

The nervousness of the Professor and his wife lest their anti-Nazi views might become known to the authorities was illustrated by a tragi-comic episode. Situated in Ballsbridge in Dublin there was the long-established Swastika Laundry which stamped its swastika emblem on clothes entrusted to them for washing. One day Mrs Schenck was tidying away my clothes and discovered the swastika on my shirt. I was aware of panic-stricken whispering with her husband, for they feared I might be some sinister agent of the regime. Their fears were soon allayed when they confronted me and asked for an explanation. Curiously enough the Swastika Laundry retained its emblem right through the course of the war in spite of considerable criticism.[5] I shall never forget the Professor's reaction of complete shock, and the obvious shame he felt for what was being done in the name of his country, when we came across a burned-out Jewish village while on a walking expedition in remote mountainous country. As we were confronted with a scene of complete desolation, with 'Jude' and swastikas painted on the shattered village walls, it was quite obvious that until this moment he had no idea that the rumours he had heard concerning such crimes were in fact true.[6]

Life at Cambridge proved to be the fulfilment of dreams for one who wished to stretch his wings and discover what intellectual stimulus could be found through the freedom of uninhibited flight. With so many thousands of students, among whom there were many who were to become important leading figures in years to come, there was an almost limitless choice of friends. Great intellects and profound minds among the dons and teaching staff were mostly willing to share their special insight in friendly discussion. Boris Ord, the organist and choirmaster of King's College, became a

5. The Swastika Laundry in Dublin had been founded in 1912 and continued to operate under that name until the 1980s. Coincidentally its delivery vans were painted red, with a black swastika on a white background, the same colouring used by the Nazis. The swastika emblem, however, was positioned squarely rather than obliquely.
6. Brian used also to relate how, out of curiosity, he had attended a Nazi rally in Heidelberg. His particular memory was of how excruciatingly tiring it was to have to hold up his hand, like everyone around him, in a prolonged Hitler salute, not daring to lower his arm under the penetrating gaze of the watchful SS and other party members.

personal friend.[7] Through the University Madrigal Society, of which he was the conductor, I developed a life-long enthusiasm for sixteenth-century music. Professor Edward Dent took an active interest in encouraging the 'Echo Club', which met in his rooms for the performance and discussion of student compositions.[8] I didn't get to know Ernest Rutherford personally but I was privileged to attend his lecture concerning his recent revolutionary discovery of the splitting of the atom (not that I can claim to have understood much of their complex mathematical content).[9] In biochemistry (one of my favourite subjects, along with geology) my mentor was Professor Hopkins, who could be said to have invented this new subject.[10] (It has developed so much since then that I now hardly understand a word of it!)

I have observed over the years how scientific subjects tend to breed the most active and keen musical amateurs. Cambridge was no exception. The physiology department provided an example with Frank Winton, who had written one of the standard textbooks on the subject, being a fine cellist; and Willie Rushton, another physiology lecturer, played the bassoon, while his wife was an oboist. Understandably I formed a special relationship with them, and we frequently met in the relaxed social atmosphere of the University Music Club. During these intensely active years, so crowded with activities of all kinds, it was somehow possible to be involved in half a dozen or so university and college music societies, fulfil my duties with the College Chapel choir, practise the piano regularly, and attend the requisite number of science lectures and practical classes.

Cambridge offered many opportunities for widening one's experience of music and of hearing the leading exponents of the time. The great pianists Schnabel, Gieseking, Rubenstein, Horowitz and Cortot gave recitals there, also the Léner Quartet. There was the first performance of Vaughan

---

7. Boris Ord (1897–1961) was organist and choirmaster at King's College from 1929 to 1957.
8. As Professor of Music at Cambridge from 1926 to 1941, Edward J. Dent (1876–1957) reorganised the music degree to broaden it from being a degree primarily designed for church organists into a broader musical education relevant to the wider musical profession. Brian Boydell would later reflect this approach in the fundamental changes he introduced as Professor of Music to the music degrees offered at TCD. Dent was one of the foremost British musicologists of his day, his publications concentrating in particular on Mozart operas, English opera, and the music of Busoni. See further *NGroveD2*, vol. 7, p. 219.
9. Rutherford (born in New Zealand in 1871) had become Professor of Experimental Physics and director of the Cavendish Laboratory at Cambridge in 1919. He died at Cambridge on 19 October 1937 (at the beginning of Brian's third undergraduate year).
10. Frederick Hopkins (1861–1947) was jointly awarded (with Christiaan Eijkman) the Nobel Prize in Physiology for Medicine in 1929 for the discovery of vitamins (which, as Brian recalled from Hopkins' lectures, he as inventor of the term always pronounced with the first syllable rhyming with 'light', not 'lit').

Williams' opera *The Poisoned Kiss*,[11] and the University Music Club was wildly adventuresome in organising student performances of contemporary experimental music and rarely heard music from all ages. London was easy to get to, and I travelled there to hear Rachmaninov himself playing his Second Piano Concerto, and Prokofiev playing his Third. The former, who was without doubt the finest pianist I ever heard, sat at the keyboard almost as though he were a stone statue, hardly moving at all (such a contrast to flamboyant pianists like Pouishnoff).[12] With his shaven head and well-worn dress suit (which looked almost moth-eaten) he gave little impression of his outstanding ability until he started to play. Indeed, I thought he looked more like an itinerant ex-convict than one of the world's greatest pianists. When I heard Prokofiev playing his Third Concerto I came out from the Queen's Hall in a rage at the idea of treating the piano as a percussion instrument to be thumped brutally with discords. When later I became so very enthusiastic about his music I couldn't believe how I could have completely failed to appreciate its lyrical melodiousness, as well as its intensely stimulating drive.

In addition to all this activity, a great deal of time was devoted to very serious intellectual discussion about every subject under the sun. One forum for this was the (unfortunately named) Clare College Dilettante Society, where members read papers on any topic so long as it had nothing to do with their academic subject. Another voyage of discovery for the newly stretched wings was the Cambridge branch of the Society for Psychic Research, where we attended seances and critically examined those who professed to be mediums. I was also at that time very involved in the pacifist movement, attending meetings of the Peace Pledge Union and haranguing the crowds in the Market Place from a soap-box.

Among my friends were several literary scholars, including the young American poet John Berryman, and a future Professor of English Literature at Columbia University, Andrew Chiappe.[13] Most of us students were confined to pretty strict parental allowances, and never seemed to have any money to spend. Andrew, on the other hand, appeared to be immensely wealthy. Entering his luxurious rooms, it seemed as though one waded ankle-deep through the sensually soft pile of his scarlet carpet. They were furnished with that meticulously sensitive and sophisticated taste that one

11. Cambridge Arts Theatre, 12 May 1936.
12. The Ukrainian pianist Leff Pouishnoff (1891–1959) settled in the United Kingdom in 1921. He was particularly renowned for his interpretation of the music of Chopin and Liszt.
13. Both John Berryman (1914–72) and Andrew J. Chiappe (1915–67) attended Clare College, Cambridge, on fellowships after graduating from Columbia University. See also note 16 below.

might associate with Oscar Wilde. Here we sipped vintage port and listened to the first available complete recording of Mozart's *Don Giovanni*,[14] and discussed Yeats, Joyce and Irish literature – a passion that satisfied my nationalist leanings. With my musical friends we listened to records in each other's rooms, and developed wild enthusiasms for several composers regarded then as the avant-garde, including especially Alban Berg. Peter Warlock's setting of poems by W.B. Yeats, known as *The Curlew*, became a veritable cult.[15] Another cult work was Berg's *Lyric Suite* for string orchestra. On strictly limited and carefully planned occasions we would listen to the newly available recording of *The Curlew* with all lights extinguished. A period of meditation would follow during which no one would breathe a word that might disturb the magic spell.[16] The only subject we never deigned to discuss was sport in the form of team games. In the somewhat tribal life among Cambridge students we snobbishly despised the enemy tribe of 'toughs'. The members of the boat club were, in our opinion, the worst. They did after all from time to time derive their amusement by wrecking the rooms and defacing the pictures of students whom they considered to be an 'aesthete'. (Dark memories of the Hitler Jugend.)

Increasingly, during my three years at Cambridge, I learned to recognise those science lectures which were of real value and those that were so badly delivered that one could learn much more from a textbook. (One geology lecturer actually delivered his lectures by reading from his own published book.) Since attendance at lectures was not compulsory I was able to devote

14. Presumably the 1936 HMV recording with John Brownlee (Don Giovanni), Salvatore Baccaloni (Leporello) and Ina Souez (Donna Anna), conducted by Fritz Busch with the Glyndebourne Festival Orchestra and Chorus (DB 2961–2983, on twenty-three 78rpm discs; reissued on CD in 2001 by Naxos, 8.110135-37).

15. The English composer Philip Heseltine (1894–1930), who used the pseudonym Peter Warlock, had met Yeats while he was in Ireland between 1917 and 1918 to escape possible conscription. *The Curlew*, for tenor solo, flute, cor anglais and string quartet, dates from 1920/22. Brian would later get to know Warlock's son Nigel Heseltine in Dublin (see Chapter 4, below).

16. In the opening stanzas of his poem 'Friendless' (published in the collection *Love and Fame* in 1970) Berryman refers to Brian and his enthusiasm for Warlock's *The Curlew*:

Friendless in Clare, except Brian Boydell
a Dubliner with no hair
an expressive tenor speaking voice
who introduced me to the music of Peter Warlock

who had just knocked himself off,* fearing the return
of his other personality, Philip Heseltine.
Brian used to play The Curlew with the lights out,
voice of a lost soul moving.

*Warlock's death is believed to have been suicide (as was Berryman's).

more and more time to music. I did most of my scientific work at home during the vacations, making use of the laboratory in which I had invested so much energy and pocket-money and going on geological field trips. (With an extraordinary lack of imagination, such fieldwork was totally neglected in the Cambridge course at that time.) I realised the importance of studying my examiners; finding out what aspects of their subject appealed to them most. I also worked out what questions were likely to be asked in the final examinations by going through papers from previous years. Thus, for example, I saw that no question about the human kidney had been asked in the physiology papers for three years. I made sure that I knew everything about this organ, even to the extent of recently published research. Sure enough, I got the question I was prepared for. This undoubtedly contributed to my obtaining a first-class degree. I was thus quite adequately qualified to take advantage of my father's generous promise of a period at the Royal College of Music.

Between the final university examinations and settling in London to begin my studies at the RCM I planned to explore Europe with a couple of friends. To this end I persuaded my father to provide the greater part of the £35 required to buy a second-hand Ford V8 two-seater from a bizarre motor salesman off London's Great Portland Street. Mr Twitchings seemed wider than he was tall; and under his bowler hat the solid gold smile displayed his satisfaction at being the local boss of dubious motor dealing. I adapted the car, by making it possible to reverse the front bench-seat and removing the partition between the front compartment and the 'dickie',[17*] so that two – Charles Acton and myself – could sleep in it.[18] The third member of our party, Alan Leeke from Cambridge, brought a tent and had to contend with scorpions in Yugoslavia. We set off with the intention of driving to Greece, which was an ambitiously adventuresome expedition to undertake in those days. However, when we reached the Dalmatian coast we found that country so idyllic that we didn't proceed any further. We never had to cope with the bandits that were rumoured to pose a serious threat to travellers in the mountains between Albania and Greece. That trip could be the subject of a chapter on its own, but it is not directly relevant

17.* The 'dickie' seat was the name given to an extra occasional seat at the back of a two-seater car which folded away when not in use. [Author's note]
18. Charles Acton (1914–99) was, like Brian, educated at Rugby School and Cambridge (although he did not complete his degree in the natural sciences). They developed a close friendship, and Brian would later be among those who recommended him as music critic for *The Irish Times*, a post he took up in 1955 and held for thirty-one years. Acton's sometimes outspoken reviews and opinions (including those expressed on some of Brian's compositions) ultimately led to a frostiness in their relationship.

On the motoring holiday to Yugoslavia, 1938 (*l. to r.*): Alan Leeke, Brian and Charles Acton, with unknown Yugoslavian.

here ... except, perhaps that I returned with a BEARD: the first of several attempts that were met with such intense social disapproval that my courage failed me, and I was forced to shave it off.[19]

After returning from the trip to Yugoslavia, the end of the summer of 1938 provided further memorable experiences. Bernard Robinson, an enthusiastic amateur musician, had established with Edric Cundell, the head of the Guildhall School of Music, an annual music camp.[20] This was attended by mad-keen singers and instrumentalists both amateur and professional, including such distinguished figures as Denis Brain the horn-player.[21] It was a great privilege for an inexperienced young musician to be invited. The members of the camp, who together formed a choir and orchestra, slept in tents and rehearsed seldom-heard choral and orchestral music in an old hay-barn. Smaller groups would play chamber music and sing madrigals in cow-byres and pigsties nearby. The camp was aroused in the morning by a reveille which had to be an original composition or an arrangement provided for the occasion by the group allotted to 'orderly

19. For an account of the Yugoslavian trip from Charles Acton's perspective, see Richard Pine, *Charles: the life and world of Charles Acton, 1914–1999* (Dublin: The Lilliput Press, 2010), pp. 146–51.
20. The English composer and conductor Edric Cundell (1893–1961) was Principal of the Guildhall School of Music from 1938 to 1961.
21. Denis Brain would become the outstanding British horn-player of the post-war years and his 1953 recording of the Mozart concertos remains a classic. Although only aged seventeen in 1938, he was already beginning to establish a reputation as an outstanding player. He died in a car accident in 1957.

'duty' for the day. For our duty-day, I made an arrangement for carefully tuned motor-horns of the jingle that introduced the Gaumont British News at the cinema.

After music camp, I attended the Three Choirs Festival at Worcester, where I was present for a performance of Vaughan Williams' recent Fourth Symphony conducted by the composer, then in his sixties. He was not by any means a gifted conductor. Sitting on a high stool, with the hard front of his starched dress shirt bulging forward as he leaned over the score, he had a charming way of acknowledging the instruments when they duly entered at the appropriate moment, rather than giving them a lead; at the very end he gave a vigorous down-beat for an extra non-existent chord, which the experienced orchestra was wise enough to disregard. It was at the previous year's Festival, at Gloucester in 1937, that I had heard the Hungarian composer Zoltan Kodály conduct his exciting *Te Deum*: a work I have vainly tried to have performed in Dublin. After three days sketching in the Welsh mountains with Kenneth Stubbs, preparations had to be made for attending the RCM in London.

My friend Maurice Pettitt, who had been organ scholar at Clare College, had found a flat in Cranley Gardens in South Kensington, which we were to share in the company of my cat Boris. To have my very own cat and live in a flat in London symbolised for me a sense of complete liberation from all the rules and regulations that surrounded the first twenty-one years of my life. At the RCM I enrolled for composition with Patrick Hadley, with whom I formed a lasting friendship.[22] Many years later (in the 1960s) after he had retired from the Chair of Music at Cambridge, he used to stay with us in Dublin as a base from which he travelled the country collecting folksongs in local pubs. He proudly supposed that he was saving priceless treasures that might otherwise have been relegated to oblivion. We never disillusioned him, since he was so happy with the hobby of his old age. He used to arrive each year in his ancient open Austin car, with a spare wooden leg on the back seat.[23] Our children were spell-bound when he showed them how he kept his sock in place with a drawing pin.

---

22. Patrick Hadley (1899–1973) had taught composition at the RCM since 1925. His appointment as a lecturer in music at Cambridge University in 1938 would have coincided with Brian's leaving Cambridge and moving to the RCM. Hadley was elected to the Chair of Music at Cambridge in 1946, a position he held until his retirement in 1962. An admirer of Frederick Delius and a friend of Ralph Vaughan Williams, his compositional output is limited, consisting largely of vocal works, including cantatas and anthems written for the choir of Caius College, Cambridge. See further Eric Wetherell, *'Paddy': the life and music of Patrick Hadley* (London: Thames, 1997).

23. Hadley had lost his right leg below the knee following an injury received while on active service in the First World War.

When I was studying with him at the RCM, Paddy used from time to time to go on the binge and be unable to undertake his teaching. For such occasions he had an arrangement with Herbert Howells, who would attend to his pupils in his absence.[24] This arrangement resulted in the best lesson I ever had in composition. I had just completed a song-setting, which I brought to Paddy. 'That's a very slimey-crawly bass', he said, 'let's have some decent manly jumps and get rid of these chromatic intervals'. I took his advice and rewrote the song. Next week Paddy was on the booze, so I brought the song along to Herbert Howells. 'That's a very angular bass – especially for such a tender romantic poem! What about some sensuous chromatic intervals to create an emotional mood?' The complete contradiction between the opinions of two respected teaching composers puzzled me, until I came to realise that, apart from pure technique, effective creative expression can be developed only through rigorous self-criticism. A critical opinion from others, provided they have the experience and expertise to know what they are talking about, can indeed be most helpful: but such criticism must be subjected to careful personal scrutiny to have any useful validity. If taken as infallible doctrine, there is the danger (so often observed) of the pupil becoming a clone of the master. Very many years later, as a result of this thinking, I used to advise my own students that any opinion about a work of art tells you more about the personality of its author than it does about the work concerned. I found it quite alarming when one had gained a respected title such as 'Professor' that one's opinions were so often taken uncritically as having the force of some divine oracle.

As a second subject to composition at the RCM I decided to learn the oboe – right from the beginning. My teacher was a delightful retired player from Henry Wood's old Queen's Hall orchestra called Shepley.[25] He belonged to the rapidly dying species of orchestral player typical of the profession before the new breed of 'educated' players replaced them. He turned out to be a breeder of champion singing canaries, and invited me to his house to see and hear them. Apparently they nearly always trill on minor thirds – never major thirds. In addition to the classes at the RCM I was studying the piano and singing independently. I continued the rigorously

24. Hadley had apparently developed a reliance on alcohol as a relief from the consistent pain he experienced from his war injury. Herbert Howells (1892–1983) is probably better known today as a composer of Anglican service settings and anthems, but before the 1940s his output was primarily instrumental, including two piano concertos (1913, 1925), a cello concerto (1936) and the Concerto for String Orchestra (1938).
25. The Queen's Hall, opened in 1893, was London's principal concert venue until it was destroyed in the London Blitz in 1941. It was the home of the 'Promenade concerts' conducted by Henry Wood from 1895.

disciplined piano lessons with a pupil of Solomon, with whom I had been studying during my Cambridge days.[26] On a couple of unnerving occasions my progress was checked by the great master himself. The technical demands of the Solomon style of playing were so exacting that I lost my nerve and abandoned my earlier ambition to become a concert pianist. In future years I was very glad to have taken this step.

As a promising singer I was sent by a mutual friend to Lady Harty (Agnes Nicholls).[27] After my audition, she declared that I hadn't the faintest idea how to sing, and that before she would consider taking me on I would have to study the technique of voice production with Louise Trenton. Louise, an American widow who had retired from public singing, proved a delightful and stimulating teacher – though extremely exacting. I had to have a lesson every day, and never let a day pass without at least an hour's practice at technical exercises. Unlike the Solomon training, she was always most encouraging, and I laid the foundations on which I was later to begin my professional career in music by teaching voice production.

At the RCM there was a student society for the performance of contemporary music. By taking an active part I added experiences of permanent value to the many that were to influence my future. I remember singing songs by Schoenberg, Berg and Bartok, and hearing a very earnest student with pebble spectacles introducing us to the music of Anton von Webern. Two further experiences from the London period stand out in my memory. There was Toscanini's season of Beethoven concerts[28] and a Sibelius Festival conducted by Thomas Beecham. I was swept up in the new craze for Sibelius. After each concert we would stay up most of the night discussing what we had heard.

This fruitful time in London was to be interrupted after just one year: for the war broke out in the autumn of 1939. The day that war was declared was made memorable for me by an incident which was both embarrassing and comic. My friend Maurice Pettitt and I had joined my family for a late

26. 'Solomon' was the professional name used by the London-born pianist Solomon Cutner (1902–88). A noted child prodigy who went on to develop an international reputation, he was particularly renowned for his performances of Beethoven's sonatas and concertos.
27. Agnes Nicholls (1877–1959) was one of the outstanding English sopranos of the early twentieth century. Her roles included Sieglinde in *Die Walküre* and Brünnhilde in *Siegfried* in Wagner's *Ring* at Covent Garden in 1908, and first performances of music by Edward Elgar. She married the Irish-born composer and conductor Hamilton Harty in 1904, styling herself Lady Harty following his knighthood in 1925.
28. Toscanini conducted the complete cycle of Beethoven's symphonies together with two performances of the *Missa Solemnis* with the BBC Symphony Orchestra as part of the 1939 London Music Festival.

summer holiday in Achill. My two sisters were there also. On the way back to Dublin, on a day full of foreboding, we had arranged to call in for tea at Killyon House in County Meath, the home of Colonel Shaen Magan. Shaen was a living caricature of a retired colonel. His remarks, delivered as though to a regiment on the parade ground, could be heard throughout the length and breadth of County Meath. We arrived just in time for Chamberlain's announcement of the declaration of war. As we crowded round the wireless, the first sound we heard was a rousing performance of 'God Save the King'. Everyone, with the painfully obvious exception of the two rebels – my sister Yvonne and myself – stood stiffly to attention, with eyes fixed on the round hole of the 'loud-speaker' as though one might see the King himself if one looked hard enough. When the momentous announcement had been made, the Colonel addressed us in a confident roar: 'Great little army the French, *great* little army. All be over in six weeks!'

The outbreak of war completely disrupted life in London and cut short my period of study at the RCM. I gave up the flat I had shared with Maurice Pettitt and had to move all my belongings to Ballybride, the family home in Shankill (near Bray, County Wicklow), including my Bösendorfer piano and Boris the cat. The former was less of a problem since it was looked after by professionals, but Boris had never been outside the flat in South Kensington. I constructed a travelling cage for him from a wooden box with wire netting over the top and set off with him to Euston station. As we boarded the Irish Mail, Boris was so terrified by the alarming racket in a busy railway station that he forced his way out of the box and fled down the corridor of the train, finally darting into a compartment. Luckily the window was shut and I was able to catch him. I then proceeded down the corridor asking the occupants of each compartment whether they objected to the company of a cat. 'Oh I don't think that would be very convenient, dear, do you?' Eventually after travelling the length of many coaches, a dear old lady welcomed us in exuberantly: 'A pussy cat – how delightful – do bring him in.' Boris sat on her lap most of the way to Holyhead. The boat journey passed without incident, though not without anxiety, and Boris was eventually released in Ballybride. Of course he'd never experienced the countryside before, and promptly disappeared for several days. He eventually returned and lived to a ripe old age, lording it over all my various households until shortly after we moved to Baily in 1955.

CHAPTER 2
BACK IN IRELAND

Brian's Type 40 Bugatti fitted with the gas producer (with Lionel Kerwood?), c. 1941.

BACK IN IRELAND after a dozen or more years of education in England I felt rather like a piece of jetsam washed up on its beach of origin, which after so long adrift in salty currents seemed like a foreign shore. What made the shore more foreign than I had hoped it would be was an attitude which pursued and haunted me for very many years. Even now, after fifty years at home, the spectre is not entirely laid to rest. This was the reluctance of the majority of Irish people to accept me, with my background, as a true Irishman. I have already referred to this when describing the legacy of the public school experience. The full force of being branded as an outsider – even a 'West Briton' – was not immediately as strongly apparent as it later became, since for some time my circle of friends were either part of the Anglo-Irish community or intellectuals and artists with an international outlook. It was when I became more involved with the wider Irish community through musical and other public activity that the feeling of being excluded from full acceptance became increasingly acute. Mind you, I realise now that to some extent I had myself to blame. A portion of that patronising British superiority that I so much resented at Rugby had invaded my subconscious thinking. In retrospect there were occasions when I didn't entirely hide a certain arrogance based on the fact that I had had the privilege of a far wider educational experience, particularly in the field of music, than most of the Dublin musicians with whom I came into contact. I shudder when I think of some of the arrogant and tactless criticisms which I was guilty of levelling at Dublin musical life before developing a more mature relationship with people of varying views. Dublin musical life was indeed rather primitive in the early forties when compared to the richness of London, Heidelberg or Cambridge; but I needn't have been so rude about it.

The impact of tribal membership was not always predictable; in fact a bizarre episode in Northern Ireland resulted in a reversed reaction. It was when I was earning a large part of my living by adjudicating competitive music festivals, and was in Derry for the Londonderry Feis – the one that displayed a Union Jack on the platform to advertise its opposition to the rival Gaelic one in the same city. The chairman of the organising committee, an old friend of my father's, came up to me during the first day and said, 'I wonder, Brian, whether you'd be good enough to follow our usual custom whereby the adjudicator plays "God Save the Queen" at the end of the evening session?' With my distaste for national anthems and the tribal emotions they engender – and very particularly in Northern Ireland where the British national anthem seems to be performed as a provocation – I had no wish to be involved. With what I thought was a brilliant inspiration of tact, I explained that since we didn't perform it in the Republic, I hadn't played it for ages, and might well make a mess of it. Two days later the kindly old fellow drew me aside and said, 'You know, Brian, I'm afraid it's being noticed that you have not been playing "The Queen" each evening. I wonder whether, for the sake of your father, you might reconsider your decision.' I then felt that I had to admit to my distaste for national anthems, and declined to oblige him. Many years later, an ex-student of mine was a member of the committee of the same festival. He told me how my name had been suggested as a possible adjudicator for the following year, and an elderly committee member said, 'Oh but we couldn't possibly have that Republican. Don't you know that he actually refused to play "The Queen"?'

When I first came back to live in Dublin, I knew very few people of my own age, and even fewer who shared my outlook and enthusiasms. I had a few anchors from previous years: my sister Yvonne, with whom I have always had a very close and sympathetic relationship; my cousin Alan, who brought me into contact with the theatrical world, including Hilton Edwards and Micheál Mac Liammóir; Charles Acton, whom I had known since Rugby days (though he went to live for some time down in County Wicklow),[1] and Lionel Kerwood, a Cambridge friend who soon came to Dublin to complete his medical training at TCD.[2] We were later to share a house in Rathfarnham.

Then there were the more senior Trinity people whom I had met and continued to meet at my parents' house. Among them were Bedell Stanford, R.B.D. French, H.O. White, George Hewson and David Webb. Stanford, who was Regius Professor of Greek, became an increasingly notable and dignified figure in the college and indeed in the country as a whole as a senator and Pro-Chancellor of the University. He was very interested in music and sang in the university Choral Society. R.B.D. French (always referred to as 'RBD') was a very popular tutor and lecturer in the English department, of which H.O. White was Professor. George Hewson, a very fine organist, was the Professor of Music (whom I was later to succeed). David Webb, who was to become Professor of Botany with a distinguished international reputation, has been a close friend of our family ever since. Then there was William Fearon, who had a tremendous influence on my future. Indeed, ever since he had encouraged me with a gift of apparatus for my laboratory in 1929, he guided my enthusiasms in many varied directions. Many have said of William Fearon that if he had not dissipated his energies in so many different directions he would have been a very great biochemist. As Professor of that subject in TCD he wrote one of the best early textbooks on what was then quite a new subject.[3] He was also for many years a member of the Irish Senate, representing TCD. He also wrote a

---

1. On Charles Acton and his family house at Kilmacurragh, Co. Wicklow, see Pine, *Charles*.
2. Lionel Kerwood, who graduated with Brian from Clare College, Cambridge in 1938, remained in Dublin until 1948. In 1954 he emigrated to Canada where he worked as a doctor and psychiatrist.
3. William Fearon (1892–1959). His *An Introduction to Biochemistry* was first published in 1934 (London: Heinemann) and went into at least four subsequent editions up to the 1960s.

play about Parnell which was put on at the Abbey Theatre;[4] he collected vintage motor cars and drove a Lancia Lambda with great enthusiasm, enjoying the use of the exhaust cut-out which by-passed the silencer so as to intimidate other motorists; he had a great interest in organs, spending much time in assembling one himself; he had written a pantomime song for which he had refused an offer of £5; he had been a friend of George Russell (AE), and numbered an extraordinary variety of diverse characters amongst his friends.[5] I well remember him bringing J.B.S. Haldane and Wee Georgie Wood the comedian on a visit to the zoo on top of the open tram.[6] He introduced me to Philip Dore, who played the cinema organ at the Savoy. We shared a great interest in fireworks. He would attend displays armed with a pocket spectroscope. Pointing it up at a spray of brilliant red stars from a rocket, he would exclaim, 'Ah! … Strontium!' The firework craze nearly led to my early demise, but that is a story more appropriate in another context.[7]

Fearon's infectious interest in motor cars was to have a marked influence on my life-style. When I needed to equip myself with a means of transport, I was thinking of picking up a cheap second-hand 'baby' Fiat. When I asked his advice, he became quite agitated and insisted that I get a REAL motor car. He sent me round to see 'Sonny' Wilders, the scrap merchant in Lad Lane, who had a 1929 Model 40 Bugatti which he might part with for £15. I duly bought it, and during the course of the following year every possible thing went wrong with that machine which had been cruelly maltreated by its previous owner. Often stranded in the depths of the country, one just had to repair the fault or walk many miles home, for there were very few cars on the country roads in those days. With the advice of an elderly and kindly mechanical expert by the name of Nugent, and Grattan Norman who was gifted with mechanical genius, I learned a great deal about motor cars. I soon managed to get hold of a 1926 Type 13 'Brescia' Bugatti for another princely sum of £15, spent many hours reconditioning it and became involved in motor sport.

My involvement with motor cars became one of the many absorbing interests which occupied my time during the war years: in fact, how I

---

4. Fearon served as a member of Seanad Éireann from 1943 until his death; his play *Parnell of Avondale* opened at the Abbey Theatre on 1 October 1934 and ran for fourteen performances.

5. George Russell (1867–1935), also known as 'AE', was a noted Irish poet, writer, artist and mystic. A friend of W.B. Yeats, he was a leading figure in the Irish Literary Renaissance.

6. J.B.S. Haldane (1892–1964), geneticist and populariser of science; George ['Wee Georgie'] Wood (1892–1979), British music hall and variety actor and comedian.

7. See below, pp. 69–70.

found time to do anything else I now find hard to believe. When petrol became almost unobtainable towards the end of 1940, Lionel Kerwood and I sought the cooperation of Grattan Norman in finding out how to run cars on producer gas, using charcoal as a fuel. A producer gas plant should not be confused (as it often is in the memory of some) with the balloon filled with town gas with which some cars were equipped during a short period in the war years. The producer gas apparatus consisted of a steel cylinder about four feet high and two feet in diameter, with an air-tight fuel port at the top end, and a restricted water-cooled air intake at the bottom. Charcoal was burned in the cylinder giving rise to a mixture of carbon monoxide and the unchanged nitrogen from the air. This is producer gas. The very dusty hot gas had to be cooled and filtered by a number of devices varying in design which were inserted in the pipe-line leading to the engine. The cooled gas, which one vainly hoped was free of dust, was introduced to the engine manifold through a mixing valve controlled from the driving seat by a Bowden cable. This introduced the right amount of air for optimum combustion.

Initiating the gas production and starting the engine was a major problem. A draught had to be established through the system by means of a suction-fan. At first we adapted old pre-electric mechanical vacuum cleaners by attaching a handle to one of the wheels which activated the fan. Later we made blades which were fixed to the small twelve-volt electric motors obtained from scrap 'Klaxon' horns. This improved type of fan was incorporated in the gas system. The fan was turned on and a taper of

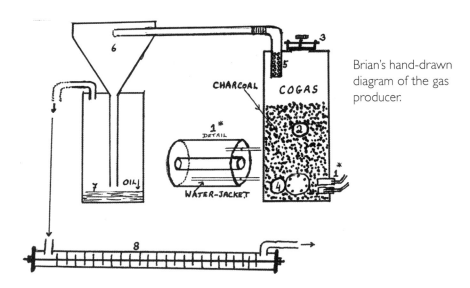

Brian's hand-drawn diagram of the gas producer.

newspaper, lit with a match, was inserted into the air inlet of the furnace. After about ten minutes or so the fire was judged to be providing sufficient combustible gas to try to start the engine. Efficient batteries were hard to come by in those days, so that one seldom could depend on what then was referred to as the 'self-starter', and had to indulge in exhausting exercise with the starting handle.

Before we developed the electric fan and were using the adapted vacuum cleaner, we foolishly never considered the fact that carbon monoxide was streaming out from the contraption as we vigorously twirled the handle. With heavy breathing brought on by exertions with the starting handle, one often inhaled vast quantities of the lethal gas. After completing what proved to be the very first crossing of the country achieved on producer gas, from Dublin to Achill, Lionel Kerwood and I couldn't think why we felt so very ill, with splitting headaches (and he a medical student!). The journey had taken two days, during which we had had to dismantle the engine and remove all the dirt from inefficient filtering, and assemble it again. That was in Athlone. We had had great difficulty getting started after re-assembly, involving re-sealing of all gas-joints with manganese jointing mixture, and vigorous exertions with the starting handle. Once we managed to get going we didn't dare stop for relaxed refreshment, and ate our sandwiches on the move, consuming considerable quantities of the black jointing mixture transferred to the sandwiches from our filthy hands. This, we thought, was the cause of our illness.

What with charcoal dust, engine oil and manganese jointing mixture, we were always absolutely filthy whenever undertaking an extensive journey. When we had to dismantle the engine in Athlone and spend the night there, we were curtly refused accommodation at the Prince of Wales Hotel. Accompanied as we were by my equally filthy fox terrier, I suppose we could hardly blame them. Occasionally I used to stay with Alec Wallace at the Old Head Hotel in Louisburgh, County Mayo. Mary, my wife-to-be, was manageress there at the time and well remembers Mrs Wallace giving instructions that all the chairs should have newspaper covering the seats when they heard that a visit from me was imminent.

Leading on from our pioneering experiments, and as petrol became virtually unobtainable, Lionel, Grattan and I established the commercial firm of Norman, Boydell and Kerwood, manufacturing and fitting COGAS producer plants to clients' cars. Continuing experiments and developments led to great improvements. These included injecting water into the furnace to make a certain proportion of water-gas, with its more powerful hydrogen content. Unlike our rival firms, who relied on a small amount of petrol to get started, we were able to boast that our apparatus needed no petrol whatsoever: for we injected waste oil into the furnace before starting, the resultant 'carburetted water gas' proving more readily combustible.

My connection with the motor business didn't last very long, for I soon came to realise how embarrassingly crooked the business tended to be. I was however never off the road – even going off on our honeymoon in June 1944 in my 3-litre Sunbeam running on gas. By that time virtually every motor accessory had become unobtainable. We finally arrived home with an ominous pink blister of inner tube bulging out through a hole in my very last tyre-cover. As the general petrol starvation increased, some wealthy people managed to keep on the road by paying an exorbitant price on the black market. To avoid drawing attention they would have a producer-gas plant mounted on their car. The gardaí stopped one such motorist who declared that he was legitimately travelling on gas: whereupon it was pointed out to him that his producer apparatus had fallen off his car ten miles back down the road. Such episodes led to the banning of all private cars except those of doctors and some others whose dependence on motor transport was essential to the community. That was why I converted my two-seater Sunbeam into a small lorry. I had a slightly legitimate excuse, for I had helped with a small financial contribution to set up a White Russian refugee named Nic Couriss in the business of making charcoal in Collon, County Louth. My 'lorry' was for delivering the product of Oriel Charcoal Ltd. One needed such bulky supplies of charcoal for any extended journey on gas, so that I always appeared to be delivering our product. I never felt guiltily dishonest about this since with the special improvements we had developed, I never used a drop of petrol, even for starting.

Nic Couriss became a close friend. A remarkable survivor from unbelievable horrors during the Russian revolution, he had escaped to Turkey where he managed to exist by making charcoal; so he was well equipped for his new role in 'Oriel Charcoal'. He lived in the old Court House at Collon with his exceptionally charming wife Ksana, who had the unmistakable bearing of the old Russian aristocracy to which her family had belonged. The other occupant of the Court House was Prince Lieven, who seemed to us then to be immensely old. He spent much of his time developing a special heating stove which burned waste sawdust that the local sawmill was only too glad to get rid of. When we could only obtain a miserable smouldering fire from the damp turf which was the only available fuel, the Court House in Collon was always snugly warm – at least when his special contraption was persuaded to work. After the war, when there was no longer a demand for charcoal, Nic turned to growing mushrooms. In this he was a pioneer in a market which has since become a major industry. The other means of support for the family consisted of taking in members of the diplomatic services as paying guests, and teaching them Russian. After his wife died, Nic made the unexpected decision to become ordained as an Orthodox priest.

A short selection of extracts from the log-book in which meticulous details of every journey and the mechanical work done on the three-litre Sunbeam were recorded will give some idea of the problems and adventures endured by a determined motorist during the war years. The descriptions of extended journeys are usually accompanied by a table consisting of eleven columns: Place; Time; Time of stops; Total time less stops; Time between places; Mileometer reading; Total miles covered; Miles between places; Average speed; Amount of fuel in lbs. added at each refuelling stop; Remarks. A graph incorporating these figures illustrates the table. These details are not included in the following extracts.

Achill, 12 August 1942: Battery was very low and would not turn the engine. Car was dragged to the top of the hill, by Mr Patten's cottage, with the help of a donkey, and then started down the hill.

Achill, 13 August: Children had turned the headlights on, and jammed the self-starter button in. Battery was completely flat. Major Fryer's 6-volt battery was borrowed and one field-winding shorted on the fan. In this way the fire was started. Charcoal was very damp. Meanwhile two 6-volt batteries were borrowed from Anthony O'Malley, and a connection was made with several strands of fencing wire. The car was started down the hill.

Drive from Achill to Dublin, 10 September 1942: A highly successful run … one puncture outside Roscommon. Cylinders nos. 3 & 4 were receiving considerable quantities of dirt. Several changes of plugs in these cylinders were necessary. When the road permitted, a steady 45 mph could be maintained, rising at times to 53.

Dublin, 19/20 November 1942: Fan ceased to function and charging stopped. After a long puzzle it was discovered that the Sunbeam has an insulated return. When the fan was earthed to the insulated return it went so well as to fly to pieces. Work abandoned.

Dublin, 8 December 1942: Hood blew away!

Dublin, December 1942: Near the Pro-Cathedral the accelerator butterfly came adrift, so that the car had to be driven at full throttle as far as Rutland Place, using the ignition switch as a kind of speed control.

Drive from Dublin to Achill, 1 January 1943: A dreadful drive. Owing to damp charcoal, the car refused to start. Being New Year's Day it was two hours before a tow could be obtained. The car was started, and spare charcoal dispatched from the N[orth] Wall.[8] By this time it was 12.30; so after lunch we set off for the West. The car ran very badly, doing less and less to the fill of charcoal – it being noticed that she burned out very near the top.

Near Moate, the luggage caught fire, and two bags of smouldering charcoal had to be thrown away. Near Athlone, the car was going so badly that we decided to stay the night.

2 January: The producer was cleaned out and some awful-looking charcoal purchased for spare.

Car started easily and ran fairly well as far as Roscommon. Speed then gradually fell off, and refuelling became more and more frequent. At about 8.00 p.m. we crawled into Westport with no charcoal left. Having failed to get my own charcoal from the station, some was purchased in the town. After two hours' stop the car refused to start – even down a big hill. Braheny towed me round and round the town, and eventually she started, but would not pick up for several minutes.

Charles [Acton] and Thurloe [Conolly][9] had to push her up the hill outside Westport, and we crawled along in 2nd and 3rd gears, refuelling every six or seven miles until we reached Dugort very late that night, with no more fuel left than would have carried us another 100 yards. (Assisting the inadequate engine-power I was at the controls.)

[*Achill, 3–13 January 1943*: Few details are available here, owing to a general feeling of disgust. The car persistently refused to start, and when it was either towed or pushed it went very badly indeed.]

---

8. The North Wall refers to the docks area of Dublin to the north of the River Liffey.
9. The artist Thurloe Conolly (1918–2016), who married Brian's sister Yvonne in 1946. See also Peter Murray, *The Language of Dreams*, and obituary in *The Irish Times*, 30 April 2016.

13–15 January: Engine taken down. Complete overhaul.

Achill to Louisburgh, 26 January 1943: Car went very well as far as Westport, and then refused to go more than 25 mph – missing consistently. No remedy was found. On Wednesday we made charcoal with Alec Wallace for the run home. Plugs were cleaned and brakes adjusted.

Louisburgh to Dublin, 28 January 1943: Another terrible drive. Leave Old Head at 10.00 a.m. Car went progressively worse; we were constantly changing plugs and refuelling. Eventually it was decided to let out the old charcoal and refill, in case of clinker trouble. The red-hot charcoal was dumped in a blazing serpent on the road. Little or no improvement was noted. Darkness fell shortly after Athlone. By this time we were travelling mostly in 3rd gear at about 20mph, and refuelling every 8–10 miles. Near Moy Valley we saw that there would not be enough fuel to get us home. We luckily managed to pick some up from a sawmill nearby. Imaal was eventually reached at about 1.00 a.m.[10]

Achill Island was a magical haven where a number of my friends and I frequently sought the refuge of isolation from urban pressures and from the madness of a world at war. As an island off the west coast of Mayo (but connected to the mainland by a road bridge over the narrow sound), the timeless grandeur of its dramatic landscape had been carved out by the full forces of the Atlantic throughout millennia. Coming to terms with the power of the sea and the hardships of tempestuous nature had formed the character of the local people, who displayed an inspiring simplicity in their way of life. (A characteristic which was sadly to be eroded as more and more of the islanders sought easy riches as labourers across the water when the English labour force was depleted.) It was a refreshing privilege to become friends with fishermen who were in touch with the timeless forces of nature, as a contrast to city people whose thoughts were taken up with the ephemeral negativeness of rival political ideologies.

I had come to regard Achill as a very special place many years before the war, since the family often spent holidays at the Strand Hotel in Dugort. Tom Sheridan and his Canadian wife Muriel owned this simple, almost primitive, hotel, which served as a hospitable refuge during the war when the rigours of camping in the unpredictable Achill weather became too much for us – as on the occasion when Lionel Kerwood and I undertook

---

10. Imaal was Brian's house in Rathfarnham, Co. Dublin. See further Chapter 4 below.

Brian refuelling his Sunbeam car, July 1942.

a marathon walk all the way around Croaghaun, the highest mountain in Achill. As we wearily came over the pass to descend to our camp in Keem Bay we saw our tent floating out to sea. A freak 'hurricane' occasionally swept down the valley carrying all before it. On this occasion it blew the tent away, but left our bedding soaked through and a suitcase full of rainwater with socks and other clothing floating around it. We also often stayed with Tom and Muriel during the Christmas holidays, when we spent much of the time watching the mighty waves dashing on the rocks, and painting in the glass porch of the hotel.

My first wartime holiday in Achill was with Lionel Kerwood shortly before petrol became unobtainable. We set off in my Model 40 Bugatti early in August 1940, complete with a small tent, a few cooking utensils and my fox-terrier dog. Our first camp was among the sand dunes on the

Mannin peninsula in Connemara; a dream-like place of peace and isolation looking out over the sea to the Twelve Bens and conveniently near to Clifden for provisions. After a few days there we drove northwards towards Achill. As we passed through Leenane we spied a rare Austro-Daimler sports car parked outside the hotel. Driving a Bugatti we were naturally fascinated with this sight of another rare example of famous motor cars and stopped to examine it.[11] We were soon aware of a tall figure in a bowler hat standing beside us. His age and his well-developed paunch didn't seem to indicate that he had anything to do with the car; but he spoke to us: 'Are you interested in my Austro-Daimler? A bit disappointing really; I have never managed to get it to do much over a hundred and five.' This turned out to be Mr Punch, the owner of a boot-polish factory in Cork who had a vast collection of vintage cars including at least two Lancia Lambdas.[12]

Later in the day, after we had passed through Mulranny, we were halted at a crossroads by the Local Defence Force. Some children, just for the fun of it, had reported seeing parachutists descending and the Local Defence Force was called out to hunt down the supposed German spies. Unshaven as we were and driving a strange-looking foreign car complete with our 'parachutes' in the back (our tent), we were quite obviously their prey. During the course of an argument in which our perfect English seemed to be some help, we asked them what they would have done, armed as they were with nothing more lethal than blackthorn sticks, if we had had a machine-gun handily secreted under the supposed parachute. The logic of the scenario was too much for their innocent training and they retorted with confidence that they would have arrested us and brought us to Castlebar for interrogation.

If you pass through the Achill village of Dooagh, which is the most westerly village in Connacht, the motor road going westward ended in those days at the entrance gate to Corriemore House, the home of the eccentric Major Fryer. Thereafter the road petered out into a track suitable for little more than a donkey and cart. It ascends to the old amethyst quarries and then drops steeply down into Keem Bay. Few people penetrated that far except locals tending their sheep and cattle on what was traditionally common land. The track ended at the ruins of the old coastguard station,

---

11. The Austro-Daimler car company existed from 1899 to 1934. Ferdinand Porsche, later to found the car company that still bears his name, was technical director until 1923. Austro-Daimler produced what have been recognised as some of the outstanding cars of the 1920s and 1930s.

12. In 1851 Abigail Punch had opened a tea and coffee trading business in Cork. Her nephew George Punch established the shoe polish manufactory in 1912; it had become a household name by the 1920s.

beautifully sited on level ground overlooking the bay. Between the ruins and the sea, just beside a stone shelter used by the fishermen during the salmon-netting season, a level grassy patch tops a little cliff that juts out above the silver sand just ten yards or so above the high tide. Having successfully negotiated the cart-track in the Bugatti, this is where we pitched our tent and established a handy sheltered kitchen in the fishermen's hut. For extra sleeping comfort we excavated small hollows in the ground and filled them with bracken. These hollows are still there today. Unfortunately, in the very frequent wet weather they filled with water. We soon discovered that when it rained the cart-track became a slimy stream, and we couldn't get the Bugatti up the hill again until we had walked to Dooagh and borrowed shovels to make the track passable.

Shortly after the war some speculator bought the old coastguard ruins and made the cart-track into a motor road. His idea was to build a hotel on the superb site: a plan which was by no means popular with the local people who regarded the area as common grazing land. After the repairs to the road had been completed, the next task was to drain the sodden site. A load of drainage pipes was stacked in readiness. After a weekend the labour force arrived to start the job. All the pipes had disappeared; but every cottage in Dooagh had a new chimney pot. The hotel was never built.

We soon became very friendly with the fishermen who came over from Dooagh to net the mackerel shoals. They helped us to salvage and repair an abandoned currach so that we could have our own boat. We learned the secret of preparing the tar in a cast-iron cauldron over a turf fire, judging the right moment for painting it on the canvas which formed the skin of the boat by spitting into the boiling tar and observing the effect. A currach, though it may appear flimsy enough, is the safest craft on a rough sea; riding the waves rather than being swamped by them, as a heavier boat might be. The chief disadvantage was that, having no keel, the wind would catch the bow and slew the currach off course. The other disadvantage was more the fault of our stupidity. We succeeded one day in fulfilling our ambition to catch a really big conger eel. Monsters were reputed to live out by the point to the west of the bay and we landed a six-footer there. We had been warned that these monsters can bite your hand off, and the best precaution is always to have a large sharp knife handy with which to sever the spinal cord behind the head. In the excitement of the drama we completely forgot the construction of the boat and missed the neck of the squirming eel, plunging the knife through the canvas bottom of the currach, which began to fill with water. There we were, right out at the mouth of the bay and several hundred yards from the shore with the conger eel lashing around in the deepening water and snapping at everything in sight. With our bare feet up on the seats away from the terrifying teeth we only just made it, with the water within six inches of the gunwale.

At the summit of the headland six or seven hundred feet above Keem Bay to the west there was a look-out post established as part of national wartime defence. With no military personnel quartered on the island, volunteers from Dooagh were employed to man this post in shifts of six hours for each pair. This duty involved a three-mile walk each way from the village and included strenuous climbs. Since officers hardly ever came all the way from Castlebar to inspect the post, the volunteers soon lost interest in this arduous and apparently useless activity and frequently neglected their duties. Unfortunately an officer did turn up one day to find the look-out post deserted. The volunteers were all carted off to detention in Castlebar. One of them was the village postman and butcher. The life of the village was put in such disarray that he had to be released. The look-out post, along with certain other vantage-points along the western cliffs, had a special function in certain gales. The local people knew well what winds were likely to bring wreckage ashore, and beach-combing could be a profitable occupation during wartime scarcity. When the winds were suitable, these vantage-points would be manned. The first who spotted wreckage drifting towards land would make a signal to the others, claiming his booty. The claim was always respected, though there was always the risk that the object would turn out to be valueless. With luck it might be a cask of some scarce chemical like acetone. More than once it was a human body. Then there was a crate of condoms (or 'French Letters' as we called them then). Unfortunately they had perished in the sea water and the Achill birth-rate is said to have increased alarmingly. They didn't bother about the plentiful timber wreckage, so that we had ample fuel for a fire in the fishermen's hut. For a time we cooked our meals on the remains of a cabin door which, with a three-figure number on it, most probably must have come from the ill-fated *Arandora Star*.[13]

With the great difficulty of getting the car over the hill on the track to the village, our currach was an easier form of transport for supplies. To reach the village involved negotiating a narrow channel between rocky islands at the exposed eastern mouth of the bay. In stormy weather this could be an

---

13. The *Arandora Star*, carrying German and Italian internees and prisoners of war from Liverpool to Canada, was sunk off the north-west coast of Ireland by a German U-boat on 2 July 1940 with the loss of over 800 lives.

exciting experience. I say 'exciting' advisedly; for we had what the fishermen rightly regarded as a foolhardy disregard for physical danger, which we found stimulating. It would be quite wrong to describe such escapades as courageous. On one such occasion we rigged up a primitive kind of sail and having safely negotiated the boiling sea around the rocks sailed into Dooagh harbour with the assistance of a westerly gale. We were met by an angry group of fishermen who were furious with us for our madness. Knowing the dangers of the sea they wouldn't dream of venturing out in such weather.

I think it is true to say that I have never been really frightened by natural or impersonal situations. On the other hand, what really scares me is to be faced with the threat of violent human antagonism, such as one feels when faced with a gang of bullies. In situations of the former kind any feeling of fear becomes replaced with one of challenge and the excitement of overcoming the threat of danger. This is surely what must be at the back of the minds of those who enjoy such activities as arctic exploration, climbing precipitous mountains, sailing around the world, or motor racing. Feelings of fear can also be suppressed when, as a member of a team with the single-minded purpose of winning a physically taxing athletic challenge, one plunges into a rugby scrum without thought of the possibility of being trampled on by studded football boots. I suspect that this same suppression of fear must often have made it possible for soldiers in warfare to enact such unbelievable feats of 'bravery'. But what is bravery? For me, a really courageous act of bravery is one where there is the opportunity to consider the consequences of the action with cool reasoning, before the stimulus of hurling oneself into the fray suppresses fear. I do not regard our foolhardy escapades with the currach in the wild seas of Achill as being brave: just an intensely exciting experience.

Another episode, which happened some years later, provided further insight into the nature of what some might mistakenly call 'bravery'. I was staying in Glenbeigh in County Kerry near the Behy river. Sea trout would run up this 'spate' river in a flood, and as the water level began to fall, the fishing was at its best. It had rained all one Saturday and cleared up in the evening. I knew that if I went out at dawn on Sunday morning, the water would be ideal. On the upper reaches of the river, high up in the valley and surrounded by bogland with not a sign of human habitation, I put on my long thigh waders, waterproof fishing coat and tweed hat. With landing net slung over the shoulders and a carefully chosen cast of flies ready on the rod, I approached the river. The conditions were ideal. Within a short time I had landed two good sea trout. Then there was an almighty pull on the line: I had hooked one of the occasional salmon that were reputed to ascend the river. It jumped clear of the water so that I could see that it was a grilse (young salmon) of about 7 lbs. After a minute or so during which my light trout tackle could make no impression on the fish, it turned and bolted downstream towards the sea. I looked down the bank. It was so overgrown with sally bushes that there was obviously no hope of following the fish on dry land. Without a thought of danger I took the only alternative course and jumped into the swirling waters. At one moment I was bumping over boulders and then, arriving in a deeper pool, I was out of my depth with my mouth just above the surface and the rod held high over my head. The salmon halted its headlong rush and stopped in the deep pool. The technique is to get below the fish, persuading it to move upwards against the current and the tension of the line. I crawled out onto the bank only to discover that my water-logged clothes were so heavy that I could scarcely manage to stand up and play the fish. No sooner did I apply the classic pull from below but the fish turned and made off downstream once again. There was nothing to do but plunge in and follow it again. This drama was repeated through several deep pools. After travelling thus downstream for about half a mile, I arrived in a deep pool once again with the salmon still on my line. Only then did I realise that I was completely exhausted and had the utmost difficulty keeping my mouth above the surface of the water. I was going to drown. I somehow just managed to make it to the bank, complete with hat, landing net, fishing bag and all the rest of the gear. But the salmon had bolted once again and broken the cast in its dash to the safe haven of the sea.

Was I brave? Not at all. It was an intensely exciting experience, even though it ended in disappointment. Any disappointment at failing to land the fish was somewhat tempered by my admiration for the cleverness of the fish, and also by hearing locally that the only salmon ever landed from the Behy river were caught on extra-heavy tackle of at least 25 lbs breaking-strain.

To return once more to Achill ….
The basking sharks that came into the bay in warm summer weather could be quite alarming. Though they are harmless and docile, they could easily overturn a currach with a careless swish of the tail-fin. Charles Acton was staying with me one summer and we were out fishing in the boat when one of these huge fish surfaced very close to us. Charles has never been

known to exert himself physically if he could avoid it. On this occasion he grabbed the oars and in panic rowed madly away from the scene with a burst of physical energy, which I never saw him display before or since.

Lionel Kerwood and I became intoxicated with 'boulderage' – rolling great boulders down the side of a mountain, or over a cliff. We took it very seriously and constantly aimed at more ambitious and dramatic undertakings, even spending most of the day dislodging an 'enormoid' weighing several tons with the help of crowbars and a hydraulic car-jack. We soon learned a lesson which could provide valuable advice to anyone who might be tempted to indulge in this fascinating occupation: never do boulderage down a convex slope, since you can't see all the way down to be sure that no living creatures are in the line of fire. On one occasion, before we had realised this danger, we spent a whole afternoon above the cliffs on Saddle Head, having developed the art of choosing slate-like rocks which were of the right shape to go hurtling down like spinning cartwheels. Late that evening when cooking the supper in our hut an irate shepherd appeared at the door. He had been tending his sheep on a precarious path half way down this cliff just beyond where the slope hid our view. Not knowing when the boulders would stop hurtling down from above, he didn't dare emerge from a safe shelter under a rock. What annoyed him most was that he had run out of cigarettes. The fact that we had killed two of his sheep seemed a minor concern, satisfactorily settled by giving him the price of the sheep.

After camping for two summers in Keem Bay I got to know Stella Frost, a sensitive water-colour artist who owned an isolated cottage west of Dooagh.[14] She was only too glad to allow fellow artists the use of her well-equipped dwelling when not using it herself. I spent the month of August there in 1942 and the following year. It was not so far from Major Fryer's Corriemore House, where he ran an eccentric hotel. When prospective guests arrived expecting a porter to appear and carry in their baggage, the Major would watch them, observing whether they considered themselves too grand for such a demeaning task. If they failed to satisfy his test he forthwith refused to take them in. The few who qualified for admission would seldom know when the next meal would appear, and were expected to assist in entertaining casual visitors who dropped in for his open-house sessions of morris dancing on Sunday afternoons.

The story went that Major Fryer had been in the British army Medical Corps stationed in India and he had cured a member of the family of a

14. An Achill landscape by Stella Frost (1890–1962) hangs in the collection of the Crawford Gallery, Cork. She edited *A Tribute to Evie Hone and Mainie Jellett* (Dublin: Browne & Nolan, 1957).

very wealthy Maharajah. It was forbidden for a member of His Majesty's forces to receive any monetary reward for such services. When offered a real chest of jewels, just like Aladdin would have conjured up, he couldn't resist such a reward. He retired from the army to spend the remainder of his days enjoying his quite eccentric idea of luxury. One of the Major's eccentricities took the form of an inability to understand why artists or gardeners did not regard an invitation to beautify his property as an unpaid privilege. He broke off relations with his neighbour Stella Frost, who besides being an artist was a professional gardener, because she declined to spend six months in residence designing and replanting his estate. He had been a friend of the British sculptor Jacob Epstein (whom he referred to as 'Eppie') and offered him the unique opportunity of executing an immense monumental sculpture on the cliff-face of the mountain behind his house. When 'Eppie' declined, the friendship came to an end.[15]

Since we were his nearest neighbours in Stella Frost's cottage, he enjoyed an occasional visit from us. The conversation was usually entertaining and there was the added advantage of being able to have a real hot bath. During the first summer there he invited us to dinner for his birthday. I can't remember who was staying with me in the cottage that year – probably Lionel. We had been out fishing all day and were eagerly looking forward to the birthday dinner. We duly arrived at half-past seven to discover that the Major had only just got up and was going to have his breakfast. The post had arrived with a parcel from Arnotts containing a new pair of grey flannel trousers which he had ordered.[16]

Considering it unseemly to be dressed like a businessman in smart clothes, he promptly took his penknife and made the trousers more suitable to his taste by slashing each leg. When he had finished his breakfast he started to read for our entertainment the stories he had written and published over the years in *Punch*. This recital went on and on and on while we were getting more and more desperate with hunger. At last, near midnight, dinner was announced. This turned out to be the sort of dainty repast that later became known as 'nouvelle cuisine': one tiny sliver of meat meticulously decorated with a single baby carrot, a brussel sprout and a leaf of lettuce. The sort of dish more suitable for an exhibition of minimalist abstract design. The following year I received a similar invitation. This time we

---

15. Jacob Epstein (1880–1959) was born in New York but became a British citizen in 1911. He was a pioneering figure in modern British sculpture and a major influence on the younger Henry Moore and Barbara Hepworth. His often controversial works include the tomb of Oscar Wilde in Paris (1914) and *St Michael's Victory over the Devil* at the new Coventry Cathedral (1958).

16. Arnotts of Henry Street is Dublin's oldest department store, established in 1843.

were wise and had a substantial meal before turning up about half an hour after the appointed time. He was standing on the entrance steps in a rage over our lateness and herded us straight in to the most enormous meal of roast 'mountainy' mutton. Many years later I became very friendly with his son Grattan who was a pioneer as an artist in pottery, having studied with the legendary Bernard Leach.[17] Grattan didn't have a great deal of use for his father![18]

Memories of motoring and Achill holidays have carried us beyond the chronological story. I must return to the beginning of 1940. My father rightly considered that I should start to earn my living, and I was installed as the biochemist in the laboratory of John Plunkett & Co. at a salary of five pounds per week. My cousin Alan was also working there, for his father (my 'Uncle Will') was my father's senior partner. During particularly busy periods, such as the hourly estimation of the colour and protein-content of amber malt during the period it was being roasted, Alan acted as my assistant.[19]* Apart from such busy periods, the work was mainly concerned with the routine estimation of the moisture content of home-grown wheat, which in the damp Irish climate had to be dried on the malt kilns for storage by Bolands Flour Mills. To occupy my time more interestingly, I became involved in research with the aim of reducing the growing time needed to convert barley to malt and in searching for vitamins and nutritional trace-elements which might lie hidden in the malt combings which were disposed of as cattle-feed.[20]*

To stimulate my research, it was arranged that I should be brought around the extensive Guinness laboratory by their head chemist (I think his name was Tullow). The youthful arrogance of the recent Cambridge graduate with a first-class degree in biochemistry was talked about in shocked voices for a long time after the remark I made criticising what I considered to be an out-of-date method of estimating sugar content. The

17. Bernard Leach (1887–1979) was one of the most influential British potters of the twentieth century. He lived in Japan between 1911 and 1920 studying under traditional Japanese potters. Returning to England, he established his pottery at St Ives, Cornwall, producing simple, utilitarian ceramics influenced by Asian traditions. His *A Potter's Book*, first published in 1940 (London: Faber & Faber), was hugely influential.

18. The potter Grattan Freyer (1915–83) and his wife Madeleine (1909–99) had both trained with Bernard Leach. They founded the Terrybaun Pottery in County Mayo in 1950. See Peter Lamb, 'A Kiln Fired by Turf: Grattan Freyer and the Terrybaun Pottery', *Irish Arts Review*, vol. 16 (2000), pp. 63–72.

19.* Lightly roasted 'amber' malt was an ingredient in Export Stout. I believe it is no longer used today. [Author's note]

20.* Malt combings are the small rootlets that develop as barley grains sprout during the malting process. They become detached as the finished malt is dried on the kiln. [Author's note]

latest Cambridge teaching was that Benedict's reagent had superseded older methods. I observed a chemist involved in this test and exclaimed 'What! You don't mean to say that you still use Fehling's solution?' After some years, any who may have remembered my cheeky insult could have the laugh on me; for I hear that in the light of some years' experience, Benedict was found to be far less reliable than trusty old Fehling.

Towards the end of my first year as a maltster's biochemist, a refugee who had done research in an Austrian brewery arrived in Dublin. It was arranged that I should meet him. He listened attentively as I described my tentative research ambitions, and then turned to me with grave advice: 'I'm afraid, my dear boy, that most of this work has been attempted by many of our biochemists. My advice to you is to spend a few years reading in the library. Then you might come and discuss your ideas with me, and we might outline some plan for useful future research.' I was so deflated that I decided there and then to abandon any idea of pursuing a career as a biochemist.

This decision was not as difficult to make as it might seem, for I was then becoming more and more involved in Dublin musical life and the artistic community. But I had to face the problem of earning a living. Somehow or other – I'm not quite sure how it came about – I was invited to take over the art classes at St Columba's College, a public school of Anglo-Irish background situated in the foothills of the Dublin mountains. I had no qualifications whatever for such a job, other than being a keen amateur painter. It was a part-time position, so that I was able to fit it in with continuing routine work at the maltings. I was eventually able to give up this latter work as I developed a reputation as a singer, oboist and teacher of voice production: the beginnings of a musical career. Joseph Groocock was the inspiring teacher in charge of music at St Columba's, and I was careful not to invade his domain. We became very firm friends, and we, and our families, have remained so ever since. I was very much later able to take advantage of the benefit of his outstanding teaching by having him appointed as a part-time member of the staff of the School of Music in TCD. I have never come across anyone, anywhere, with such outstanding ability to impart his penetrating knowledge of counterpoint, fugue and the music of J.S. Bach.[21]

I entered enthusiastically into the unknown territory of teaching 'Art' to teenage schoolboys, becoming caught up in many new ideas about education

---

21. Joseph Groocock's *Fugal Composition: a guide to the study of Bach's '48'* was published post-humously in 2003 (ed. Yo Tomita, Westport, Connecticut/London: Greenwood Press). Groocock died in 1997. See further *EMIR*, pp. 448–9, and numerous references in Part II: Diary (below).

in the arts, such as those pioneered by Herbert Read.[22] The major problem was how to free young people from the shackles of self-conscious attempts to produce photographic realism – the legacy of having to draw umbrellas – and bring out a freedom of fluid line in drawing related to a developing sense of balanced composition. These were some of the problems. To try to find an answer to them, I sought the help of Mainie Jellett, and became her pupil. Her lessons were inspiring, and her broad-minded tolerance of all the experimental ideas in contemporary creative thinking encouraged me to pursue my painting far more seriously than I had ever done before; soon becoming involved with many of the more adventurous painters in Dublin – particularly those associated with the White Stag Group.

My activities at St Columba's were not confined to the duties for which I had been appointed. With my great interest in natural history, particularly geology, I was goaded into action by the lack of encouragement given to the boys to develop an awareness of their natural surroundings. Much to the irritation of some of the more traditional members of the staff, who considered that I was distracting their pupils from serious study, I formed a Natural History Society, and organised geological field trips. I also invited experts in their various fields, including such distinguished scientists as Frank Mitchell,[23] to give lectures to the Society.

When some masters had to be absent through illness, I was asked to take over certain classes. I was even drafted in to take the senior class in English, for which I had even less qualification than the teaching of art. In this case I was however able to infect some of them with my enthusiasm for Yeats and Joyce. When the science master was ill, I was well qualified to take over; though my method of teaching was largely responsible for my leaving the college under a cloud of disgrace. I have always believed that class teaching should be made as enjoyable and lively as possible, avoiding the pompous academic approach such as had almost ruined any enjoyment of Shakespeare at Rugby. Young people often retain important basic

22. A leader of the radical avant-garde in the 1930s and 1940s, the literary critic, philosopher and art historian Herbert Read (1893–1968) exerted a strong influence on the role of art in education. He believed that everyone has inherent artistic qualities, and that the teaching of refined aesthetics could lead to social harmony. His theories of what might today be described as 'soft' anarchism and his concept of the organic in art are reflected in Brian's non-conformist and artistic views.

23. Frank Mitchell (1912–97), Professor of Quaternary Studies at TCD from 1965 to 1979, President of the Royal Irish Academy (1976–9), and also President of both the Royal Society of Antiquaries of Ireland and of An Taisce, was an outstanding naturalist, geologist, botanist and geographer. His publications include *The Irish Landscape* (London: Collins, 1976), *The Shell Guide to Reading the Irish Landscape* (Dublin: Michael Joseph, 1986), and *Archaeology and Environment in Early Dublin* (Dublin: Royal Irish Academy, 1987).

knowledge if it is related to some entertaining relevant anecdote. Not being so very much older than the boys in the class I was teaching, and knowing well the sort of stories they found amusing amongst themselves, I didn't see any reason why I should hypocritically assume the dignity more usually expected of a pedagogue and not share their sense of slightly naughty fun. In a biology class, I told the story of a master at Rugby, who having drawn on the blackboard some strange parasite, turned to the class and provided an unforgettable spoonerism: 'This animal has sore fuckers'. A wretched little boy wrote this down in his notebook, which was later inspected by his horrified parents who wrote a pungent letter of complaint to the reverend headmaster.

In parallel with my painting studies, I took regular lessons with Dr John Larchet in preparation for taking the examinations for Bachelor in Music (Mus.B.) at TCD (where at that time there was no teaching in this subject).[24] Unlike Mainie Jellett, Larchet was not a really inspiring teacher, but exceptionally sound in his ability to impart technical facility, which was what was needed for the examination. Beyond the field of purely technical matters, we held somewhat opposing views concerning creative composition. With admirable workmanship, he followed in the Charles V. Stanford/ Hamilton Harty tradition of music based on Irish melodies, or tunes with an Irish flavour, dressed in the harmonic idiom of Germanic romanticism. I was much more interested in the newer European developments in musical language, and was already reacting against self-conscious nationalism. I must say however that Larchet exhibited a remarkable though hardly enthusiastic tolerance of my 'modern' tendencies, and was always most supportive in my efforts to build a reputation as a composer. Many years later, he was largely responsible for swinging the opinion of the assessors when I was appointed to the Chair of Music in the University of Dublin (TCD).

Having by now decided that the main thrust of my career should be as a musician, I set about obtaining reasonable qualifications with a Licentiate of the RIAM in the teaching of singing, and a Bachelor of Music from the University of Dublin. I also became increasingly involved in Dublin musical life.

---

24. An influential figure in Irish musical life, John F. Larchet (1884–1967) taught composition at the RIAM between 1920 and 1955 and was Professor of Music at UCD from 1921 to 1958. He was a composer principally of miniatures and an arranger of Irish melodies, while as music director at the Abbey Theatre from 1908 to 1935 he composed the incidental music to plays by W.B. Yeats and others.

CHAPTER 3
MAINLY MUSICAL

M Y FIRST IMPORTANT musical contact in Dublin was Havelock Nelson, who with one or two others had recently formed what soon became the chief amateur orchestra in the city.[1] At first it was named the Dublin Junior Orchestra, since its original aim was to provide a training ground for Signor Grossi's Musical Arts Society orchestra. This was a semi-professional body which in the absence of any professional symphony orchestra at that time was the sole purveyor of orchestral music in Dublin.[2] Under Havelock's enthusiastic leadership the junior orchestra soon outstripped its senior in public acclaim and changed its title to the Dublin Orchestral Players (DOP), which still flourishes today after more than fifty years.[3] When the orchestra was founded just after the outbreak of war in 1939, Havelock invited me to join as second oboe and cor anglais, sitting next to a kindly English professional who had retired to live in Dublin. This was Harry Baxter, who played the first oboe part. We rehearsed once a week in the parish hall of St Andrew's church in Suffolk Street, each member putting sixpence in a tin box to cover the rent of the hall. The first public concert was given in the Abbey Lecture Hall on 5 June 1940. In 1943 Havelock left Dublin for the position of accompanist at the BBC in Belfast, and I became the permanent honorary conductor, continuing in that post until other commitments obliged me to retire in 1966.[4]

1. Havelock Nelson (1917–96) had studied at the RIAM and read medical science and music at TCD, completing his Doctorate in Medical Science in 1943. He later obtained a MusD from TCD in 1950. He was appointed staff accompanist at BBC Northern Ireland in Belfast in 1947, where he spent the rest of his life active as a central figure in local musical life. See further *EMIR*, pp. 732–3; Alasdair Jamieson, *Music in Northern Ireland – Two Major Figures: Havelock Nelson (1917–1996) and Joan Trimble (1915–2000)* (Tolworth: Grosvenor House Publishing, 2017); and Part II: Diary (below).
2. The Italian violinist Feruccio Grossi (born *c.* 1876) had taught in Cork in the 1920s and played in the band for the short-lived Cork radio station (6CK), which operated from 1927 to 1930. He then moved to Dublin where he became deputy leader of the studio band at 2RN (later to become RÉ) and taught at the RIAM.
3. And, indeed, still today (2018) after more than seventy-five years.
4. *Recte*: Nelson left Dublin in late 1943, not to take up the position of accompanist at the BBC (which was in 1947) but to accept a commission in England in the medical branch of the Royal Air Force. See *EMIR*, p. 732 and Jamieson, *Music in Northern Ireland,* p. 6.

Apart from the stimulus of the challenge to maintain the spirit of Havelock's leadership, to have one's own tame orchestra proved to be of incalculable value to me as a composer and provided my basic experience as an orchestral conductor. The organisation of an amateur musical society made up of so many diverse and musically active personalities was a most valuable training, needing as much imagination and diplomacy as musicianship. What was one to do, for instance, about the first clarinet player? He was a very senior retired professional who knew far better than I how the standard classical works should be played and totally disregarded my gestures and interpretive suggestions. He went his own way, completely disrupting the ensemble. Furthermore, sitting firmly in the first player's seat, he effectively closed the door on younger players who needed the encouragement of a chance to play some of the more rewarding solo passages. To overcome this problem, and correctly anticipating his reaction, I introduced the idea that, provided suitably competent players were available, there would no longer be permanent first and second players in the wind section. They would rather share the more rewarding first part by changing places for certain items in the programme. When P.K. was thus asked to play second clarinet in one of the less important works, he was so offended that he resigned, leaving his place to be filled by an excellent younger musician (John Miley) who had patiently been waiting in the wings.

Another problem of a major kind which faces the conductor of any amateur music society was unfortunately not resolved with such success. Does an amateur orchestra exist for the enjoyment of the faithful core of players who have paid their subscriptions and attended with regularity over the years and who have passed the age when there is an incentive to improve their technical ability; or should the aim of the society be concerned with a continual improvement in the standard of performance? It is very difficult to persuade young talent to join a group of ageing senior amateurs, with a result that the standard of performance gradually deteriorates. To overcome this problem I initiated what I thought was a brilliant idea. In each concert there would be one item in which the best players, selected by audition, would form a smaller group for the performance with a higher standard of some lightly scored piece such as an eighteenth-century sinfonia. The scheme seemed likely to provide the necessary incentive for some of the older players to do some practice. The auditions were duly held; but, much to our embarrassment, a player with a wealthy and influential husband, who had generously provided financial support for the orchestra over the years, was so obviously hopeless that we couldn't possibly admit her to the select group.

The husband, who was convinced that his wife was a top-class player with a superior musical background, took it as a calculated personal insult. The lady resigned forthwith and it was made clear that we no longer could rely on their valuable financial support. He even went so far as to influence the press critics to produce scathing reviews of our hoped-for triumph.

A rather similar situation happened when Joseph Groocock was conductor of the University of Dublin Choral Society. For their performances they relied on an amateur orchestral group which understandably welcomed members of the college staff or their spouses. For many years the cello section had been led by a lady whose brother had become Provost by the time that her ability as a cellist had deteriorated disastrously. On the advice of Joe Groocock, the student committee decided that she must be persuaded to retire. Undergraduate honorary secretaries of college societies rarely have the sensitivity and tact to write the right kind of letter in such circumstances. This situation proved no exception. The Provost, who was not very musical and believed that his sister was the finest cellist in Dublin, was furious. Poor Joe was summoned to his presence and accused of engineering a sinister plot to undermine his sister's reputation.

The DOP played what might appear to be its most significant role in Dublin musical life during the first ten or so years of its existence. Not only did it provide a training ground for many orchestral players who later became members of the professional radio orchestras, but it supplied the demand for symphonic music during the period when very few concerts of this kind were available, and it introduced many works to Dublin for the first time. Most significantly these included new works by Irish composers; also the first Dublin performances of standard classics such as the keyboard concertos of J.S. Bach and Mozart's Bassoon Concerto, and – believe it or not – the first European performance outside Russia of Prokofiev's *Peter and the Wolf*. At their tenth anniversary concert in June 1949 Hugh Maguire (who later had a distinguished career in England, becoming leader of the BBC Symphony Orchestra) made his first appearance as a soloist in a Mozart violin concerto; and the orchestra provided the opportunity for numerous other young Irish musicians who later became distinguished players to make their debut as concerto soloists. In those days the DOP had the field to itself and apparently gave pleasure, since it managed on occasion to fill the large and rather unattractive Metropolitan Hall in Abbey Street (which has now disappeared: it was acoustically splendid but looked rather as though someone had tried to convert a railway station into an evangelical temple). As conductor of the orchestra at the time, I know that

Final rehearsal for the DOP's tenth anniversary concert on 16 June 1949 at the Metropolitan Hall, Lower Abbey Street, with the string section playing Sibelius' *Romance in C for Strings*, op. 42. Note that both Brian and two of the cellists are smoking, despite the 'Smoking strictly prohibited' sign!

COURTESY OF *THE IRISH TIMES*

many of the performances were very scrappy; though I do believe that they were inspired by an infectious pioneering enthusiasm; and it is surprising the number of people who have since expressed their gratitude for the pleasure they got from our concerts in those far-off days when the availability of music was so much less plentiful than it is today.

Perhaps the greatest publicity hit for the DOP in those years was the concert in March 1950, given in the Metropolitan Hall.[5] I well remember the thrill of arriving to conduct the concert and seeing a queue of people waiting to get in which stretched most of the way to Marlborough Street. The reason for this great crowd was a combination of novelty in the form of what I believe was the first and only performance in Ireland of the symphony by Beethoven which we don't mention, 'Wellington's Victory', and the loyalty the public felt for the most popular pianist of the time, Charles Lynch, who was to play Beethoven's third concerto. Both attractions were backed up by a carefully contrived publicity drive. Beethoven, in this so-called 'Battle Symphony', asks in the score for French and English cannons, representing the opposing forces at the Battle of Vittoria. We wrote a letter to the *Evening Mail* requesting the loan of a pair of cannon for a forthcoming symphony concert. This extraordinary, unexplained request gave rise to banner headlines such as 'Musicians go to war!', and 'Mr Boydell in the bomber command', and a pseudo-serious leader in the *Evening Mail*. One of the more amusing aspects of this affair, which didn't come out into the open, was the strong division of opinion on the committee between those who deemed it highly inappropriate to play the second movement (which features variations on the British national anthem), and a mischievous group of us who wanted to play it and see part of the audience standing up and another section hurling abuse. Caution prevailed and it was omitted.

Another particular attraction offered at this concert was a performance of Haydn's 'Farewell' Symphony enacted in the traditional manner with house lights down and candles on the music stands. As each player finished his or her part in the final movement, the candle was snuffed and the player left the stage, finally leaving the first desk of fiddles and the conductor with just our two candles. Just as on another occasion in the Cork City Hall, there were alarming accidents as members fell off the stage in the darkness, injuring either themselves or their instruments.

Inadequate staging in those makeshift days of scarcity was apt to be hazardous. The small Abbey Lecture Hall, where we frequently gave our less ambitious concerts, had such a small stage that it had to be extended

5. The concert took place on 2 March. See Part II: Diary (below).

in order to accommodate the orchestra. The conductor and his wife, and a couple of volunteers who were fortunate enough not to be bound by normal working hours, would be seen driving through the streets of the city with a horse and cart carrying timpani, music stands, double basses, and a pile of trestle tables with which to extend the platform. On more than one occasion, as this gimcrack affair started to sway during a vigorous *allegro*, the general anxiety nearly resulted in a complete collapse of the performance.

As we emerged from the period when we benefited from the position of being the only regular providers of public orchestral concerts in Dublin, and when neither of the schools of music had student orchestras, it was necessary to diversify the role of the orchestra in order to ensure the vitality of its future. The DOP now developed the idea of bringing orchestral music to schools, and also to those provincial towns which had never had the opportunity of hearing live symphonic music. Apart from special visits to Cork, and joint concerts with the Studio Symphony Orchestra of Belfast (which Havelock Nelson had founded there on the model of the DOP in Dublin), these 'country' concerts were confined to towns within a radius of Dublin which allowed the players to travel in private cars and return the same evening. (This was after the war, when petrol had once again become available.) The enthusiastic reception in towns such as Drogheda, Carlow, Athlone, Mullingar, Portarlington and Dundalk more than compensated for the anxiety suffered by those whose responsibility it was to see that a large group of assorted characters would arrive in time to work out how the orchestra should be accommodated in a hall that had never before coped with such an array of musicians – let alone be in time for the concert itself. A clairvoyant soloist correctly predicted that the car in which he was travelling would end up in a ditch; and why was it that it was always certain members of the brass section who would last have been seen entering a pub, on the way?

Quite apart from the general social upheaval during the war, Dublin musical life had hardly begun to develop when considered in the light of today's flood of live events. Apart from a short experimental period, it wasn't until the end of the forties that we had regular orchestral concerts here; and the depletion of the English orchestras meant that very little good music was available on the wireless (as we called it). Those of us who wished to explore what the world of music had to offer had to resort to gramophone records; and they were then so limited in scope, and the long-playing record or the CD hadn't been dreamed of. However, did we listen with pleasure through all that hissing and scratching, and jumping up every three minutes or so to turn over the record? We did of course: in fact some of the most moving and exciting musical experiences I remember include evenings spent with my friend Ralph Cusack the painter, during the war years.[6] Ralph and I were both avid collectors of records, and he had the most extensive collection of anyone I knew. Long sessions beginning on Saturday afternoon and stretching to dawn on Sunday morning and often continuing again after a couple of hours' sleep, were spent exploring new paths in music as we listened to his EMG gramophone with the thorn needles and the enormous exponential horn about five feet long. The thrill of exploration was so much more fun in the days of scarcity: the mine of treasures was so difficult and often impossible to excavate.

One source of our mine of treasure was the record shop in Johnson's Court presided over by the vast adipose figure of Mr Moiselle and his daughter Ellie, who was constantly brewing cups of tea that you could trot a mouse on in days when no one else could get hold of more than an ounce of tea in a week. I remember the excitement when the first recording of the twelve *Concerti Grossi* of Handel came out (just imagine regarding that well-known series of works as a rare treasure to explore and you'll realise how rich and 'spoilt' we are today!).[7] The records were duly ordered, and after allowing for the expected delay for consignments of that kind to get through the chaos of 'the Emergency', I called to see if they had arrived. Mr Moiselle was as usual seated on his wooden chair behind the counter with a stained cup of tea in his hands and his body melting over the sides of the chair like hot candle-wax. My enquiry elicited a sadly familiar dialogue. 'Eh, Ellie, did them *Grossi* (*Gross-i* to rhyme with 'tie') things come in for Mr Boydell?' And then Ellie's voice from the tea-brewing cubicle somewhere at the back of the shop: 'Ah sure Father Hickey of Castleknock was in yesterday and took the only set that came in'. I never met Father Hickey of Castleknock – somehow he always seemed to get there first. If only he had known how many records in his apparently colossal collection were swiped from under the nose of another contester in the greedy race to obtain such scarce musical treasures!

How was it that we obtained such pleasure and excitement from the old '78' records, which no one would deign to listen to now? I think the

---

6. A cousin of Mainie Jellett, Ralph Cusack (1912–65) lived outside Roundwood, County Wicklow. He returned to the south of France (where, for health reasons, he had been living before the war) in 1954 and published the novel *Cadenza* in 1958 (London: Hamish Hamilton). See also frequent mentions in Part II: Diary (below).

7. The first complete recording of Handel's *Concerti Grossi* op. 6 was made in the late 1930s by Boyd Neel with the Boyd Neel Orchestra.

answer is that we used our imagination. The gramophone was regarded as a reminder, or an evocative taste of the real thing. Mind you, I had had the good fortune to experience a great deal of live music of the highest standard before the war, when I was a music student in London; and that must be part of the experience necessary to be able to enjoy inadequate recordings. I do believe that the depth of our enjoyment of things is in some way related to the effort put into our appreciation of them; and the exercise of our imagination is an important part of this effort.

To give an idea of the insatiable appetite we shared during the many regular marathon sessions with Ralph's gramophone, I quote a list of what we listened to on one weekend in April 1941, which I had noted in a diary of the time.

Saturday 5 April
Afternoon:
Mahler, *Kindertotenlieder*
Vincent D'Indy, Symphony in G major, op. 25
Roussel, Symphony in G minor

Evening:
J.S. Bach, Klavier Concerto in A
J.S. Bach, Violin Concerto in A minor
Handel, Concerto Grosso [op. 6] no. 10
Vivaldi, Concerto Grosso no. 6[8]
Hahn, *L'heure exquise*
Fauré, *L'automne* and *Clair de lune*
Hahn, *D'un prison*
Milhaud, *Le printemps*
Milhaud, *Concertino de printemps*
Prokofiev, Violin Concerto no. 2
J.S. Bach, Klavier Concerto in F minor
J.S. Bach, Brandenburg Concerto no. 4

Sunday 6 April
Morning:
Gretchaninov, *Credo*
Archangelsky, *Credo*

8. It is not clear which of Vivaldi's concertos this refers to. The occasion of this listening session in April 1941 predates Bernardino Molinari's 1942 recording of Vivaldi's 'Four Seasons' (op. 8, nos 1–4) with the Orchestra dell'Accademia di Santa Cecilia issued in Italy, which is widely credited as being the first recording of Vivaldi.

Afternoon:
Part II of J.S.Bach's *St Matthew Passion*

Evening:
Haydn, String Quartet in G, op. 3 no. 5
Mozart, Violin Concerto in G, K216
Prokofiev, Violin Concerto no. 2
Brahms, Symphony no. 3.

I'm not quite sure how I first got to know Ralph Cusack. It was when, as a returned exile, I was exploring and developing a new network of friends and kindred spirits. Ralph was undoubtedly one of the most stimulating people I have had the privilege to meet, and we became very close friends. He was however an uncomfortable friend to have. He was one of those whom I regard to be of immense value in a community, who held passionate opinions and never hesitated to express them no matter whom he was confronting. Not everyone took kindly to the violent torrent of abuse which he would deliver when faced with hypocrisy or humbug. The trouble was that if you disagreed with him about any of his most ardent prejudices he would react with violence which was often totally uncontrolled. It is difficult to compose a descriptive portrait of Ralph which gives a positive impression of his great value in the community without stressing what would seem to be the negative effects of the very many dramatic events in which he featured: for it is the drama of these extraordinary events that stands out in retrospect and can too easily fail to reveal his loyal and inspiring friendship and his generosity. It was indeed a privilege to share in his burning enthusiasm and be associated with one whose determination to fight for worthwhile causes was of inestimable value to creative artists. Above all, he was so intensely alive. The foundation of the annual Exhibition of Living Art (the Irish equivalent of the famous 'Salon des refusés' created by the Impressionists) was very largely due to his dynamic influence; and this was but one of his many achievements which enriched the arts in Ireland.[9]

Bearing in mind my anxiety not to paint a distorted picture, I cannot resist describing just a few of the bizarre events which are quite unforgettable. If you didn't match Ralph's unbounded enthusiasm for a piece of music or a work of art, you were frequently in danger of physical harm. When I

9. The first Exhibition of Living Art opened in the gallery of the National College of Art in September 1943. See reviews in *The Irish Times*, 16 September and 1 October 1943.

conducted the first performance of my *Symphony for Strings*, with the DOP, he was sitting in the front row of the gallery at the Abbey Lecture Hall next to Thurloe Conolly, who was always very reserved about any show of wild enthusiasm.[10] Ralph had formed the opinion that my work was the GREATEST composition EVER created by an Irish composer. As I turned to the audience to take my bow, he was applauding wildly with enormous vigour. Then I saw him observe his neighbour's polite clapping and, shocked by his apparent lack of enthusiasm, bring down his fist violently on top of Thurloe's head. There was also the notorious occasion when a very distinguished art critic was invited over from England to open the Exhibition of Living Art. At a reception at the Victor Waddington Galleries on the day before the opening, the critic expressed some opinion that so angered Ralph that he knocked him out with a couple of well-aimed fisticuffs and the distinguished visitor was unavailable for the opening ceremony.[11] After losing his temper with one of his close friends, which was not an infrequent event, Ralph would become extremely depressed and ashamed, and almost maudlin in his attempts to apologise. It was often on such occasions that he threatened to commit suicide. Some of us suspected that his attempts to kill himself were unconsciously carefully calculated, for they were invariably hilariously unsuccessful, even if alarming at the time. I remember him on one such occasion striding out to sea in the lagoon on the road to Howth with the intention of drowning himself. The tide was nearly out, and after wading out for a hundred yards or so the water was only deep enough barely to reach his knees. In a fury of frustration he raised his face to the heavens and brandishing clenched fists yelled out to God, 'It's an outrage against humanity!'

Ralph's unbounded enthusiasms sometimes led to unforeseen complications. He had an uncle, Josh Watson, who had long ago been a violin pupil of Joachim.[12] Many years ago he had taught several of the senior Dublin violin players. Having been abroad for many years he decided to return to Dublin to enjoy his retirement. Ralph was adamant that the Dublin public should not miss the opportunity of hearing a surviving Joachim pupil before it was too late for him to perform. He insisted that I engage him for

---

10. The first performance of the *Symphony for Strings*, op. 26 took place on 30 October 1945.
11. Victor Waddington (1907–81) opened his Galleries in South Anne Street, Dublin in 1927, promoting contemporary Irish and European Modernist and avant-garde artists.
12. Captain Joshua Watson of Herbert Park, Dublin, owned the 'Vieuxtemps-Hause' Stradivarius violin in the early twentieth century. See W. Meredith Morris, *British Violin Makers*, 3rd edn (Gretna, Louisiana: Pelican Publishing, 2006), p. 278. Joseph Joachim (1831–1907), outstanding Hungarian violinist.

a concerto with the DOP. Just in case the aged violinist did not live up to Ralph's opinion of his playing, I cautiously decided to ask him to play the solo violin part in Bach's fifth Brandenburg Concerto so that he would have the company of flute and keyboard soloists, rather than shouldering the full responsibility of a concerto on his own. The concert was duly advertised and Josh arrived for the first rehearsal with the orchestra just a couple of weeks before the performance was due to take place. After five minutes it was horribly obvious that he was no longer capable of achieving anything like a professional standard and didn't seem to realise his severe limitations. What were we to do? I appealed to Ralph who, after all, had initiated the idea. Fortifying himself with the greater part of a bottle of whiskey, he climbed up a drainpipe on Josh's house in the middle of the night, broke into his bedroom, and ordered him with menacing threats to become forthwith ill with 'flu and cancel his engagement. With some difficulty I eventually persuaded Nancie Lord, who had been one of Josh's pupils, to take his place, and the situation was saved as far as the public was concerned.[13] Those of us directly involved in the drama had to suffer repercussions of a more private nature for some time to come.

As already recounted, Ralph's enthusiasm more usually resulted in great positive benefits: such as, for example, his central role in founding the annual Exhibition of Living Art. Another less public action resulted in an unforgettable musical experience shared by a few dozen or so friends who, like him, had been bowled over by the performance by the Griller Quartet at the RDS of Ernst Bloch's First String Quartet – a work we had avidly studied during several of Ralph's gramophone sessions.[14]

One evening, shortly after the RDS performance, we were listening to that work on records and were once again overcome by its magic. Although it was well past midnight, Ralph suddenly announced that he was there and then going to ring up Sidney Griller and ask him to give a private performance for a specially invited audience during the forthcoming return visit of the quartet to Dublin. Sidney Griller, awoken from his sleep, agreed to it in exchange for one of Ralph's paintings. The opportunity of hearing a much-loved musical work in the company of a small group of like-minded

---

13. Nancie Lord was leader of the RÉ Orchestra between 1945 and the establishment of the RÉSO in 1948. She continued as a member of the RÉSO under its new leader, Renzo Marchionni.

14. The String Quartet no. 1 by the Swiss-American composer Ernest Bloch (1880–1959) dates from 1916; his String Quartet no. 2 (1945) attracted Brian's interest at the time he was composing his own String Quartet no. 1 in 1949 and is mentioned a number of times in the Diary (Part II) below. The Griller Quartet, established by Sidney Griller in 1931, was one of the first British string quartets to gain an international reputation. It disbanded in 1963.

enthusiasts creates an atmosphere seldom if ever achieved in the public concert hall: a privilege that leaves an unforgettably inspiring memory, as indeed this occasion proved to be.

One of the professional bodies that provided during the early forties what was virtually the only orchestral music with a really high standard of performance was Terry O'Connor's Dublin String Orchestra.[15] In addition to the enjoyment they provided for us, they introduced many new contemporary works to Dublin, including first performances of Fred May's *Lyric Movement for String Orchestra* (RDS, 1943) and my *Fantasia on an Old Catalan Chant, Pregaria a la Verge del Remeí* (RIAM, 1942).[16] When they gave the first Irish performance of Benjamin Britten's *Serenade for Tenor, Horn and Strings* in the ballroom of the Gresham Hotel (to a background of rattling cutlery and washing-up from the adjacent kitchen), the auspicious occasion was marred by an unfortunate incident at its conclusion. The work ends with an atmospheric off-stage horn solo. The player on this occasion was Harry Wood from the RÉ Station Orchestra. To obtain the best effect, Harry was placed in a small pantry adjacent to the stage. The horn is silent for a considerable time before this final moment, so Harry settled down in his pantry to read the *Evening Mail*. When Terry gave the signal for the final entry, there was an embarrassing silence. Harry had fallen fast asleep. Repeated gestures followed by loud whispers failed to rouse him. Eventually a viola from the back desk nearest the pantry had to creep across and prod him with her bow. His concluding peroration then staggered into life too late to save the intended atmosphere of magic.

Many performances which benefited from the outstanding musicianship of Charles Lynch, Ireland's leading pianist during the forties and fifties, provided their own special anxieties. Before the war this distinguished Cork-born pupil of Petrie's and friend of Arnold Bax had made a name for himself in London as one of the leading exponents of contemporary piano music.[17]

---

15. Terry O'Connor had been a violinist in the cinema orchestras of the Bohemian Picture House in Phibsboro (Dublin) and the Capitol Cinema in Dublin before joining the band of the newly established national radio station 2RN (later RÉ) as leader in March 1926. She founded the Dublin String Orchestra in 1939, remained as leader of the RÉ Orchestra until 1945, and directed the Rathmines and Rathgar Musical Society until 1976.

16. Although his output was relatively small, Frederick May (1911–85) was one of the most original Irish composers of the mid-twentieth century. Like Brian and Aloys Fleischmann, he looked to the European avant-garde rather than identifying with an Irish national expression. His String Quartet in C minor (1935/6) is recognised as a defining work in Irish musical Modernism. He is mentioned periodically in Part II: Diary (below); see further *EMIR*, pp. 638–40.

17. On Charles Lynch, see further *EMIR*, pp. 606–7.

If one were to be critical of his playing, it could be said that he was such a brilliant sight-reader and had such a prodigious musical memory that he didn't always prepare his performances with the thorough practice that a less gifted musician would need. Anyone involved in the organisation of concerts in which he was involved would have been critical on another score: for he was quite incapable of the reliability expected of a professional artist. This failing was certainly not the sort of arrogant pose adopted by many who wish to be thought of as such great artists that mundane matters are beneath them. Charles's brain just didn't function as far as the practical world was concerned, and he was as genuinely incapable of timing appointments as he was of managing his finances. He had apparently inherited enough money to be accustomed to comfortable living and, having no permanent home, always stayed in the best hotels. When travelling by train he insisted on a first-class carriage. On the numerous occasions when he failed to turn up for a rehearsal or undemanding appointment, it came to be assumed that he was in the waiting room at Limerick Junction drinking tea: for coming to Dublin, when he had to change trains at the Junction, he refused to board a train that had no first-class carriage, and resolutely waited until suitable transport arrived. On one such occasion I had to keep the audience happy at a meeting of the Dublin Music Club where he was due to play by organising a musical 'question time' until he arrived – as unruffled as a serene cow chewing cud in a sunny meadow. Curiously enough, I never knew him to be actually late for his more important engagements; but his habit of arriving with only a few minutes to spare was the cause of many potential heart-attacks among concert promoters.

I shall never forget the first performance of my Cello Sonata in September 1945. It was to take place at a concert in the National College of Art in Kildare Street, in memory of the artist Mainie Jellett who had recently died. Betty Sullivan, to whom it was dedicated, was the cellist, with Charles at the piano. For some reason in those days it was very difficult to obtain a hotel room in Dublin. I eventually went to Buswells Hotel, close by the concert venue, and enquired whether by any chance they might be able to provide a room for Mr Lynch, who was to give a concert next day. 'Well, if it's for Joe Lynch we are of course happy to make a special arrangement.' I never breathed a word about the honoured guest not being the popular singer of that name, and immediately phoned Charles at the Metropole Hotel in Cork to tell him the good news. Next morning, the day of the only rehearsal at which Betty would have the opportunity of working with her partner, the telephone rang just before the nine o'clock train was due to leave Cork. It was Charles. 'Are you *quite* sure my accommodation in Dublin is securely arranged?' As he was speaking, I heard the train whistle and the chuff chuff of it pulling out of the station. He arrived just in time for the actual performance, and sight-read the manuscript piano part. A bit hard on Betty, and for that matter on me too!

The other similar occasion was when he was due to play the César Franck *Symphonic Variations* with the DOP. (He was always most generous in his willingness to play with amateurs for a very small fee.) He had been invited to do a rather special concert tour on the Continent, where he was to stay with various titled aristocrats – just the style of living which suited his taste. He was enjoying himself so much that nothing was heard of his whereabouts during the course of several weeks. The date for his appearance with the DOP was fast approaching; so, just in case, I arranged for a stand-in. That is something one hates to have to do, since it often puts people to great trouble with little or no reward. It was Valerie Walker who kindly volunteered on this occasion. In the middle of the night just two days before the final rehearsal the phone rang. 'This is Charles Lynch speaking from The Hague. I do believe I am to play the César Franck at a concert with you fairly soon. When do you need me?' I told him that the final rehearsal was to be the evening after next, and he said that he 'hoped to catch the Channel boat next morning'. On the day of the rehearsal I tracked him down having tea at the Shelbourne Hotel. I confirmed the arrangements, and just before ringing off he said, 'Oh, by the way – have you got a copy of the music?' It was obvious he hadn't looked at the work for months.

In his later days Charles had obviously run through whatever fortune he may have inherited, having spent it on taxis and expensive hotels, and he was chronically short of money. One time he was staying in the best hotel in Kenmare and didn't have enough to pay the bill. He rang up Aloys Fleischmann (then Professor of Music in University College Cork), who was always so kind to him, and Aloys quickly collected subscriptions and drove all the way to Kenmare to bail him out.[18] After settling the bill, there was a little left over in the rescue fund. Charles promptly ordered a taxi to drive him to Dublin.

Martin McCullough told me a delightful anecdote about Charles' financial innocence.[19] Several friends in Cork began to think that it was

---

18. Aloys Fleischmann (1910–92), composer and Professor of Music at University College Cork from 1934 to 1980, became one of Brian's closest musical colleagues. Brian had the highest regard for him and he was the one Irish composer with whom Brian felt he could – and often did – discuss his own new compositions while in their final stages of completion (see for example Part II: Diary (below), 8 January). See further *EMIR*, pp. 389–93.
19. Martin McCullough of McCullough's music shop, later McCullough Pigott.

rather embarrassing for Charles to have to keep asking for a few shillings to buy a packet of cigarettes or a cup of tea. So they arranged a subscription and lodged the proceeds in a bank with strict instructions that he could withdraw only limited amounts of petty cash. After a month or two his account was heavily overdrawn, and the manager sent him a fairly stern letter. Charles thought it rude and insulting, and threw it into the waste-paper basket. A few days later a telegram arrived summoning him urgently to the bank. Off he went with his familiar music case at his side and reluctantly presented himself to the manager. After carefully explaining that Charles could not overdraw this modest financial assistance, and observing the total lack of reaction, he said, 'Mr Lynch, I don't think you really understand what I'm trying to explain to you!' Whereupon Charles reached down to his music case, drew out a volume of Liszt's piano music, opened it at a fearsomely black-looking page of rapid notes and said, 'Well … I don't think YOU understand THAT!'

Looking back on all the anxieties caused by Charles' unreliability, one could be forgiven for wondering why we continued to engage him for concerts. He was of course an outstanding pianist and made a really valuable contribution to Irish musical life; but apart from that he was such a lovable and generous man. However angry you might feel in the middle of the many crises he precipitated, your heart would always melt when you met him after the crisis was over.

When we try to recapture memories of our enjoyment of music before an undoubted revolution in the standards of performance was brought about by modern recordings and improved communication, we tend to remember the dramatic disasters rather than the moderate successes. I believe we did indeed put on, and get away with, some pretty appalling performances in Dublin during the forties, as well as experiencing much excellence: but it was all part of immensely enjoyable participation.

Perhaps the most dramatic musical disaster in which I took part was when I was picking up the odd penny as a freelance oboist in the scratch orchestra assembled each year for the Grand Opera season in the Gaiety Theatre. Since there wasn't enough room in the orchestra pit, the oboes were put sitting in the equivalent of the Royal Box at the side of the stage, along with the harp player. She was constantly losing her place and would cry out, 'Oh my God, Mr Boydell, have we passed letter D?'[20] Since you can't reply when playing a wind instrument, I couldn't be of much help

---

20. Rehearsal letters (as in 'letter D' here) are inserted into orchestral scores and instrumental parts to facilitate the conductor and players resuming at a given point, following an interruption in rehearsal.

to her. When, with the aid of an instinct earned by many years of similar panic, she finally managed to play her entry at the right moment, her breath, pent up with anxiety, would be expelled in an audible sigh of relief: 'Ah – I got it – I got it – by the skin o' mi teeth!' On this occasion my friend Billy Boucher was conducting *La Gioconda* (he was later to become Head of Music of the BBC in Belfast).[21] In the middle of an important aria, which was being sung by the famous and revered star of the time, Patricia Black, the complete orchestra collapsed in total disarray. I can still see the expression of dark fury on Patricia Black's face as she glared at poor Billy from the stage. Forgetting, in the heat of the moment, that singers in an opera don't have the music in front of them with the letters that indicate to orchestral players where they are, he whispered loudly, 'Start again at letter S.' The singer had of course no idea where letter S occurred. Added to this, there was a further complication. Financial stringencies meant that there could be only one full rehearsal with orchestra and singers before the opening performance. At the final rehearsal, the night before, it was discovered that there were no orchestral parts for the trombones. New parts were hurriedly copied overnight, and the trombones had to sight-read their music with no rehearsal at all. Furthermore, the copyist, working late at night, had omitted to put in the essential rehearsal letters. When Billy brought down his baton for the fresh start at letter S, there was total shambles and cacophony. Even if we had all had the essential letter S in our parts, some of us had not been quick enough in the uptake to find it in time. There were a couple of further cacophonous catastrophes before we all got under way again.

To turn from the memory of a disaster to a very positive experience – at least as far as I was concerned – I must recount another musical occasion. One need hardly stress the difficulties facing a young composer when trying to make his music known to the public. If, like Benjamin Britten for instance, you have the good fortune to be taken up by a publishing firm as a financial investment, you are well away. (Remember Gerard Hoffnung's quip 'If Britten can make it, Boosey's can hawk it'.)[22] In Ireland, there was the advantage that there weren't all that many composers around to crowd the competitive field; but, on the other hand, we had no publishing firm with

---

21. Further on Edgar ('Billy') Boucher, see *EMIR*, pp. 109–10. Ponchielli's opera *La Gioconda* was first performed in 1876.

22. Gerard Hoffnung (1925–59) is probably best known for his books of musical cartoons and for the 'Hoffnung Festivals' held at the Royal Festival Hall in London. The quip cited here, referencing the prominent English music publishers Boosey & Hawkes, is from *Punkt Contrapunkt*, of which Brian had a 45rpm recording. *Punkt Contrapunkt*, which formed part of one of the Hoffnung Festivals, was a mock-serious discussion and performance of a parody of Webern's 12-note music.

anything more than very restricted local distribution, and few performers of sufficient professional standard to be able to tackle contemporary idioms. As oboist and pianist, and conductor of an amateur orchestra which could manage a limited range of simpler pieces, I was fortunate enough since I could undertake the public performance of a few of my own compositions, and those of my colleagues. We Irish composers really had to wait for significant opportunities to arrive with the establishment of the RÉSO at the end of 1948, followed by the professional chamber choir (the RÉ/RTÉ Singers) in 1953 and the RÉ/RTÉ String Quartet in 1958.

With so many of my friends, and indeed myself, involved with the visual arts, it often occurred to me to make an envious comparison with those creative artists who don't need the act of performance to bring their work to life. This prompted the thought that I saw no reason not to mount the equivalent of a 'one-man show' in the form of a concert of my chamber music, to be given with the cooperation of my friends. The idea bore fruit with a concert given in the Shelbourne Hotel on 30 January 1944 before an invited audience. That concert would not have taken place were it not for the quite overwhelming generosity of many of my friends; and indeed of my father James, who in spite of his disappointment at my not fulfilling his ambition of my serving the family business, paid for the large room in the Shelbourne. The string quartet, consisting of Carmel Lang, Hazel de Courcy (later Lewis), Maire Larchet and Betty Sullivan: a string trio with Morris Sinclair, John MacKenzie and Betty Sullivan; and Doris Cleary (later Keogh) the flautist, all gave up many hours of devoted effort at rehearsals with no reward at all beyond whatever satisfaction their loyal enthusiasm in supporting a fellow artist may have brought them. The singer to whom I had dedicated the *Three Songs for Soprano and String Quartet* was my pupil Mary Jones. We decided on that very occasion to get married. Apart from the *Songs*, the other works were the Quintet for Oboe and String Quartet (1939/40) in which I played the oboe part; *The Feather of Death* – a setting of surrealist poems by Thurloe Conolly – in which I sang the baritone solo; and the String Trio. All except the Oboe Quintet were first performances.

The poet Patrick Kavanagh was at the concert, and wrote as follows in the *Irish Press* of 4 February 1944 (under the name of 'Piers Plowman'):[23]

Last Sunday evening I was present at a performance of new music by a young man called Brian Boydell. Mr Boydell is a man of talent. Shortly

---

23. Patrick Kavanagh (1904–67) wrote for the *Irish Press* from 1942 to 1949, initially contributing the gossip column under the pen-name Piers Plowman cited here (Kavanagh came from a rural, farming background) and later writing as film critic.

after the war broke out he was one of the first to invent a gas-producer plant, which I believe has been quite successful. At the recent exhibition of 'subjective art' he was one of the exhibitors and, to give him his due, he was as 'subjective' as the best of them.[24] On the oboe he is one of the most delightful performers I have heard – oftentimes playing his own work. As far as I remember, another of his accomplishments is that of being technical instructor – in woodwork, I think. [I don't know where he got that idea!] Now he has taken over control of the Dublin Orchestral Players, and on next Sunday week he is conducting this orchestra in a programme at the Abbey Lecture Hall.

Broadcast talks about music, designed to assist the ordinary member of the public in an appreciation of music, are commonplace today; but before the war they were unheard of in the programmes of RÉ. Many of us, however, tuned in to the BBC to listen to Walford Davies' excellent pioneering work in this field.[25] I believe I was the first to suggest to our own broadcasting station that a series of talks on music appreciation would be a good idea, and I was duly engaged for an experimental series. For the very first broadcast, I devised what I thought would be a dramatically arresting beginning. The idea was that I should start off in a rather stuffy academic manner, and a friend of mine, pretending to be a casual member of the public who happened to be wandering around the passages of the studios on the top floor of the GPO (where RÉ operated from in those days) and having heard the rather highbrow beginning of my talk, should break into the studio and start arguing with me – whereupon we would continue in dialogue form.

On the appointed occasion, I started off as arranged; but when I came to the cue for my friend to burst into the studio, he didn't appear. We had, of course, forgotten about the sturdy presence of the garda whose duty it was to sit outside the studios and defend them against any possible incursion of revolutionaries intent upon taking over the national radio station. Glancing through the observation window of the sound-proof studio, I could see the altercation taking place, and realised that no argument was going to satisfy the solid figure of the law in time to create the planned illusion. To be faced with the unexpected task of improvising an entirely new script on the occasion of my very first broadcast was a challenge I wouldn't care to repeat!

24. The Exhibition of Subjective Art, mounted by the White Stag Group, was held at 6 Lower Baggot Street, Dublin, in January 1944.
25. The English composer [Henry] Walford Davies (1869–1941) gave many non-specialist broadcasts on classical music for BBC radio from 1926 to 1939 under the title 'Music and the Ordinary Listener'. He succeeded Elgar as Master of the King's Musick in 1934.

SYMPHONIC MUSIC FOR YOUNG LISTENERS

BRIAN BOYDELL

No. 5. Wednesday May 24th. 1950 5.30 - 6.0
        The Finale of Beethoven's seventh symphony.

        There now only remains the last movement, or 'Finale'
for us to study before I tell you something about the Symphony
as a whole. This finale has such tremendous drive and vitality
that the music carries us along with it - it is a movement
which hardly needs explanation to help you to enjoy it; but
in the hopes that you might enjoy it even more, I will point
out one or two things about it.
        Like the first movement, the last is in Sonata form: though
unlike the first movement, there is no Introduction section for
the finale. The ideas of the first subject group burst in upon
us without warning; though of course the previous three
movements have acted in a way as Introduction, since they have
prepared our minds for this burst of energy. When you hear
the beginning of the finale, you will realise that it would be
quite unthinkable to start this movement without the other
movements preparing our mind for it.
        Here is the opening of the finale, which introduces us
to the material of the first subject;

RE ORD   Opening to bar 20

        We now have a transition, which leads towards the
second subject's entry. In this transition, which we can think
of as part of the first subject group, we meet another tune which
is to be rather important in the Coda at the very end.

RECORD.   Bar 20 - 36

        As the transition continues, we hear parts of the main
first subject tune being used for the modulation which brings
us to the new key for the entry of the second subject:

RECORD   Bar 36 - 63

        Now we have the second subject, the main tune of which
is rather skittish - appearing softly on the first violins,
with sudden loud interruptions that give us the same kind
of surprise as the violent changes between loud and soft in
the scherzo. Before the closing section of the Exposition,
it dives right down and up through the string section
of the orchestra while the wind instruments hold a chord above.
You will hear this at the very end of the illustration which
I will now play you of the second subject.
RECORD
        Bar 61 to letter D

Typewritten script for RÉ radio broadcast, 24 May 1950. See his comments on
giving this broadcast (Part II: Diary, 24 May, 1950). © RTÉ DOCUMENT ARCHIVES

In those early days of broadcasting nobody bothered much about the necessity of providing a typescript before the broadcast (which of course was always 'live', recording techniques having not yet arrived on the scene). When doing a series of weekly broadcasts for schoolchildren on the subject of music that told a story, I used to arrive at the studio about five minutes before the broadcast, with a bundle of gramophone records under my arm. There was no special engineer to put on the records: I managed that myself, just giving hand-signals to the engineer behind the glass panel, who twiddled the appropriate knobs; and I chatted away without any script to read from. On one occasion, I was nastily caught out when talking about Smetana's tone-poem *Die Moldau*, which describes the great river which flows through Bohemia. In the days of 78rpm records each side lasted a little over three minutes; and you usually had to turn the record over to continue with Side 2. I would cover the delay necessitated by turning over the record by chatting about the music that was to follow. Unfortunately, some extended pieces of music were issued with what was known as 'automatic coupling' – so that they could be stacked one above the other on a gramophone turntable provided with this facility, and at the end of side 1, the next record would automatically drop into place with the minimum of delay. If you follow the idea, you'll understand that Side 2 was not on the reverse of Side 1 (as in the ordinary system), but on another record. Anyway, at the conclusion of Side 1, I proceeded to turn the record over, describing how the river, as we proceeded downstream, was about to pass a village and we would hear the lively dance-music of the peasants' merry-making. On dropping the pick-up head on the reversed record, I was horrified to hear totally inappropriate music emerging. I was right in the middle of the same composer's *Bohemia's Meadows and Forests* – which was on the reverse three sides of the three records. I thought it better to allow the music to continue, and hurriedly made some feeble excuses, such as 'Well they've not really got going with their merry-making yet – just thinking about the solemnity of the Saint's-Day they are celebrating'. I continued in this vein for the whole side of the record, not quite sure what kind of music was going to turn up next (since I didn't know that piece very well). I was expecting a series of critical or angry letters following this broadcast; but apparently nobody even noticed!

The experience in the way of broadcasting which I relish most concerns one of the numerous occasions shortly after the war when the rumour would fly round Dublin that the Head of the BBC Third Programme was over, looking for likely material for this most prestigious programme. To make contact – or even hopefully to sign a contract – one should turn up at the Pearl Bar that evening. I was never very happy about this kind of touting – but in the face of urgent persuasion, I duly arrived at the Pearl Bar at the appointed time.[26] As my eyes adjusted to the dim light and penetrated the thick haze of tobacco smoke, I became aware of Paddy Kavanagh, in the last stages of inebriation, completely bewitching a fine London lady with quite incomprehensible alcoholic rubbish. This frightfully respectable emissary of the BBC had never heard anything so 'delightfully Irish' in her life before, and just managed to obtain Paddy's signature on a contract before he disappeared beneath the table for the rest of the evening. I saw my chance, introduced myself, and asked whether the Third Programme would be interested in a talk about contemporary Irish composers, about whom little was known in England at the time. 'I'm sure that would be *most* interesting, Mr Boydell; but, you see, I was given strict instructions by our programme committee not to arrange for anything of a purely parochial nature'. Now I am quite sure that every one of us has been faced with the situation where it would be wonderful to be quick-witted enough to produce just the right reply on occasions such as this. We usually think of the perfect riposte about twelve hours too late. Only twice in my life do I remember having the good fortune to think of the right remark to counter such a patronising insult – and on this occasion, it just happened to fall out of my mouth when I replied, 'But you do have talks about English composers, don't you?' Needless to say, I was not asked to sign a contract. But the nice end to that story is that about twenty years later I was asked to give a talk on the BBC Third Programme about contemporary Irish music; and I told that story just as I have told it to you.

I think it's now about time to come to some conclusion about what general picture emerges from this jumbled jigsaw of musical anecdotes. The first conclusion is obvious to those of us who experienced life in Dublin more than forty years ago. The richness and vitality of the crowded calendar of musical events, and the stimulus of a focus for this activity in the later National Concert Hall, were beyond our idealistic dreams in the lean years of comparative starvation during the forties. But it is nice to think that the enormous amount of energy and enthusiasm which went into our somewhat amateur endeavours in those days may have had something to do with the astonishing development of public interest in music since then. As far as orchestral performances are concerned, I think the most significant step forward was achieved when Jean Martinon was appointed conductor of

26. See also Part II: Diary (below), 12 May 1950.

the RÉ Orchestra at the end of the forties.[27] It was an astonishing revelation to observe how a really top-class conductor could miraculously transform the standard of playing into something that some of us at the time dimly remembered as having experienced in great European cities before the war.

If I may interpolate another anecdote in this context, I do so with the excuse that I thereby learned a valuable lesson, which might with advantage be handed on to younger musicians. It is that even under the most extreme provocation one must never argue with a newspaper critic by writing a letter to the editor of the paper that employs him. The press holds all the trump cards, will always win, and probably make a fool of you into the bargain. Those of us who were involved in the enthusiastic early stages of the newly founded MAI were fanatically inspired by Martinon's miraculous work with the orchestra;[28] but John O'Donovan, who wrote for a short-lived paper known as *Radio Review*, just hated *all* French musicians and their music, and wrote a vitriolic review of one of Martinon's concerts, which we had considered one of the most inspiring musical experiences we had enjoyed for many years. We met together in a spirit of outraged anger, and decided some protest should be made. Freddie May, the composer, volunteered to write a letter over our names to the *Radio Review*. Unfortunately, without thinking, he wrote the letter on a sheet of notepaper from the desk of his father, who worked for Guinness, and our protest was headed by large letters which suggested that it had emanated from the brewery. The editor couldn't resist that opportunity in defending his critic, and made such fools of us that there was no doubt in the minds of the public who had won that contest.

To return to whatever picture may emerge from the various experiences I have described, the second conclusion is not so much a conclusion, as food for thought about a paradoxical problem. In the light of all the enthusiastic enjoyment of music and music-making during what might now be considered the rather primitive days in the development of Dublin musical life, I often wonder about the very difficult problem of standards. It is so easy to say that one should only be satisfied with the very best – but that means that there remains that much more which will give us no satisfaction. The more critically demanding we become, the less there is left to enjoy. On the other hand, the struggle to improve continuously on our previous achievements

---

27. The French conductor Jean Martinon (1910–76), who was the first conductor of the RÉSO upon its establishment in 1948, had already conducted its precursor, the RÉ Orchestra, for three concerts in 1946 and for a six-month contract from April 1947. See Pine, *Music and Broadcasting*, and *EMIR*, p. 630. Martinon was also a composer (see Part II: Diary (below), 16 January 1950).
28. On the founding of the MAI, see Chapter 5 below.

is one of the most inspiring ideals of the performing musician; and the deepest satisfaction in listening to music is directly related to a continuous development of our powers of perception, so that we grow to learn how to distinguish greater artistic perfection from more superficial experiences. And yet, in the light of my own experience, I nurse a sneaking, heretical feeling that our accepted standards of performance (that is, taking the world at large) are getting uncomfortably high; and many of us are enjoying fewer performances, and gradually edging out amateur enthusiasm. I find it most depressing to listen to the kind of remark so commonly heard as audiences emerge from a concert: 'Wasn't that absolutely *appalling*?' Do audiences today go to concerts in order to emulate critics (well, many critics) and prove how destructively clever they can be? How many have forgotten that music can be a life-inspiring enjoyment?

I can't really provide an easy answer to this paradoxical question; and leave it as a thought to ponder.

CHAPTER 4

DANGEROUS INTELLECTUALS
AND SPIES

THE NAME OF PATRICK KAVANAGH has arisen during the course of the previous few pages. Memories of him slouching along Pembroke Road in a wide-brimmed hat and an old tweed overcoat open down the front remind me of his usual greeting: 'Hello, Brian! And how's yourself and the clarionette [with each syllable clearly enunciated]?' These memories also remind me of the first of various regular meeting places where I would enjoy the company of my new Dublin friends and many stimulating and often eccentric characters.

In those days nobody seemed to have thought of the idea which later became a status-symbol of fashion: to live in a mews flat adapted from the coachman's quarters behind the large houses of well-to-do city dwellers. When Tony Reford and Philip Seaton converted No. 16 Heytesbury Lane behind Waterloo Road, in 1940, they were pioneers in this style of dwelling. They were both medical students who, like my Cambridge friend Lionel Kerwood, had come to TCD to complete their training. Tony, reflecting to some extent a problem with which I was familiar, was a reluctant student of the subject dictated for him by his father: for he really wanted to be an artist; I still possess a couple of fine woodcuts which he did at the time. The difference between our problems was that, whereas my father accepted my choice of career – even with disappointment – Tony's father would only pay the bills while he was a medical student. Tony and Philip managed the conversion of the mews dwelling mostly with their own hands. When it was just habitable, Tony asked me to supper. It was a very cold night, and we sat shivering on tea chests and a couple of deckchairs thickly covered in cement dust, as the last bit of fuel was consumed in the process of frying sausages. When the cold became too much for us, the tea chests and the deckchairs were sacrificed to revive the fire, and, without any furniture left, we sat talking till late at night on the floor.

Philip Seaton was a philosophical idealist. He later became a psychiatrist. For one summer vacation he somehow managed to hire a 'gipsy' caravan from the travelling community. The bargain included the horse to draw it,

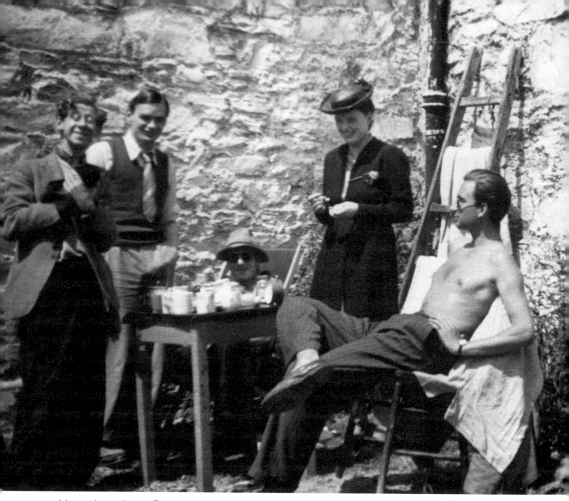

Heytesbury Lane, Dublin, June 1940 (*l. to r.*): Tony Reford, John Beattie, Philip Seaton (seated), Dorothy Beattie and Nigel Heseltine.

which stopped at every cross-roads and patiently waited to be told which way to go, lest the driver were asleep. There was a dog too, who had been trained to supply the traveller with sustenance by stealing chickens along the way. Hosts of fleas and bed-bugs made up the remainder of the bargain. At a fairly alcoholic gathering (it was possibly their house-warming party), Philip's caravan was parked in the yard below. Memories of such parties are understandably rather hazy, but I distinctly remember Nigel Heseltine, who tended to become physically aggressive when drunk, throwing Charles Acton out through the upstairs window.[1] Fortunately for Charles, the caravan was below, and the canvas roof broke his fall and prevented serious injury.[2]*

1. On Nigel Heseltine (1916–95), see below p. 70.
2.* My 'distinct memory' must indeed be hazy. I have recently (1993) corresponded with both Charles and Nigel, neither of whom remembers the episode. Perhaps it was someone else who was propelled through the window. Charles does, however, remember being chased by Nigel down Heytesbury Lane. [Author's note]

It was probably through Lionel Kerwood that I was introduced to his fellow medical students in Heytesbury Lane. They were all frequent visitors to my home in Shankill where they were assured of a generous welcome from my mother, who enjoyed the company of young intellectuals with stimulating and unorthodox views. I don't think my father was so keen on their presence. Lionel and I, apart from our shared interests in photography and developing producer-gas plants to meet the emergency of petrol starvation, became enthusiastically involved in many of the sort of mad escapades that wild young men of our age indulged in. We had so many enthusiasms in common that from April 1941 we rented together a small house in Rathfarnham. Imaal, as it was named, was later to become a sort of clubhouse for artists of all kinds, including a few penniless scroungers who were largely responsible for a horrifying account that had mounted up at the local butcher's. We shall return to Imaal later in the story.

Meanwhile, one of the pursuits which Lionel and I had become involved in was the inheritance of William Fearon's enthusiasm for fireworks. An extraordinary feature of the war years in Ireland, when most things became difficult to obtain, was that all the chemicals necessary for making fireworks and explosives were plentifully available. We experimented with all kinds of recipes, producing a variety of colours and dramatic bangs and demonstrated our successes in elaborate displays. One problem that we never solved was making a really successful rocket. To overcome our inability to produce what should be the prime ingredient of any good firework display, we experimented with firing a 'Roman candle' from a mortar. In one of the early attempts the mortar consisted of a piece of copper piping. The propellant exploded too violently and sent fragments of copper shrapnel spinning over the garden hedge, resulting in the death of one of the neighbour's turkeys. A mortar was then made from iron piping encased in concrete. Now the problem was timing the fuse. Sometimes the Roman candle would burn out before it was projected by the mortar, or it would be fired into the air before it was properly alight. So we decided to fire the mortar charge at the right moment by electricity, using fuse-wire and a car battery.

We were having a grand display to which we had invited William Fearon. Philip Seaton and Nigel Heseltine had joined Lionel and I for a test rehearsal. It was a very warm day and we had taken off our shirts, casting them down on the grass of the field in front of the house where the display was to be mounted. I was loading the charge into the mortar using a broom-stick as a ram-rod. Quite mad of course, since the propellant contained potassium chlorate which can explode under impact. Whether it was the impact of the broom-stick or a short circuit in the electrical set-up I don't know; but the mortar exploded, sending the broom-stick about two hundred yards down the field and a large lump of concrete straight into Philip Seaton's body. I received the full blast on the side of my face and was knocked unconscious.

I was later told how my unconscious body was being carried up to the house, with blood all over my face, at the moment when William Fearon arrived in his ancient Rolls-Royce that looked rather like a hearse. Fearon, who was very short-sighted, saw the bloody cortège and glanced towards the field. Thinking that our discarded shirts were dead bodies, he promptly fainted. I had a nasty time in hospital having small pieces of gunpowder removed from my eyes and face. At least, however, I had the excuse of a very sore face to succeed in what was my fourth attempt to overcome social disapproval and grow a beard. I have had one ever since.

Nigel Heseltine has already been introduced to this story. He was the son of Philip Heseltine, the real name of the composer Peter Warlock. It was rumoured that he was a deserter from the British army enjoying refuge in neutral Ireland.[3]* But none of us minded in the least what might have been the murky past of any of our friends. It was what they could contribute to our community now that mattered. Whatever the truth of his past, the number of his unbelievable exploits in many distant lands, which he related for our fascinated entertainment, could hardly have been fitted into the limited life-span he had experienced. He was a good poet, and published in Dublin a volume entitled *A Four-Walled Dream*. I set one of these poems (*The Lamenting*) to music in 1942. It was a very complex setting for baritone and string orchestra in the style of Alban Berg's early songs. I considered it as an experimental exercise. It has never been performed.[4]

Nigel went into partnership with Shelah Richards, the actress, and they produced a series of new plays at the Olympia Theatre. Ralph Cusack painted the scenery, and I was given my first professional job as a composer writing and performing incidental music for these productions. My first

---

3.* Nigel has recently published *Capriol for Mother* (London: Thames, 1992) in which he describes the life of his father and his family background. He tells how he voluntarily opted out from the training as a future officer in the British army, which had been imposed upon him by his grandmother. This would explain the origin of the rumour. [Author's note]

4. *The Lamenting* was performed by Aylish Kerrigan (mezzo-soprano) with Dearbhla Collins (piano) within the context of a lecture-recital on the early songs of Brian Boydell presented by Dr Kerrigan at the Brian Boydell Centenary Conference held in the RIAM and TCD on 23–4 June 2017. Although indicating string accompaniment, the music exists only in manuscript piano score.

assignment was an overture for Paul Vincent Carroll's *The Strings are False*, written for the very odd assembly of instruments in the small Olympia band. Every night during the run I had to be present to conduct this overture before the curtain went up, having had considerable difficulty at rehearsals throughout the previous week trying to get the theatre band to make something of what was then regarded as very modern music.

> The lights go down. A red glow, like a distant fire in the sky, spreads over the curtain. War in music fills the Olympia. The author of the striking overture to *The Strings are False*, Paul Vincent Carroll's new play, is Mr Brian Boydell, school-teacher and composer of modern music. I doubt if an Olympia orchestra has ever had to play such music before, and it must certainly have come as a surprise to many people visiting the Olympia.
>
> How difficult it was to do justice to the overture may be judged from the fact that in ideal circumstances it would be played by an orchestra with thirty string instruments, whereas the Olympia orchestra has only two violins, there being a predominance of brass instruments [which] however seem to lend themselves to creating in music that sense of universal upheaval that the author must have had in mind when he wrote the piece, and what with the thunder of drums and the clash of cymbals, a very realistic impression was given of aerial bombardment and anti-aircraft fire, with the pathos and tragedy descending on human lives.
>
> *Times Pictorial*, 28 March 1942

The other assignment was incidental music to be played on two pianos throughout Frank Carney's *The House of Cards*. Billy Boucher and I were the pianists; and of course we had to attend at the theatre every night. I afterwards orchestrated some of this music and presented it with the DOP as my *Satirical Suite*. One section of noisy factory music (influenced by Mosolov's *The Iron Foundry*)[5] gained some notoriety under the title *Hammond Lane Serenade* (the Hammond Lane Foundry was the principal iron works in Dublin).

> The scoring was so witty, that the audience could not restrain their mirth, and laughed outright ... The pièce de resistance in the Suite was

---

5. *The Iron Foundry* by Alexander Mosolov (1900–73), premiered in Moscow in 1927, uses ostinati and discordant chromatic chords to portray the sound of a factory. See also Part II: Diary (below), 14 May, note 13.

'Hammond Lane Serenade', reproducing with almost deafening realism the atmosphere of an iron foundry.

Evening Herald, 24 May 1944

The Hammond Lane Serenade had a tendency to amuse.

Irish Press, 24 May 1944

The sound effects of an iron foundry are cleverly reproduced in Hammond Lane Serenade, but they are just the noises that drive the listener out of his senses. Why the composer wishes to perpetrate such a clangour, and apparently take pleasure in it, is beyond me.

Irish Independent, 24 May 1944

I experienced very considerable difficulty getting paid for those jobs, resorting first to sending postcards as a reminder. After several weeks I took to posting the cards without any stamp, and eventually received my modest due.

The concert at which my *Satirical Suite* was first performed was the same one (described above) in which Bach's Fifth Brandenburg Concerto was played with Nancie Lord taking the place of Joshua Watson. Also in this memorable programme was the first performance of *A Short Overture for Orchestra* by John Beckett, who was then seventeen years old. Two-and-a-half years later I was to give the first performance of three songs of his in a recital that I gave at the Gresham Hotel, at which I also introduced my *Five Joyce Songs*. Joseph Groocock was my accompanist. I put great faith in John Beckett as a composer, but during the 1950s his remarkable musical talent led him in another direction. He became an outstanding harpsichord player and interpreter of baroque and early music.[6]

Several keen amateur musicians lived close to Heytesbury Lane, and we would frequently gather together for evenings of chamber music. Edward Oldham, who had a flat in Pembroke Road, was one of this circle. A gentle and most un-military man, he was, I believe, the British Naval attaché; though we were never aware of his activities in this area. Perhaps he didn't have much in the way of duty to occupy him with naval matters. He was a good violinist, and played in the DOP. Paul Egestorff was the chief pianist. He and his wife Edie had a flat round the corner in Morehampton Road.

---

6. Despite his early interest and promise in composition (he had studied composition at the RCM in London from 1945), John Beckett (1927–2007) would go on to establish an international career as a harpsichordist and conductor of early music, most notably as co-founder with Michael Morrow in 1960 of Musica Reservata. See *EMIR*, pp. 71–2 and Charles Gannon, *John S. Beckett: the man and the music* (Dublin: The Lilliput Press, 2016). See also Part II: Diary (below), especially 23 January 1950.

He was a pupil of Mainie Jellett and a fine painter.[7] There were several others who played flute, recorders and other instruments necessary to complete an ensemble. I went along with my oboe and also played piano from time to time. Edward had a touching adoration for old English baroque music, and became quite overcome when we played Purcell. As each evening progressed, there would be more frequent calls from Edward, uttered in quiet tones of religious awe: 'I think we should now have The GOLDEN!' As he played Purcell's famous sonata of that name, his deep emotion was reflected in the passion of his vibrato, which became wider and more wobbly as his passion overcame him, while tears dropped down on the strings of his violin.

These chamber music evenings resulted many years later in a charmingly touching outcome. When I was Professor of Music in TCD, a solicitor got in touch with me saying that a client of his, a widow named Mary Taylor, wished to leave a substantial sum of money for me to administer in what I might consider the best way to encourage the art of music. I was able to found the Taylor Music Scholarship for entrants to the School of Music in College. It transpired that she had many years ago been inspired by our musical evenings, which she had attended in her young days. She had ever since wished to make some material contribution to the practice of the art which she came to love.

The first floor of 25 Lower Baggot Street was occupied during the early 1940s by René Buhler; sometimes, but not always, accompanied by his wife Zette (the painter Georgette Rondel). There seemed to be a strange arrangement whereby René shared his wife for regular periods with Nick Nicholls, the English painter (who was a member of the White Stag Group). Roger Roughton, a surrealist writer, often occupied the back room where he made a point of wearing a bowler hat in bed. In the flat above lived the painter Stephen Gilbert and his wife (the Canadian-born sculptress Jocelyn Chewitt).[8] Apart from one possible candidate, the inhabitants of

---

7. Paul Egestorff (1906–95) exhibited with the White Stag Group, the Irish Exhibition of Living Art, the Royal Hibernian Academy, and the Water Colour Society of Ireland. He held a solo exhibition at the Grafton Gallery in 1949 but later ceased painting.

8. The artist Georgette Rondel (1915–42) was born in France, moved to London in the 1930s and came to Dublin in 1939 with René Buhler and Nick Nicholls; she died in London at the age of twenty-seven. Nicholls (1914–91), born in England of an English father and Irish mother, was a self-taught artist; he returned to London in 1946. The British painter and sculptor Stephen Gilbert (1910–2007) had lived in London and Paris before moving to Dublin in 1940 after he had been declared unfit for war service; he and his wife settled permanently in Paris after the war. Jocelyn Chewitt (1906–79) had studied at the Slade School of Art in London, and in Paris; she married Gilbert in London in 1935. For more on the above artists, including examples of their work, see Kennedy, *The White Stag Group*.

the building were all what we might now call blow-ins from outside Ireland.

René, a German-Swiss, exuded an aura of warm friendliness which endeared him to everyone he met. This stood him in good stead, for he had no apparent means of earning a livelihood beyond giving occasional lessons in German and French and acting when hard pressed for cash as a salesman for vacuum cleaners. When he called in his role as salesman at the house of the Manning Robertsons in Raglan Road, Mrs M.R. presumed him to be a friend of her daughter Olivia, the writer. She immediately invited him in for a meal. The household was so taken with his charm that it was said that he could always be sure of a good substantial meal if he were in need.[9] The story was told that when he was living in Paris before the war, he rang up Picasso expressing his enthusiasm for the great artist's work and asking for an appointment to meet him. Picasso reluctantly agreed. When René turned up at the studio the artist was so taken with his charm that they became great friends. There were many such stories like this which we could well believe; for everyone loved René and he was welcome practically everywhere he cared to go. He was not however welcome with the authorities. With no apparent means of support and his foreign background he was naturally regarded as a spy. It was also rumoured that he was carrying on a relationship with the wife of a very important and influential minister of the government. (If you ask me privately, I might tell you who this was!)

Besides his own wife and that of the minister he had a girlfriend who worked in the British Passport Office. It was she who alerted us when an application was made by the Irish police for a visa for him to enter England. This signalled to us that he was about to be deported. I happened to be in the Baggot Street flat one day when the detectives arrived to arrest him. Enquiring whether Mr Buhler was in, I told them that he would probably be back soon. 'We have our orders; and although we know he's a very nice chap we have to attend to our duty and take him away.'

Realising that this meant the removal of René from our community, I asked the detectives whether I could arrange a farewell party at the Unicorn Restaurant to say goodbye to their victim.[10] They considered this suggestion carefully, and came to the conclusion that it would be all right; though they

9. Manning Robertson (1887–1945), born at Huntington Castle, Co. Carlow, established his career as an architect and town planner in London before returning to Ireland in 1925. He was town-planning consultant to Dublin Corporation and a founder member and first chairman of the Irish branch of the Town Planning Institute (1942).
10. The Unicorn, an Italian restaurant founded in 1938, still exists at the same location off Merrion Row near St Stephen's Green. It would for many years be one of Brian and Mary's favourite restaurants in Dublin.

had to decline my invitation to join the party. I went out to the Unicorn, where there was a phone, and rang up all René's friends whom I could contact. I was very conscious that a clicking sound indicated that the phone was being tapped. I then booked a large table for the wake of our friend. Meanwhile René had returned to the flat, where he was arrested. I was just in time to explain the arrangements I had made. We proceeded to the Unicorn with the detectives apologetically explaining that they would have to sit at a nearby table lest some attempt might be made to rescue their prisoner. William Griffith, who owned the restaurant, was not directly concerned, so he could not be accused of bribing the law. He stood them a meal on the house, and they joined in drinking a farewell toast to our friend. There were about a dozen of us there, and after the dinner we ordered three taxis to drive us, along with the detectives and their prisoner, to the Bridewell jail. We saw him to his 'hotel' with a bottle of whiskey to keep him happy for the night. Next morning we got up early and saw him off at the mailboat in the company of an unsavoury collection of thugs who had arrived under armed guard in the 'Black Maria'. The next we heard of René was that he was given an important job in the British Secret Service as a translator: so it seems most unlikely that he was, as some people thought, a German spy.

Vaughan Briscoe, who lived in one of the flats above René, is quoted by Brian Kennedy as explaining the continual surveillance of 25 Lower Baggot Street by the Garda Special Branch:

> … if only because of the famous parties in No. 25 Lower Baggot St. it was not unknown for Cauvet Duhamel, of the French embassy, and Dr Karl Peterson (German 'Press Attaché') to be present at the same time tho' at different ends of the room, and things got pretty hairy at times. There were, to my certain knowledge, at least two 'spies' always around – really not much more than paid agents posing as students and reporting to various embassies.[11]

My own memory of these parties is perhaps understandably hazy, since a great deal of drink was consumed. One occasion however does stand out in my mind. The befogged details may well be quite inaccurate, but the atmosphere of dramatic tension evokes a feeling of the wild spirit of our unorthodox behaviour. Ronald MacDonald Douglas, a playwright and writer, always dressed in a kilt of the Douglas clan and carried a dirk in his

---

11. Brian Kennedy, *Irish Art and Modernism*, p. 93.

stocking.[12] Posing as the chief of his clan, he was believed to be a communist agent – which was about the worst thing you could be accused of in those days. By some extraordinary chance someone else claiming to be the head of the Douglas clan turned up at the same party, dressed identically. They spied each other, drew their dirks from their stockings and became locked in combat, as we attempted to drag them apart. This is just when we really needed the help of the Special Branch, who always turned up at those parties.

Unfortunately they lay in a helpless heap in a corner: for with the help of an expert at mixing drinks we made a practice of dosing the detectives with appropriate concoctions to render them incapable of carrying out their duty. I don't remember the precise outcome of this episode. We must have managed to drag them apart, for no murder was reported.

We were told that the Special Branch had rented a flat on the opposite side of the street where they had a powerful pair of binoculars trained on our activities which could be seen through the large Georgian windows. On one occasion I failed to get my car started on producer gas and René offered me half of his capacious double bed (for Zette was on one of her regular visits to Nick). Some years later I was told that my name was on the Garda files as a dangerous homosexual.

Some of the activities of the detectives were so ludicrously clumsy that I can only believe that they were mainly concerned with putting on an appearance of being very busy in ensuring the security of the State. Mind you, plenty of really serious espionage was going on at the time, but I feel quite certain that none of my regular close friends were involved. Charles Acton was under suspicion and detectives questioned my father and my uncle about my relationship with him. Both of us had spent some time as students in Germany and we were unashamedly involved in the pacifist movement. Charles, however, had rented his family home, Kilmacurragh in County Wicklow, to a German named Charles Budina, who ran it as a hotel. For a short time Charles arranged to continue living there, acting as a barman for the guests.

In an extraordinary arrangement shortly after the outbreak of hostilities, when warfare was still conducted under gentlemanly rules reminiscent of a game of cricket, German nationals with Nazi sympathies who lived in Ireland were allowed to return to the fatherland to join their 'team'. They

---

12. Ronald MacDonald Douglas (1896–1984), Scottish nationalist and author, *inter alia*, of *The Scots Book. A Miscellany … about Scotland and her People* (London: A. Maclehose & Co., 1935), was arrested for high treason in 1936 in Edinburgh, accused of planning an armed insurrection against England. Released on condition he leave Great Britain, he came to Ireland where he lived for about thirty years.

were given unmolested passage through England in a sealed train. Budina was one of these; but he had left the management of the hotel and the responsibility for certain other activities in the hands of an agent. One of these 'other activities' was apparently a radio transmitter in the attic sending regular messages to Germany. Charles was quite unaware of these goings-on. I should say that the Kilmacurragh story may well be complete rubbish: but this is how I heard it. It would go a long way to explaining the interest of the detectives in Charles' activities and his association with me.[13]

One of the more ludicrous incidents happened when Lionel Kerwood and I, having missed the last tram to Rathfarnham where we were living, were walking home from town. (This was before we developed the producer-gas plant.) It was a foggy night and as we came to the green triangle at Harold's Cross I saw a photographic subject which was irresistible: a streetlight throwing fingers of light and shade through the fog as it shone through the railings. I set up a tripod, mounted the camera, and spent some time calculating the correct exposure. At that moment we saw a very large garda riding purposely towards us on a bicycle without a light. Jokingly we taunted him for having no light. Without deigning to reply, he dismounted with heavy dignity. 'You'll have to come along with me to the Station in Terenure.' When enquiring for the reason, it became apparent that anyone taking a photograph in the middle of the night must be some lunatic up to no good. We were of course gathering weather information for the Luftwaffe. We were escorted to the Terenure barracks where the sergeant laboriously wrote down our address and a long list of personal details. When I pointed out that he had wrongly spelt the name of our house, Imaal, he had to clump up the stairs to the office above, fetch a new official form, and begin all over again. It was rather late when we eventually reached Rathfarnham.

A couple of weeks later a detective arrived at St Columba's College where I was teaching. Asking for the headmaster (or 'warden') he informed him that he was very sorry, but had to report that the school was employing a German spy. Sowby, the warden, was apparently able to convince the detective that I was innocent of such activity, and my name was cleared – for a time at least. We were followed by detectives wherever we went in the city. We got to know them quite well and would turn around from time to time and give them a friendly wave. It's quite an experience to be shadowed by detectives. It can be entertaining when you know that you have nothing to hide!

---

13. For more on Charles Budina, Charles Acton and Kilmacurragh House, see Pine, *Charles*, Chapter 6, *passim*.

Those who, during the war, had the most radical influence on the future of the visual arts in Ireland centred on the White Stag Group, the leading initiators of which were the painters Basil (or 'Benny') Rakoczy and Kenneth Hall, who had settled in number 34 Lower Baggot Street. The genesis of the group and how both Irish artists and others seeking refuge in neutral Ireland became associated with it is described by Brian Kennedy in his *Irish Art and Modernism*. There is not a great deal that I can helpfully add to this well-researched description, apart from the colourful background to the activities of this group, which I have already described. I was myself no more than a fringe member, being increasingly more concerned with music than with the visual arts. In fact, it is hardly correct to speak of membership at all; for the White Stag Group did not have an official membership list or publish specifically stated aims. It consisted rather of a loose grouping of those who wished to break away from established academic conservatism and explore contemporary European influences. Many of the Irish artists who became associated with the group had previously found an outlet for their work in the Dublin Painters' Gallery on St Stephen's Green. Among these was Mainie Jellett, whose greatly respected and influential encouragement gave a sense of positive cohesion to the group. There were also Ralph Cusack and Thurloe Conolly. It was chiefly through them that I became involved.

My other contact was through Noel and Margot Moffett, who were also on the fringe of the group. Noel was an architect with views considered very advanced at the time. He was also an excellent photographer of the creative kind. His wife Margot was of great assistance as someone whose practical head was well screwed on. She acted in an unofficial secretarial capacity, undertaking most of the practical aspects of arranging the Exhibition of Subjective Art which was held at number 6 Lower Baggot Street in January 1944. Margot and Noel knew Herbert Read and persuaded him to come over to Dublin to open our exhibition, write an introduction for the catalogue and give a series of lectures.[14] Brian Kennedy states that 'at the last minute Read was unable to come to Ireland'. As a member of the organising committee, I can say that it was our understanding that he was not allowed to come to the country because the authorities considered his 'communist' views too dangerous for Ireland. In place of an eagerly anticipated occasion we had to resort to asking Margot to read the text of his opening speech. His advertised lectures also had to be read out in the

---

14. Herbert Read (see also Chapter 2, note 22, p. 39, above) had been one of the organisers of the London International Surrealist Exhibition held in 1936.

'A Surrealist Writer'. Pencil portrait of Brian by Thurloe Conolly, 1943.

absence of the great man himself.

At this time I was preparing for the recital of my chamber music at the Shelbourne Hotel, which I have described. I was also shortly to be married to my singing pupil Mary, who sang at the recital, and who helped me to look after visitors to the Subjective Art Exhibition. Music was taking more and more of my time. Although I continued painting throughout the year – notably in the Aran Islands on our honeymoon there[15] – and exhibited at the Living Art Exhibition during the following autumn, I was gradually coming to the conclusion that I could not devote the time needed to develop my ability as a painter to the degree of mastery I would wish to aim at. Furthermore, I was becoming increasingly aware of a serious lack of facility in draughtsmanship. Towards the end of 1944 I made the decision to devote my energies to music. Much as I may have been tempted, I have never painted since.

I may have decided to devote my energies to music, but I have never wished to confine my life to a single track. Motor sport was still an enthusiasm, especially since petrol was once again becoming available and I was able to enjoy my Brescia Bugatti.

A new interest developed through Nelson Paine, whom I had first known as an amateur flute player. He had formed the Dublin Marionette Group with which both Mary and I became involved from the autumn of 1943. Mary manipulated the puppets and made costumes and I provided incidental music and read speaking parts. This led to my writing a surrealist play, *Revelation at Low Tide*, which we put on at the Peacock Theatre in November 1944 along with Synge's *Riders to the Sea* and Prokofiev's *Peter and the Wolf* presented as a puppet ballet. The characters in my surrealist play consisted of Kryptomena, Teasel and Pencille (who lived in sea shells), Mr Crankbox, The Hollow Monitor and the Inhabitants of the Mud Flats (including a tar machine with smoke billowing from its chimney). Using the distortion of the viewer's sense of scale – a special possibility with puppet performances – a huge blackened human hand, the hand of the fearful God of the Old Testament, removed the characters bodily from their life on the mud flats when they had offended against the conventions of respectability. Most of the critics failed to find any meaning or sense in my play. I didn't intend that there should be any logic or sense in what was just a dreamlike surrealist evocation of a disturbing mood-picture.

I have described above how Lionel Kerwood and I set up house at Imaal, Rathfarnham Park, in 1941, and how this later became a sort of clubhouse

---

15. Brian and Mary were married on 6 June 1944.

for artists and scroungers of all kinds. After a couple of years Lionel became very involved with a girlfriend and moved out by degrees to a flat in town. His place was taken by Thurloe Conolly, a painter and member of the White Stag Group, whose work I greatly admired. He was later to marry my sister Yvonne, who was also a regular visitor to Imaal. The most permanent members of the household were the cats: Boris, the large tabby whom I had brought back with me from London; and two gingers: Gimble and Erasmus. The gingers resolutely declined to be properly house-trained and if they didn't 'do it' defiantly under the grand piano, staring at you as though to say 'Don't you dare disturb me in my natural functions', they would make use of a spare room which we seldom used. I shudder to think what the place must have smelt like to those not so thoroughly inured to cat odours.

Another component of the general aroma must have been cooking smells. Preparing meals during wartime scarcity was fraught with complications. The gas supply was reduced to very low pressure except at certain specified hours. It was illegal to try and cook outside these official periods on what became known as 'the glimmer'; though many took no heed, and with an eye watching through the window for the 'glimmer man', who could turn off your gas supply completely if he caught you disobeying the rule, we did what we could. My holidays in Achill had taught me the use of the traditional cast-iron pot-oven, which is heated by red-hot embers of turf. Standing on three short legs, the pot stood above a layer of hot embers, with more pieces placed on the heavy lid. This is easy to manage on the ample hearth of a traditional cottage fireplace, but not so suitable for the neat tiled hearth of a suburban bungalow. Palatable white bread was unobtainable and I learned how to cook excellent soda-bread in the pot-oven; and there is nothing to compare with a joint of mutton roasted in this way. Of course, being in the living-room rather than the kitchen, the whole place became bespattered with turf ash and mutton fat. 'Great man for the grease!' my cleaning lady used to exclaim when she attempted her weekly clean-up of the house.

Outside the house, which was situated on a respectable avenue of new suburban houses, there was a very small area which more respectable inhabitants would have cultivated as a neatly mown lawn, or even a rose garden. For us, it was just the right space to use for cleaning out the producer-gas plant on the car and storing scrap exhaust pipes, which were to be used in constructing COGAS producers by our firm of Norman, Boydell and Kerwood. The whole area in front of the house, including the concrete footpath, was coated with a blanket of charcoal dust cemented with waste engine oil so that the rain would not wash it away. The extraordinary thing is that we never actually received any complaints from the respectable neighbours. I wonder did they perhaps consider us dangerously mad?

Most evenings after the laboriously prepared meal had been demolished, the inmates of Imaal (whoever they happened to be at the time) would enthusiastically settle down to our special form of creative entertainment. If we weren't listening to music on the gramophone, this took the form of what we liked to call 'Surrealist Expression' in writing and drawing. Following ideas spawned by the original French surrealists, the thing was to write short pieces inspired by the unfettered imagination, or execute fantastic drawings evoking dream images in the manner of Dali, Tanguy or Chirico. Sometimes these would be executed as communal efforts, in which an unfinished beginning to a drawing or piece of writing would be handed on to another member of the group who would add some more and in turn pass the unfinished product on to someone else. The completed literary 'masterpieces', whether solo or communal, were then read out and received either with uproarious laughter or extremely intense seriousness; and the drawings were appraised in turn. A certain competitive element crept into the proceedings as we strove to produce something more outrageously comic or disgusting: a convenient form of rebellious catharsis for those of us who had quite recently broken free from a polite and civilised upbringing.

The activities of what we later, with tongue-in-cheek, called 'The Rathfarnham Academy of Surrealist Art' continued for some time, though rather sporadically, after Mary and I were married and I relinquished the lease on Imaal in favour of our new house in Cabinteely. The regular members of 'The Academy' became dispersed; perhaps largely because (from our point of view) we wanted to break free from the club, which could easily have invaded and dominated our new married home. We did however meet from time to time and spend an evening producing a few more outrageous 'surrealoids'. Perhaps the best introduction to what we were up to is provided by *Osmograph*, a communal effort by Nick Nicholls (the painter), Thurloe Conolly, Charles Acton, and myself, dating from February 1943:[16]

> Osmograph – thy footstool screams
> Casting spleen shadows on my thigh stones
> And on my thighs the last laugh remains

---

16. See also Murray, *Language of Dreams*, pp. 13–15.

Embedded like a pearl among black swine:
And yet thy riders, hollow and sand red
Pass and repass thy shining footstool, dead.
Bleeding from the nostrils I searched
Amongst the base remains of the hollow riders
And my finger stuck in coils of tendon strings
Revealing hidden stubfoot clusterscreech.
My heart was a lampen string, close-knit,
My heart was a singing web, red-lamped,
My heart was a rose leaf, rabid and thong-tied.
And thine? Or wert thou fused
With singing firetoned commentaries of jade,
Or pared with suctous razor clouds?
O I'm all right, right, tight, tight as the trivet
That burns in your heart
And safe as the wing that bears the bird
With a song like a song that you've never heard.
Don't listen any more:
God has blessed the mustard,
And I am dead.
We are all dead,
Perched on riderless footstools,
Screaming very quietly.

Caricature of Brian by 'Pyke', *Evening Herald*, 10 November 1945.

COURTESY OF INDEPENDENT NEWS AND MEDIA AND THE *IRISH INDEPENDENT*, AND THE BOARD OF TRINITY COLLEGE DUBLIN

CHAPTER 5
BACK TO MUSIC AGAIN

TOWARDS THE END of the 1940s I was becoming more deeply involved in musical pursuits. To earn a living and support a family led me to pick up what lucrative employment I could find. I obtained the position of Professor of Singing at the RIAM, where I was occupied for most of the day teaching. (What a wonderfully inflated title for a junior singing teacher!) As an oboist there were occasional professional jobs in orchestras that would be assembled for oratorio or opera performances. I was increasingly on demand as a bass soloist in oratorio and my experience as the unpaid conductor of the DOP gradually led to professional engagements as a conductor with the RÉ Orchestra. I have already recounted how radio broadcasting on musical topics was becoming one of my main sources of income. Then I was employed by the RDS for its vocational educational scheme, which involved travelling to all corners of the country to give musical lectures at local technical schools. I also instituted public lectures on the interpretation and enjoyment of music. One such series was given weekly in the evenings at our own home, and for another I hired a room in the Broadway Café in O'Connell Street. Mary sat at a table by the door and collected half-a-crown from those who turned up in response to newspaper advertisements. Spare moments were devoted to composition. Royalties from the very few performances obtainable in those days didn't amount to more than a pittance. Hence, with this pervading involvement in musical matters, the memoirs I have to recount from this point will be almost entirely concerned with music and musicians.

I have described how the outbreak of war brought a great influx of artists to neutral Ireland, with their more international outlook and fresh ideas, which brought about significant changes in the Dublin artistic community. There were however no musicians of significance among them to invigorate what was frankly rather a musical backwater. Music had to wait until some years after the war to receive its injection of new ideas and higher standards such as the visual arts had enjoyed several years earlier.

Meanwhile, some of us were trying to do something for Irish musical life equivalent to the inspiring excitement that had resulted from the stimulus of fresh ideas in the visual arts. Musical effort, with rival organisations each pursuing their own separate ideals, was so diffuse that in our view it urgently needed focusing into a more unified purpose. It was chiefly due to Edgar Deale, Michael McMullin, Fred May and myself, who met together in the Unicorn Restaurant early in 1948, that the idea of forming what became the MAI was born. In describing its foundation I give here a historically correct account, thus differing from some previous reminiscences where I admitted that some imaginative embroidery may have coloured the story.

Edgar Deale was Irish manager of an international insurance company. He was an accomplished composer and enthusiastically involved in choral music.[1] His profession assured us of the assistance of sound business sense. Michael McMullin was a keen observer who had written articles on musical subjects and was an outspokenly virulent critic of the official musical establishment, particularly RÉ, which was then under the control of the Minister for Posts and Telegraphs. He vanished from the Dublin scene some time in the late 1950s and no one seems to know what became of him. Freddie May, whom we regarded as the first Irish composer of real significance in the twentieth-century context, was a passionate idealist who provided much enthusiastic determination for our cause.

We immediately contacted our musical friends, asking for their support and sponsorship. With Michael McMullin acting as honorary secretary we circulated a letter, after discussing our plans with those who had agreed to become sponsors, calling a meeting to inaugurate the new Association. The letter bore the names of the following sponsors:

J[ohn] S. Beckett
Brian Boydell
E[dgar] M. Deale
James Delany (organist and choirmaster)
Brendan Dunne (composer and conductor)
Aloys Fleischmann (composer, Professor of Music at University College
    Cork, and tireless worker in the cause of music)
Arthur Franks (violinist and teacher)
Dorothy Graham (choral conductor)

---

1. Edgar Deale (1902–99) was a composer, choral singer (for many years a member of the choir of St Patrick's Cathedral and of the Culwick Choral Society) and activist for music, especially through his involvement with the MAI. He was Dublin manager of the Zurich Insurance Company. See further *EMIR*, p. 288.

Joseph Groocock (choral conductor and Head of Music at St Columba's
     College)
Victor Leeson (choral conductor, and organiser of the St James's Gate
     Music Society concerts)
Frederick May
Terry O'Connor
Joseph O'Neill (music critic of the *Irish Independent*)
Olive Smith (choral conductor, involved with the Culwick Choral Society
     – and later to become one of the chief driving forces in the MAI, first
     as Hon. Treasurer and then as Hon. Secretary)
Dorothy Stokes (accompanist, and teacher at the RIAM)
Thomas Tierney (young professional pianist)
W[illiam] F. Watt (tenor singer, well-known in oratorio performances;
     also founder of the Waterford Music Society [Waterford Music Club])
Alice Yoakley (for many years conductor of the Culwick Choral Society,
     and a distinguished teacher of piano)

At the meeting held on 13 April 1948 the MAI was founded. The original
prospectus which was circulated is a rare historic document worth quoting
in full in the way that it was laid out.

THE MUSIC ASSOCIATION OF IRELAND
Honorary Secretary
MICHAEL MCMULLIN,
15 Upper Mount Street,
Dublin.
Honorary Treasurer
MRS. LYALL SMITH,
"Clonard",
Torquay Road, Foxrock,
Co. Dublin. (Phone: 83968).
Council for 1948

BRIAN BOYDELL	MADELEINE LARCHET
EDGAR M. DEALE	NANCIE LORD
JAMES DELANY	FREDERICK MAY
BRENDAN DUNNE	TERRY O'CONNOR
ALOYS FLEISCHMANN	JOSEPH O'NEILL
JOSEPH GROOCOCK	DOROTHY STOKES
ANTHONY HUGHES	WILLIAM F. WATT

Membership is open to those who support the objects of the Association. The Annual membership subscription is 10s., and applications will be received by either of the honorary officers.

Do you intend joining? If so, please do it now by sending your name and address with your subscription.

[new page]

This Association has been founded in the belief that there is in Ireland, as in many other countries, a growing realisation of the immense importance of music to the community, and of the need for a restoration and recognition of music of a high standard as a part of normal life.

The originators of the Association, encouraged by the recent appearance of similar movements abroad, recognise that in Ireland music has for various reasons remained comparatively undeveloped, though there is a great musical potential in the nation. They believe that there is an even greater need here for a body to work for the furtherance of music, and the establishment of a tradition and standard, and that the time is now ripe for its formation. They ask for the help and support in this project of all musicians and music-lovers who are sincerely devoted to the art.

As they see it, there is a need primarily for a body of organised musical opinion, whose main function will be to formulate a co-ordinated policy for music as a whole, and to seek to influence the authorities as far as possible to carry it out. To this end the Association needs as strong a body of opinion behind it and as many members as it can get.

The following six principal objectives have been agreed upon

    (1) To further musical education.

    (2) To improve conditions for composers and musicians generally.

    (3) To work for the establishment of a National Concert Hall.

    (4) To submit recommendations on musical policy to the authorities concerned.

    (5) To encourage the formation of musical groups, societies and choirs throughout the country.

    (6) To organise popular lectures, concerts and recitals and to awaken a musical consciousness in the nation.

The Association hopes further to act as a central source for information and advice, and has before it a number of plans by which it might contribute directly to musical life. Some of these, such as the foundation of a musical publication, are of great importance, but depend upon the contribution of considerable funds. Others, such as the organisation of public classes or recitals, depend upon the co-operation of musicians and the provision of a hall.

The extent to which the aims in general of the Association may be realised depends upon the support received now from all who pretend to any interest in the cause of music in Ireland. This is your opportunity to make this cause heard. If you neglect it the fate of music will again be left to the isolated efforts of individuals and to the haphazard interest of those who are not necessarily musical.

JOIN THE MUSIC ASSOCIATION OF IRELAND AND HELP TO ADD A NEW VOICE TO THE CHORUS OF NATIONS.

Quite soon after its founding, the MAI began to have an increasing influence on the development of musical endeavour in the country. Efforts were made to organise the teaching profession and regulate professional standards by forming the Music Teachers' Association of Ireland. Composers were brought together in the 'Composers' Group' to organise concerts and look after the interests of creative writing. Concert tours throughout the country were organised so that isolated districts could have the opportunity of hearing live music. Since most country towns possessed no adequate piano, the most useful group to send on tour proved to be a string quartet. The interesting outcome of the tours by the New London String Quartet was that what most would regard as a very 'highbrow' form of music became immensely popular in the most remote corners of the land. A natural development of the country tours was the establishment of Schools Concerts, which provided at the same time a platform for young Irish instrumentalists and singers.

An important move was the provision of a Music Diary, which was conveniently housed in McCullough's music shop in Suffolk Street. Concert promoters were encouraged to enter their forthcoming events in the diary, thus avoiding disastrous clashes of dates. A monthly bulletin was circulated to all members notifying them of the events entered in the diary, and containing news of general musical interest. All the time we were lobbying the government and other possible sources of funding in our efforts to provide Dublin with a suitable concert hall.

The early stages of providing a sound basis for the future development of the Association were not devoid of anxious moments of crisis. Michael McMullin's enthusiasm for a policy of aggressive attack against the official establishment was considered by most of us to be unproductively negative. Our future was threatened with a split within our own ranks. After a somewhat acrimonious debate the more positive approach of persuasion and cooperation fortunately prevailed and the air was cleared to forge ahead.[2]

One of the immediate aims was to organise celebrations in honour of the bicentenary in 1950 of the death of J.S. Bach. The centrepiece of these celebrations was to be the first performance in Ireland of the B minor Mass with orchestral forces as demanded by Bach's score. (There had of course been performances before, but with organ accompaniment or incomplete instrumental forces.)[3] There were no instrumentalists in the country who could play the baroque D trumpet, which is an essential element of the score. Players were therefore brought over from England for the occasion. Amazing though it may now seem, there was no playable harpsichord available. We managed to persuade the National Museum of Ireland to have the instrument made by the Dublin maker Ferdinand Weber about 1770, which is in their collection, restored for the occasion. It was played by John Beckett. The conductor was Otto Matzerath from Germany, who had an enormous appetite for mussels and other seafood. The choir consisted of the Culwick Choral Society.

Two amusing incidents occurred in connection with the Bach Bicentenary. For the performance of the B minor Mass we required the services of the RÉSO. The radio authorities were willing to provide the orchestra on condition that the performance was preceded by the National Anthem. This we considered to be quite unsuitable for the occasion. Deadlock ensued until, with an inspired flash of political acumen, Edgar Deale thought of the perfect ploy by quietly remarking (at a meeting called to argue the case), 'Isn't it funny that we cling to so many British customs, such as playing the National Anthem before a concert?' The opposition blushed and the

2. See also references to the MAI in Part II: Diary (below), January 1950, *passim*. For an independent history and assessment of the MAI, see Teresa O'Donnell, 'Musical Legacies: the contribution of the Music Association of Ireland to an Irish musical infrastructure', *Journal of the Society for Musicology in Ireland*, vol. 10 (2014–15), pp. 3–22 (http://www.music.ucc.ie/jsmi/index.php/jsmi/article/view/114/135. Date accessed: 21 March 2016). See also *EMIR*, pp. 706–8.

3. The first complete performance in Dublin of Bach's B minor Mass was given by the University of Dublin Choral Society in 1908. See Barra Boydell, '"This most crabbed of all earthly music": the performance and reception of Bach's vocal music in Dublin in the nineteenth and early twentieth centuries', in A. Leahy and Yo Tomita (eds), *Bach Studies from Dublin*, IMS 8 (Dublin: Four Courts Press, 2004), pp. 22–46.

Brian with (*l. to r.*) Olive Smith, John Beckett (seated) and conductor Otto Matzerath inspecting the Ferdinand Weber harpsichord in the National Museum of Ireland for use in the MAI's Bach Bicentenary concert in September 1950.

COURTESY OF THE BOARD OF TRINITY COLLEGE DUBLIN

anthem was not mentioned again. The other episode which caused us cynical amusement was provided by the Dublin correspondent of *The Musical Times* who was a rather eccentric organist. We had organised an impressive programme of events, and when we looked at this publication, which listed events happening all over these islands during the Bach celebrations, we saw just one short entry under the heading 'Dublin'. It read: 'Organ recital by F.C.J. Swanton'.[4]

It is in some ways sad to think of how much could be achieved forty years ago by amateur enthusiasts with very little funding. The organisation of music today is in the hands of professional administrators backed by considerable funding from bodies like the Arts Council. The country concerts are managed (very efficiently) by Music Network; the composers' interests are looked after by the CMC and the Association of Irish Composers; the National Concert Hall, which our propaganda eventually brought into being, was built and is managed by the government and its professional appointees. The Schools Concerts are still [1994] organised by the MAI, but with accountability to the Arts Council which provides the funding. As I said, it is in some ways sad; for the days when amateur enthusiasm and voluntary work could achieve a great deal are almost a feature of the past. And yet, the fact that so much musical effort is now promoted by professional administrators and supported by semi-state funding must owe something to our efforts of forty years ago.[5]

The injection of new blood into Dublin musical life came with the expansion of the RÉ Orchestra in 1948. Valiant attempts by Michael Bowles, who had been in charge of music in RÉ, to establish a full symphony orchestra with regular public symphony concerts were enthusiastically welcomed by the public, but had met with little encouragement from government sources; especially in the way of necessary funding.[6] Positive action was now initiated under the aegis of León Ó Broin, an enthusiastic music-lover who was secretary to the Department of Posts and Telegraphs, which was in charge of RÉ; and Fachtna O'Hannrachain [*sic*], its new

---

4. F.C.J. Swanton (1895–1974) gave many Irish first performances of contemporary French organ music, including that of Maurice Duruflé (1902–86). See also Part II: Diary (below), 29 May 1950.
5. The MAI formally ceased to exist in 2007, effectively a victim of its own long-term success, resulting in the establishment of bodies such as Music Network, the CMC and the Association of Irish Composers referred to above.
6. Michael Bowles (1909–98) was the main conductor of the RÉ Orchestra from 1941 to 1948, when he resigned following disagreements with RÉ relating to the expansion of the orchestra (*EMIR*, p. 112). See also Part II: Diary (below), 20 January, 23 February 1950.

director of music.[7] Wielding the ultimate power, as Minister for Posts and Telegraphs, it was most fortunate to have an enthusiast for the arts in Erskine Childers, who was later to become President of Ireland.

The excellent idea that evolved was to employ first-class musicians from the Continent who were only too anxious to find employment outside their war-torn countries. They were to lead their respective sections, and at the same time be available for teaching young Irish musicians with a view to the eventual evolution of a full professional symphony orchestra employing Irish instrumentalists. I can think of about twenty excellent musicians who came to live in Ireland as members of the new orchestra. They came from Germany, France, Italy, and indeed from all over mainland Europe, and made a most valuable contribution to the development of music in Ireland. Some formed chamber-music groups, which provided a great stimulus to Irish composers; and through their teaching they raised the standard of instrumental performance significantly.

Some of these musicians became personal friends – even life-long family friends. Wolfram Hentschel came to lodge in our house until his wife Ingrid was able to join him in Dublin. He was leader of the cello section and played, along with François D'Albert, in the newly formed Dublin String Quartet.[8] After Wolfram returned to Hamburg in 1951 to join Hans Schmidt-Isserstedt's radio orchestra, he formed, with Uli Benthien, the Benthien String Quartet. They gave many performances of my First String Quartet in several countries and recorded it for the first gramophone recording of contemporary Irish music.[9] I later wrote my Second String Quartet for Wolfram and the Benthien Quartet.[10]

The French flautist André Prieur shared with me an enthusiasm for fishing. I was responsible for converting him from the French approach, which amounted, as far as I could see, to catching as many fish as possible by the most efficient and easy method, to the more challenging art of dry-fly fishing for wily trout. André not only founded his Prieur Ensemble, consisting of flute, harp and string trio (for whom I wrote my Quintet), but

---

7. Fachtna Ó hAnnracháin (1920–2010) was music director of RÉ from 1947 to 1961 (see also *EMIR*, p. 765, and Pine, *Music and Broadcasting, passim*). He would later become a close fishing colleague and friend of Brian's. (The anglicised spelling of his name, which Brian used throughout, is retained here and elsewhere in his text.)

8. Wolfram Hentschel joined the RÉSO from Germany in 1949 as principal cellist.

9. Deutsche Grammophon 32291, LP, *c.* 1956. On the first broadcast and live performance of this string quartet, see Part II: Diary, (below) Jan.–Feb, 1950, Hans Schmitt Isserstedt founded the North German Radio Symphony Orchestra (Sinfonieorchester des Norddeutschen Rundfunks) in Hamburg in 1945 and remained as principal conductor until 1971.

10. The String Quartet no. 2, op. 44, dates from 1957.

in 1970 formed the New Irish Chamber Orchestra. This orchestra is still active today (having dropped the 'New' from its title).[11]

When, after the war, it first became possible to bring a car to Europe and tour around, Mary and I went in the summer of 1950 for a camping holiday in France in the 1935 Lancia Augusta I had bought for £25. (I had never paid more than £15 for a car previously.)[12] One was then not allowed to bring more than £50 out of the country for holiday purposes. André's widowed mother lived in Normandy, so we arranged that in return for her giving us an extra supply of French francs, we would give the equivalent in Irish money to her. We were invited to lunch with Madame Prieur, when she was to give us our extra French money. We turned up at the appointed time in very informal camping clothes, expecting just a light snack. We were welcomed by a smartly dressed lady clad in widow's black. She had prepared in our honour a six-course meal with appropriate wines. Towards the end of this formal *déjeuner* she produced a very special bottle of Calvados, obtained from a friend in the famous local distillery, and poured out generous glasses for each of us. Now Mary doesn't like such potent fire-water: so when coffee was served and Madame went out of the room to fetch something I whispered to Mary, 'Pour it into your coffee – that'll dilute it.' She duly did so just in time before our hostess returned with the bottle of Calvados and said, 'And now you must have some Calvados in your coffee'. Whereupon she poured as much as would fit into Mary's already potent brew. So as not to cause offence, when she next left the room the contents of the cup were quickly poured into the aspidistra, which stood in a pot by the window. I wish we had had the chance of calling again to see how the plant survived; but the opportunity never arose.

Among other immigrants in the orchestra Michele Incenzo stands out in my memory. An excitable and charming Neapolitan, he was a brilliant clarinet player. He charmed us all – especially the girls, whom he would invite to his flat to sample his famed Italian cooking. Michele's taste in music was largely influenced by what opportunity it offered to display brilliant clarinet technique. He responded to the black blobs of musical notation with incomparable mastery, though he was not so impressive when it came to translating the notes into meaningful or expressive music. He persuaded me to write a piece for him, and I composed my *Elegy and Capriccio for Clarinet*

---

11. On the Prieur Ensemble and the [New] Irish Chamber Orchestra, see further *EMIR*, pp. 863 and 527–8. Brian's *Quintet for Flute, Harp and Strings*, op. 49, dates from 1960 (rev. 1966 and 1980).

12. On Brian's Lancia, see further Part II: Diary (below), especially 26 January 1950, note 37.

and Strings.[13] He gave the first performance in 1956, with the Dublin String Orchestra, which had been formed by Herbert Pöche, the German viola player. During the rehearsals, Michele was particularly delighted with the Capriccio, which has quite a showy part for the soloist. Every now and then, when Pöche was sorting out some detail in the string parts, he would run over to me, shake my hand violently, and declare in his wonderful Italianate English, 'Very nice-a modern-a music-a. I do-a my best-a!' He did. He played it brilliantly!

The story was told that Michele had an altercation with Gilbert Berg, the gentle, quiet Belgian bassoon player. Michele taught clarinet at the RIAM, where Gilbert taught the double-reed instruments, oboe and bassoon. The first student who wished to learn the saxophone applied to the Academy. Who was to teach him? The saxophone has a single reed like that of a clarinet; but the fingering is more akin to the oboe or bassoon. An argument festered away for several weeks. One day, Gilbert was driving to rehearsal in his car and saw Michele standing at a bus stop. He stopped and offered him a lift. As soon as Michele got into the car, he started the argument all over again: '… you see, the saxophone has the reed of a clarinetto …' Gilbert, fed up with the argument, stopped the car, and the gentle Belgian sternly ordered the Italian to get out. The story goes that he then got out himself, walked round to the pavement, and knocked Michele flat on the ground with a well-aimed punch on the jaw. Gilbert became Professor of Saxophone.

Besides the new members of the orchestra, there were some who came to Ireland on their own initiative, or through individual invitation. One of the first to arrive was Hans Waldemar Rosen, who had been in a prisoner-of-war camp in Wales and was invited to Dublin by an Irish singer whom he had taught in Germany before the war.[14] Hans made a very great contribution to choral music. He soon formed a chamber choir and gave us the opportunity of hearing a great deal of choral music that had not been performed in Ireland before, particularly the music of Heinrich Schütz. When the RÉ Singers were instituted in 1953 he was appointed their conductor. This ten-voice professional choir provided a tremendous

13. The *Elegy and Capriccio for Clarinet and String Orchestra*, op. 42 (1956) has been recorded by John Finucane with the RTÉ National Symphony Orchestra conducted by Robert Houlihan (CD, RTÉ Lyric FM, B002TJBQ40 (2009)).

14. Hans Waldemar Rosen (1904–94) took his Doctorate in Music in 1930 at Leipzig University, where he also studied composition and conducting. He came to Ireland with his wife in 1948, joining RÉ in 1949 as a choral conductor. From 1953 to 1974 he conducted the RÉ (later RTÉ) Singers, Ireland's first full-time professional chamber choir (*EMIR*, p. 894). See also Part II: Diary (below), *passim*.

stimulus to Irish composers; for under Hans's direction they were anxious to perform our music. The result was an unprecedented out-pouring of choral music which was assured of a sympathetic and expert performance.

Among other individual immigrants who made their mark on the Irish scene were the violinists Jaroslav Vaneček from Czechoslovakia and François D'Albert from Hungary via France.[15] The former revolutionised violin teaching in Dublin, producing a number of very distinguished pupils. He persuaded me to write my Violin Concerto in 1954, and played the solo part in a number of early performances.[16]

François was a colourful character. A transparent operator, up to all the tricks of the trade in order to promote himself: the sort of character with whom we might have had no patience at all had it not been for the fact that he *was* a really fine violinist and had an endearing personality behind the self-advertising exterior. Since you could never really believe everything he said about himself, the story of his career before arriving in Ireland may not be quite accurate. He was supposed to be a Hungarian with a doctor's degree from the University of Budapest. Wishing to escape the post-war turmoil in his country, he migrated to France, where he obtained French citizenship, apparently with the idea of eventually making it to the United States. When he discovered that there was a more generous allocation of visas to would-be emigrants from Ireland, he came to Dublin with his sister (a singer) and his mother, armed with introductions to influential figures in the Catholic Church. He soon took out Irish citizenship, and indeed subsequently fulfilled his ambition to cross the Atlantic, obtaining a post in Montreal.

I began by describing François as a 'transparent operator'. It never ceased to amaze me how immigrants from the eastern part of Europe seemed so attuned to currying favour that when they sought advancement by outrageous flattery they never seemed to realise that in the circumstances of our social customs we immediately saw through them. 'You, Brian, are the only musician I have met here whom I would completely respect as being a real expert. We must get together and show how this concerto

---

15. Jaroslav Vaneček (1920–2011) was appointed Professor of Violin at the RIAM in 1949, having previously given a recital at the RDS in 1948 with his wife Květa. In 1954 he transferred to the Municipal School of Music, where he taught until 1973 when he moved to London. Vaneček was responsible for raising the standards of violin playing in Ireland (he also taught in Belfast). He continued his solo career in Ireland, commissioning and premiering Brian Boydell's Violin Concerto in 1954 (*EMIR*, p.1027).

16. A recording of the Violin Concerto performed by Maighread McCrann with the National Symphony Orchestra of Ireland, conducted by Colman Pearce, was issued in 1997 (Marco Polo, CD, 8.223887).

should be played. If you and I go and talk to the Director of Music, I'm sure we can fix a date with the orchestra.' François approached the Sligo Feis Ceoil (competitive music festival) with the proposition of instituting the D'Albert Prize for violin playing. He was invited to name the set piece for the competition, and he offered to donate the prize. The piece set for the competition was Sonata no. 1 by François D'Albert. When the winner mounted the platform to receive the prize, it turned out to be a copy of Sonata no. 2 by François D'Albert.[17]*

For the first few years after the expansion of the RÉSO there was no permanent conductor in charge. A number of distinguished European conductors were engaged for short periods. The first of these was Jean Martinon, who was followed by Hans Schmidt-Isserstedt, Edmund Appia and others, including Sixten Eckeberg, who was of great assistance to me as a Sibelius enthusiast. He had known the composer and passed on to me much valuable information about the interpretation of the symphonies.

Martinon revolutionised the standard of orchestral playing in Dublin and was a great inspiration to us. At the time, Erskine Childers was Minister for Posts and Telegraphs. I suspect that it was largely through his influence that the Department of Education was persuaded to cooperate with RÉ and arrange for the visiting conductors to give summer courses in orchestral conducting, with a view to training an Irish conductor who could eventually take over the orchestra. Advanced tuition in composition was also offered, and I valued greatly the criticism of Arnold Bax, Alan Rawsthorne and Jean Martinon.[18]

I became very friendly with Martinon, from whom I learned a great deal, particularly as an orchestral conductor. I well remember the advice he gave me during the course of an informal meal. With his charming Frenchified English he said, 'Boydell: if you wish to succeed as a conductor you must look to the *apperience*. No *barbe*! No Bugatti! No *trousèrs du corde-du-roi*!' Rather a contrast to the advice I was later given by a much less distinguished Englishman who was engaged for the summer course in conducting and composition. At the time I was wondering whether to concentrate my energies on conducting or composition, so I asked his opinion. 'Take my advice, young man. You must choose either to be a conductor *or* a composer. You can't do both. In fact, I think I am the only well-known conductor who

---

17.* Dear François, if you should ever come across these anecdotes, please believe that they are not told maliciously. You caused us much amusement; but your fine playing contributed so much to our musical enjoyment during the time you were here. [Author's note]. D'Albert had joined the RÉSO following its foundation in 1948.

18. For more on the summer courses, see Pine, *Music and Broadcasting*, pp. 332–4.

has also achieved notable success as a composer.' He is probably no longer alive; but if I were to reveal his name, I doubt very much whether you would have heard of him.

It was rightly felt that although the short-term visits of distinguished conductors had worked wonders with the standard of orchestral playing in Ireland, the orchestra really needed an extended period under a permanent conductor who would weld the players, with their diverse styles of playing, into a unified team. With this in mind, Milan Horvat from Zagreb was appointed permanent conductor in 1953.[19] A big man, he got down to his task with enthusiasm, and with an amount of physical energy when conducting that the manuscript scores of works by Irish composers were virtually illegible after a performance. The sweat would pour from his brow all over the pages of the manuscript, so that the ink of the notes ran and merged into a hazy blotch.

Shortly after he arrived there was some criticism of his appointment. At that stage in our history, the great terror that threatened the Island of Saints and Scholars was the dark cloud of communism. I myself got into trouble when I accepted an invitation to give a lecture on music to the Friends of Soviet Russia. Nobody minded when I unwittingly lectured to a society in Dundalk, which later I gathered represented the Catholic Fascists. Anyway, Erskine Childers as the minister ultimately responsible for Horvat's appointment was bombarded with flak from country deputies in the Dáil, accusing him of appointing a communist to a state-sponsored position. This pressure on Childers wasn't helped when Denis Donoghue (who later became a distinguished professor of literature) as music critic of *The Irish Times* wrote a most uncomplimentary review of one of Horvat's concerts. Childers, I regret to say, did a very unwise thing. He sent for Smyllie the editor and put pressure on him to get rid of the music critic.[20] This move was resolved when Smyllie appealed to Denis to tone down his critical remarks where Horvat was concerned. Denis, a man of resolute integrity, replied that he would either write what he believed was right, or he would not write at all. And so he resigned.[21]

A minor incident arose during what was known as 'the Trieste crisis'. There was an acrimonious argument between Italy and Yugoslavia about the territorial rights to Trieste. The local repercussion which erupted in the

---

19. Milan Horvat (1919–2014) remained principal conductor of the RÉSO for five years.
20. Robert Marie ['R.M.'] Smyllie was editor of *The Irish Times* from 1934 until his death in 1954.
21. Denis Donoghue (b. 1928) was also a singing pupil of Brian's. See Part II: Diary (below), *passim*. A renowned literary critic, he held the Henry James Chair of English and American Letters at New York University from the 1970s.

orchestra took the form of the Italian trombone player refusing to cooperate with the Yugoslavian conductor. That can have devastating results when a trombone is involved; as indeed it proved to be when at a public symphony concert in the Gaiety Theatre the orchestra was playing Ravel's *Bolero*. When it came to the trombone's turn to play the repeated tune, the Italian came in one bar late. In spite of Horvat's frantic gestures, he resolutely refused to stop until he had finished his tune, which had been out of phase with the harmonies throughout.

From my point of view, the most memorable musical event during Milan Horvat's time as conductor of the RÉSO was the first recording of orchestral music by contemporary Irish composers ever to be released. This was undertaken by the Decca company of New York in 1956. Many of us got wind of this imminent event for the first time with the arrival of Simon Rady. This rather brash American gave the immediate impression of someone who would use the advantage of his pockets bursting with dollar bills to throw his weight around. With local pride he was shown the Phoenix Hall where the orchestra rehearsed and gave studio concerts.[22] It had recently benefited from the expert attention of BBC sound engineers. This would be where the recordings should be made. The door at the back of the hall was opened and he was ushered in for inspection. He took one look around it without either stepping inside or clapping his hands as a cursory sound test and simply exclaimed, 'This won't do!' Embarrassed confusion ensued. After a tour of all possible venues around the city, he eventually chose, with some enthusiasm, the Metropolitan Hall in Abbey Street, which was the headquarters of the YMCA. Complete with a religious text in gothic lettering above the stage, it looked (as I have described elsewhere) rather as though someone had attempted to convert a railway station into an evangelical temple. But it was acoustically excellent.

By this time I was beginning to realise that there was more to this brash American than pockets full of dollars. Being very interested in acoustics and the developing techniques of sound recording, I followed in his footsteps in order to learn what I could. I soon realised that Mr Rady was not only a master of his technical science, but had an outstanding musical ear that would immediately recognise any small blemish in performance that might pass unnoticed in a concert performance, but would become an irritant to someone listening repeatedly to a gramophone recording.

Meanwhile the orchestra had been engaged for the first opportunity its members were to enjoy of earning extra money outside their routine

22. The Phoenix Hall, in Dame Court, Dublin, was the home of the RÉSO from 1948 to 1962.

contract. They assembled for the first session in high spirits, rubbing their hands in glee at the promised share of dollars from the American whom they took to be an ignorant charlatan. Precisely at ten o'clock they started tuning up. The burly figure of Rady appeared on the balcony above the stage. In a tone of utterly dismissive sarcasm he drawled, 'Do you call that an A? … Clarinet, you're flat!' Michele Incenzo stood up waving his arms in excitable gestures of outrage and replied, 'I have-a a certificate from my *professore* in Napoli: my *clarinetto* plays a perfect 440 A! 'I don't care how many bloody certificates you have; all the wind can go home, and don't dare come back here until you can play a proper A.' The wind skulked out with tails between their legs and came back a chastened lot for the afternoon session. In the meantime the recording proceeded with strings alone for the works that did not call for wind instruments.

Who was the conductor of the orchestra? Milan Horvat was on the podium all right, but Simon Rady in the control room, surrounded by portraits of grimly serious past officials of the YMCA with letter-box mouths, was ultimately more responsible for the musical outcome. He would pick up the inter-com. telephone: 'Horvat, do that bit again. Didn't you hear the out-of-tune note from inside the second desk of violins?' And if, as he often did, Horvat allowed the momentum of the music to die by pausing too long before beginning a new phrase, out came the scissors and a small length of recording tape was snipped out in order to close up the pause.

The intriguing dishonesty of gramophone recordings was well illustrated when it came to recording my *Megalithic Ritual Dances*. The score calls for a third percussion player who is allotted quite a tricky tambourine part. In those days there were only two percussion players in the orchestra. When they needed an extra player, one would be borrowed from the Army Band. When faced with the off-beat rhythms demanded from the tambourine, the new recruit just couldn't manage the challenge. Horvat called me over. 'Have I your permission to leave out the tambourine part? Otherwise your piece will never get recorded.' His question was picked up on the microphone and Rady heard it in the control room. He had a speaker rigged up for relaying instructions to the hall. It hummed into life. 'You worried about the tambourine? Cut it out. I'll put it in in Berlin.' A few weeks after that recording session the tambourine part was dubbed onto the tape by the first percussion player of the Berlin Philharmonic.

Two LP records issued by Decca (USA), which are of historic signifi-cance, resulted from this venture. Featuring works by six contemporary Irish composers, they were issued under the title *New Music from Old Erin* and enclosed in a record sleeve depicting an old thatched 'cabin' in the west of Ireland.[23]

Several of us Dublin musicians did our best to make the visiting conductors and artists feel at home during their stay here. Apart from the experience of meeting some very distinguished personalities, we enjoyed their friendship and had many fascinating conversations, learning a great deal about the music profession in a wider context than Dublin could provide. Most were very appreciative and repaid our hospitality both with reciprocal entertaining and by offering valuable advice. One or two were, I'm afraid, rather off-hand and showed no sign of acknowledging our hospitality. I regret to say that Milan Horvat earned a name for never offering anyone even an occasional drink.

When the end of the period of his contract approached, Horvat mentioned to a limited number of people that he would hold a farewell party at the Grand Hotel in Malahide. Rather wickedly, the few who had been invited spread the news around the orchestra. Seeing their last opportunity of receiving a drink in return for many offered throughout a number of years, everyone turned up at the Malahide hotel and a great deal of liquor was consumed. At the conclusion of the evening a waiter handed the host a very substantial bill. The story goes that Horvat placed a five-pound note on the waiter's tray saying, 'That is my share.' Those standing close by refused to let him get away with it. (In all fairness, I must say that this is the story as I heard it at the time. It may well be partly apocryphal: many years later I asked Val Keogh about it. He was orchestral manager at the time, and was accredited with taking the initiative in getting the host to pay the bill. Unfortunately Val didn't remember the incident.)

As a freelance musician, a source of income which began to develop most advantageously for me from the end of the 1940s was adjudicating at competitive music festivals. The festival movement was more developed in Northern Ireland than in the Republic. This is where I gained my early experience in this specialised field, adjudicating at local festivals such as Portstewart, Holywood, Bangor, Coleraine, Ballymena and Dungannon; and then with promotion to Derry and Belfast.

---

23. The two LPs (Decca (USA), DL 9843/4 issued in 1956) included the following works: Brian Boydell's *Megalithic Ritual Dances* (1956), Seóirse Bodley's *Music for Strings* (1952) and three of the five movements from Frederick May's *Suite of Irish Airs* (1942) on DL 9843; A.J. Potter's *Variations on a Popular Tune* (1955), Thomas C. Kelly's *Three Pieces for Strings* (1949), John F. Larchet's *The Dirge of Ossian* and *MacAnanty's Reel* (1940), and Arthur Duff's *Irish Suite for Strings* (1940) on DL 9844.

With my training in many aspects of performance it was not too difficult to pick a winner. The demanding part is to 'sell' your decision convincingly to the audience. In addition, I considered it most important to encourage those who didn't figure among the prizewinners, and to be careful never to kill enthusiasm and promise. This can often be a horrifying problem. What are you to do when faced with such a worthy enterprise as a brass band formed to provide some positive incentive for deprived orphan boys, and they play at full blast so abominably out of tune that you have to cover your ears to deaden the pain?

To become constantly in demand as a successful adjudicator depends indeed on your ability to convince an audience that your judgement is infallible. You must never betray any uncertainty, however much you may be caught out of your depth. I remember looking forward to a competition for string orchestra at the Moose Jaw festival on the Canadian prairies. I was anticipating the joy of hearing some real music in a medium with which I was familiar as an orchestral conductor, a change from hearing 98 piano accordionists under the age of ten playing rubbishy pieces. The only entrant in the competition turned out to be a balalaika orchestra of Ukrainian immigrants. I know nothing about these instruments and had never heard them in the flesh before; but it would have been fatal to reveal such ignorance and contribute nothing to the occasion; so I just had to get up on the platform and waffle convincingly.

Travelling throughout Canada with three colleagues from this side of the Atlantic, as I did on two occasions (1955 and 1957), provided an exacting training in the business of adjudicating which, though at times quite unnerving, could hardly be equalled. Working together throughout a period of about three months, we would soon get to know each other's characteristic techniques and mannerisms. If one of us spoke too long when delivering an adjudication, the others, sitting at the judgement table, would sound the bell that was used for giving the signal for the next competitor to perform. On one occasion in Winnipeg I was in charge of the first competition of the evening. I had to hurry away from our evening meal in order to be in time for it. My colleagues were able to take their time. When I went on stage to deliver the adjudication, there was still no sign of them. Thinking they had been too leisurely, I went on speaking to cover up their unpunctuality. I didn't know that they had actually arrived and were waiting in the wings of the stage. Suddenly I heard behind me, 'Shut up, Boydell!'

Facing page: Adjudicating at the Portstewart Music Festival (County Londonderry), July 1949.

I jumped out of my skin and only with the greatest effort could I regain some composure.

We played a nice trick on my colleague John Churchill in Halifax, Nova Scotia. At the end of the two-week festival we were all tired out. On the last night there was a competition for men's clubs in which they were required to put on an entertainment. The musical element was more or less irrelevant: the event was indeed just an entertainment for the final night audience. John fell fast asleep during the competition. When it was over, we woke him up saying, 'You're on, John!' He yawned and staggered sleepily onto the stage where he delivered a brilliant adjudication, not having heard any of the hearty contributions from the jolly boys.

I suffered terrible embarrassment once in Canada when judging a competition for operatic arias. Most of the competitors would be aged between eighteen and the middle twenties. An elderly haggard lady with grey hair mounted the platform and gave a performance of a Mozart aria in a completely inappropriate style of late nineteenth-century Italian opera. When delivering the adjudication I couldn't let this pass, and pointed out the complete misapprehension in the matter of period style. I looked down at the audience and saw the frail competitor in tears, with her head on the shoulders of an old man who was presumably her husband. Afterwards I spoke of my embarrassment to one of the festival officials. Far from relieving my sense of guilt at having upset a competitor, I was told that the lady in question had only recently been released from a labour camp in eastern Russia, and had managed to emigrate to Canada with her husband. She was convinced that she was a great singer whose talent had been temporarily stifled by her cruel incarceration. Her appearance at this festival was to be her debut at which she would convince the world of her outstandingly brilliant talent.

The Canadian tours were very well paid: in fact, I earned more in the three months in Canada than I had ever earned in a whole year in Ireland. But it was the most strenuous work I have ever undertaken. Starting at nine in the morning, one had to judge streams of little children playing or singing pieces that frankly provided no musical enjoyment. Then off to an official lunch hosted by the Kiwanis Club (the equivalent of our Rotary clubs), which had subsidised the festival, after which we had to make appropriate speeches ('How I like Canada'). A similar afternoon would be followed by a dinner given by the mayor of the town ('How I like Canada', again). If you were lucky, the evening session, with more serious events involving adults, might end at about half-past ten. Often, the session was badly timed and midnight might approach before the last item was dealt with. The following day we might have to fly several hundred miles to the next centre and be ready to start all over the following morning. In between, an obligatory part of the job was attendance at an elaborate party to celebrate the conclusion of each local festival.

Under such conditions one naturally gets very tired. At the end of the day, if you don't go to sleep during a competition it is very easy to become short-tempered. The alternative possibility can be to look on the funny side of things and seek relief in suppressed giggles. John Churchill and I swore to choose this option and never to lose our tempers. This was well put to the test in Sudbury, Ontario. There, we wondered at the lavishness of the floral decorations in the hall. We remarked on this to the president of the festival, who turned out to be the local mortician. 'Oh, when we get rid of the stiffs from the lying-in-rest parlour there are masses of flowers left behind. Pity not to make use of them.'

The last item one evening, which started sometime about midnight, was the J.G. Stevens Funeral Trophy for brass ensemble. The only entrant was a group solemnly conducted by 'Uncle': the name we gave to a stuffy old organist who had originally come from some obscure little town in Yorkshire. Uncle conducted his motley group with the ivory presentation baton, which he had been given by the Yorkshire community who were no doubt glad to see the last of him as he set off for Canada. The title of the piece they chose was *Peony Polka*. This, and the general scenario, was enough to start a fit of giggles. Then we noticed that the young man playing the tuba had a bad cold. A big drip was forming on the end of his nose. What would he do about it? After an agonising time watching the drip grow to dropping point, he lowered the instrument, got out a handkerchief and gave an almighty blow. Rejoining the music-making, he continued his tuba part exactly at the point where he had stopped to blow his nose; regardless of the fact that his companions had progressed to a later point in the polka. Uncle, feverishly waving his heavy ivory baton, couldn't stop him. What was going to happen? Believe it or not, when the others had concluded the *Peony Polka*, the tuba solemnly insisted on completing his part all on his own, with Uncle holding his head in outraged disbelief.

And then one of us had to stand up on the stage and deliver a solemn judgement of the performance.

Another late-night drama happened in St John, New Brunswick. This festival was enlivened not only by the eccentric president who kept an alligator in his bath, but by the famous Mrs Burbank who had retired from being a trombone player in a circus. When I first came across her in 1955, she was said to be seventy years old – and proud of it. Returning two years later, she told us she was sixty-eight. She conducted three brass bands made up of children, with full military discipline. There was the Junior Band, the Intermediate and the Sub-Junior; for each of which she wore a specially appropriate dress: silver, gold and bronze respectively.

The final prizewinners' concert at the conclusion of the festival took place on the last night of our Canadian tour. Since all we had to do was make a speech during the interval, we decided to celebrate the end of our labours with a champagne dinner in one of our hotel rooms. The committee was to let us know by phone when we would be required to put in an appearance at the concert. We all fell fast asleep. One of us awoke to find that it was approaching midnight, and the phone had not rung. In a state of alarm we put a call through to the hall. 'Just coming up to the interval now' was the report. We hurriedly got a taxi to be in time for our speeches.

First after the interval was Mrs Burbank with one of her bands. As an enormously popular local celebrity she received thunderous applause. In spite of the late hour, and with many items still to go, she decided that an encore was called for. More thunderous applause. At this point we saw that her conducting stand was stacked with a pile of scores which would provide an unending stream of encores. While she was taking her bow, the master of ceremonies (who happened to be a Presbyterian minister hailing from Ballymena in Northern Ireland) snatched a bouquet of flowers from the decorations in the hall, rushed onto the stage, and presented it to Mrs Burbank. While she acknowledged the renewed applause, he deftly removed her conducting stand complete with the pile of additional scores. If he hadn't shown such masterful presence of mind, I shudder to think when that prizewinners' concert might have ended.

Back in Ireland I never encountered quite such colourful incidents as in Canada. We did however enjoy the very regular appearance of Alphonsus Flood: a very podgy, pink-complexioned tobacconist who looked remarkably like Lord Longford of Gate Theatre fame. He had quite a fine voice, but his style of performance was eccentric in the extreme. He had a repertoire of about half-a-dozen songs, which he sang with such intense emotion that his pink cheeks trembled. Anything marked *allegro* would be taken as *largo molto espressivo*, and he would gallop recklessly through the slow sections. He was sure to turn up at every possible festival, even as far afield as Blackpool in England, where I heard him sing the same old songs. His performance was always preceded by the touching ceremony of presenting the accompanist with a rosebud grown in his own garden. Approaching the front of the stage, he would open his notebook of words. It was so worn from years of use that, as he turned a page, the next one would flutter to the ground. In the middle of Schumann's *Two Grenadiers* he would suddenly have to attempt to fit the words of the Hungarian song 'Shepherd, see thy horse's foaming mane' to Schumann's music. His performances were so hilarious that the audiences came specially to hear him and laughed aloud. At first I found this most embarrassing, thinking that such a reception would hurt his feelings – especially since his efforts were so obviously sincere. After a time I learned that he thoroughly enjoyed the reception he got from the audience, believing they were laughing *with* him rather than *at* him. But it wasn't all that easy to deliver an appropriate adjudication!

I have described some of the skills that must be mastered in order to become a successful adjudicator. Some of the 'kings' of the festival world were in such demand that they earned a very respectable income from adjudicating and nothing else. I don't think they realised that, as a result, they became increasingly out of touch with the real world of concert-giving. Apart from the essential skills I have described, some of the 'kings' advanced themselves by tricks that hardly endeared them to those who saw through their way of gaining popularity. I remember one pompous adjudicator at the Dublin Feis Ceoil addressing the audience after a competition for the performance of 'modern' songs (which meant anything from after Brahms to Delius and Warlock, but no further). With careful stress he declared, 'I was a personal friend of the composer of this beautiful song. If only he could have been here today, I know that he would have agreed with me that nowhere else but in Dublin could he hear such a beautiful performance of his music. You in Ireland have a rare, if not unique, gift. Pure beauty of voice is married to sensitive Celtic insight, giving rise to an art which you must strive to protect and nurture: which is just what this wonderful festival is doing' (i.e. 'do please invite me again next year'!).

My friend Archie Potter the composer was quite direct in his criticism of bogus festival adjudicators.[24] Archie had a weakness for the bottle. Unlike most people when they have had a few too many, his speech did not become slurred: he spoke with measured precision in tones of dogmatic cynicism. We both served on the music committee of Forás Éireann, a body that looked after the allocation of money from the Carnegie Trust and the legacy of Mrs Bernard Shaw. The 'brass hats' were over from London for a special policy

24. A.J. ['Archie'] Potter was born in Belfast in 1918 and died in Greystones, Co. Wicklow in 1980. See further *EMIR*, pp. 857–9.

meeting. One of them was the music adviser to the Carnegie Trust: a very senior 'king' adjudicator. Archie was late for the meeting at which we were discussing the possibility of extending the competitive festival movement in the Republic, taking a lead from its success in Northern Ireland. The door opened and Archie shuffled in. I knew from the colour of his nose why he was late. He sat down and soon got the drift of our discussion. He then solemnly addressed the meeting:

> Talking of music festivals, I remember an occasion when a friend of mine and myself decided to enter for a competition generally known as Lieder or Leider. She was a qualified pianist with no idea how to sing; and I happen to be the only Doctor of Music of the University of Dublin who is fully qualified as a singer, with appropriate letters after my name. My friend decided to do the singing bit, and I played the piano – an instrument I know very little about.

Turning to the senior adjudicator he pointed a long wagging finger at him and declared 'And you, Sir, gave us first prize!'

Looking back over what I have written about competitive music festivals, I realise that these stories may easily give an unfair and unduly cynical impression. It so happens that most of the memorable and entertaining episodes are concerned with the less positive aspects. On the positive side, the competitive festival movement provides that essential opportunity of performing in public, which all executive musicians must experience and which would rarely be available to young students otherwise. There is also no doubt that these festivals contribute significantly to the raising of standards. Ideally, I feel that it is a pity that the competitive element should invade the art of music; but apart from the reality that the musical profession is in fact competitive, the lack of enthusiasm and the depressingly low standards of any of the experimental non-competitive festivals of which I have had experience convinced me that, however much one may dislike it, competitiveness seems to be an ineradicable stimulus for the performing arts. The chief satisfaction that I derived from many years' involvement was the thought that my comments may have been positively helpful and encouraging. It is especially satisfying when competitors from many years ago warmly express their gratitude for what I had said about their performance.

As these reminiscences approach the sixties, the scene becomes more populated by the owners of sensitive toes on which one might too easily tread. No memoir of music in Dublin can however omit a few references to

Milan Horvat's successor as conductor of the RÉSO (which was soon, with the arrival of television, to become the RTÉSO).

As far as geographical latitude is concerned, Tibor Paul certainly doesn't fit conveniently into the arctic sixties. He belonged more appropriately to the region of tropical storms. There is a potential libretto for a cloak-and-dagger opera in the story of his sojourn in Ireland. I don't intend to embark on this voluminous libretto; instead, I shall just relate a few of the more remarkable episodes.

Tibor was a Hungarian who had emigrated to Australia, where he became a naturalised citizen.[25] A strikingly handsome figure, he was, I think, the vainest man I ever met. His day would begin with a game of tennis followed by a period under a sunlamp, which gave him that alluring, well-tanned complexion which had such a devastating effect on certain middle-aged influential ladies, including the wife of the then Minister for External Affairs. His devoted fan club of adoring ladies would play a prominent part in the last scene of the 'opera', describing the extraordinary drama of his final departure.

Lest you get a one-sided and faulty impression of Tibor Paul, one must straight away stress that he was an excellent orchestral trainer and a first-class conductor of music from Beethoven to Bartok. Today's equivalent (though rather more distinguished) would be Herbert von Karajan. You can't let vain personalities like this loose on Bach or Mozart; but their personalised interpretation works well with the Romantics. Tibor Paul was just what our orchestra needed at the time to weld it into a unified instrument. This was, however, achieved at some cost. The Ulster Orchestra, for instance, was initiated largely with refugees from our orchestra who could not endure Tibor's rather insensitive disciplinary methods.

He was a very clever operator, soon edging his way into being appointed Director of Radio Music in addition to his being chief conductor. The result was that members of the orchestra had no one to whom they could appeal if they felt that they were being unjustly treated by the conductor. Kevin McCourt, the Director of Broadcasting, who had the final say, found himself out of his depth; for he was inexperienced in dealing with musicians. This is where I came in; for Kevin, knowing that I had no particular axe to grind and was on friendly terms with both parties, invited me to act as his confidential music adviser.

---

25. Tibor Paul was born in Budapest in 1909 and died in Sydney in 1973. He was appointed principal conductor of the RÉSO in 1961, having already conducted the orchestra on numerous occasions since 1958. In 1962 he was also appointed Director of Music at RTÉ. He left in 1967. See also *EMIR*, p. 826.

The first major task I was faced with was to advise on what to do about a very difficult crisis. It was obvious that Tibor Paul would not be content as king of a small provincial empire in Dublin, when he believed the world was awaiting him as conqueror. He had his eye on the United States. To this end he arranged a tour for our orchestra in the USA, so that he could display his genius. The proposed tour was carefully leaked to the press before it had been ratified by the Director of Broadcasting, and it was beginning to receive excited news coverage in the papers. Kevin McCourt then discovered that the tour was going to cost more than the total budget allowed for music throughout the whole year. The tour just had to be cancelled. Tibor, with the assistance of his influential lady fan club, had the press well primed. Headlines such as 'Director of Broadcasting cancels great opportunity for Irish Orchestra in America' appeared in all the papers.

Mind you, although Tibor may have overstepped the limits on some occasions such as this, with his powerful personality he did get things done – many things that badly needed to be done. A minor episode illustrates this aspect. He decided that the orchestra should give a concert in the cathedral in Mullingar. His secretary reported that the administrator of the cathedral had refused permission. The last time they had had an orchestra there, the cellos had defaced the marble floor with their steel cello pegs; and in any case, a cathedral was for worship and not for symphonies. 'Get me the bishop,' Tibor commanded. It turned out that the bishop was attending the Vatican Council in Rome. 'Get me a ticket to Rome!' He flew there, summoned the bishop out from the conference hall, and demanded the required permission. The concert took place as he had planned.

A memorable event during Tibor Paul's reign, which demonstrated his ability to move mountains, was his success in persuading Igor Stravinsky to visit Dublin in 1963 and conduct a number of his works. I had formed the impression from reading various descriptions of his scathing remarks about other composers that he would not be a very pleasant individual to meet. When Tibor insisted that I should be introduced to the great man, I was rather apprehensive. He was absolutely charming. If only I could have made a tape recording to accompany the photograph I have of that meeting![26] I was just introduced as an Irish composer. My name obviously meant nothing to him, but lest he put his foot in it he played safe. Beaming at me he greeted me with, 'Ah ... Brian Boydell! I have heard your music with great pleasure in New York, in Tokyo and in Paris. It is a great honour to meet you in person!' I need hardly add that none of my music had been performed in any of these cities!

---

26. See p. 111.

Igor Stravinsky with (*l. to r.*) Geraldine O'Grady (leader, RÉSO), Novemo Salvatori (principal trombone, RÉSO), Brian and conductor Tibor Paul, June 1963.

COURTESY OF INDEPENDENT NEWS AND MEDIA AND THE *IRISH INDEPENDENT*, AND THE BOARD OF TRINITY COLLEGE DUBLIN

It was only when Arthur Nachstern, a Polish immigrant violinist, was introduced to him that the veneer of charm cracked and he showed the vituperative side to his character.[27] Arthur spoke of the great pleasure he had enjoyed playing the *Firebird Suite* under Ernest Ansermet, who was credited with playing an important part in Stravinsky's early successes. The benign smile was replaced with a frowning scowl. 'Ansermet ... he was a BAD man! He ruined so many performances of my music.'

27. Arthur Nachstern (1911–99), born of Polish parentage in Odessa where he studied violin under Peter Stolarski (whose pupils included Jascha Heifetz and Nathan Milstein), had joined the RÉSO in 1947. He was to remain with the orchestra as sub-leader until his retirement.

The final scene before the curtain came down at the conclusion of the melodrama of Tibor Paul's sojourn in Ireland was perhaps the most dramatic event of all. It became increasingly obvious that there was no way of controlling the extravagance of this powerful and intimidating personality. The end of the period of his contract was, however, at hand. Tibor had not yet managed to obtain the post that would raise him to a higher step on the international ladder, and he apparently intended staying on until that goal was achieved. The Director of Broadcasting thought otherwise, seeing a convenient end to the taxing strain of trying to steer a course that would be for the greater benefit of the future. To notify Tibor of the termination of his contract proved more tricky than anticipated. Tibor got wind of what was intended and sought legal advice. On being told that the termination of his contract must be personally delivered in the office of the Director of Music, he was very careful not to be found there if any messenger from the Radio was seen approaching. After several attempts to deliver the document had failed, an alternative ploy was resorted to. It could well be argued that, when conducting a concert, the concert hall could be deemed to be his 'office'. The termination of his contract was handed to him as he left the stage for his dressing room after acknowledging the applause at the end of a concert. He collapsed with a heart attack.

We shall probably never know whether this was a genuine heart attack or not. Whichever it was, he was installed in state in the VIP room of a hospital, where the press photographers had a field day. Pictures of him surrounded by flowers, with his wife Mimi holding his hand, were on the front page of every newspaper.[28] Kevin McCourt sent him a bouquet of carnations. They were returned without acknowledgement.[29]

When RÉ, which was then under the control of the Department of Posts and Telegraphs, was entrusted with initiating an Irish television service, expert advice was sought from America and Canada where this new broadcasting medium had already benefited from several years of experience. A Mr Byrne, who had served with Canadian television, was engaged as one of the advisers.

In 1961 a decision was made to commission a special arrangement of the National Anthem, which would be played along with a pictorial

28. Perhaps a slight exaggeration! [Ed.]
29. Tibor Paul recovered sufficiently to lead the orchestra on its first overseas tour, giving concerts at the Royal Festival Hall in London on 30 November 1966 and for BBC TV at the Fairfield Hall in Croydon. He concluded his tenure as conductor of the RTÉSO with an acclaimed Beethoven cycle of concerts in Dublin in July 1967. The conclusion of Paul's career at RTÉ is discussed in Pine, *Music and Broadcasting*, pp. 448–55.

evocation of Ireland at the conclusion of each day's transmission. Fachtna O'Hannrachain, who was then Director of Music, invited a selection of Irish composers to submit arrangements from which the most suitable would be chosen. We were to be paid five pounds (as far as I remember) in the first instance; and a prize of fifty pounds would be awarded to the composer of the chosen arrangement.

I was advised to seek an interview with Mr Byrne in order to become acquainted with the kind of arrangement he had in mind. I duly presented myself at the special new offices set up in Clarendon Street. They were decorated according to the latest fashion preferred by important international business: 'Levelor' Venetian blinds, thick carpets, and a decorative lady receptionist sitting behind a white desk in the entrance hall busying herself with a clutter of gaily coloured telephones. I was asked to wait. Mr Byrne was very busy. After a suitably impressive time had elapsed, I was ushered into the presence. As I entered, his feet, shod with brilliantly polished shoes, were on the desk as he spoke on the telephone. With the practised grace of movement of a ballet dancer, he swung his legs off the desk at the same time as proffering a humidor of cigars with his free arm.

'Have a cigar!'

The telephone was returned to its cradle and he fixed me with an earnest gaze.

'Now, Mr Boydell – I wan' it BIG! I envisage the kind of music that will stir the hearts of the Irish people. Now I don't know a great deal about music, but I'm thinking of great rolls on the drums, stirring fanfares of trumpets, and a really BIG sound – to accompany a film shot of the tanks and men of the Irish army proceeding down O'Connell Street in a grand procession. Now remember, Mr Boydell, I wan' it BIG!'

Not only was I at the time President of the Irish Pacifist Movement, but I was allergic to any form of flag-waving tribal nationalism. I didn't really like national anthems anyway. My first inclination was to have nothing to do with the whole business. But as I thought about it, my cynical first reaction began to be tempered by the challenge it offered. This was the problem of attempting to clothe the undistinguished tune of *The Soldier's Song* with harmonies and orchestral sounds that would raise its musical value and lend it some sense of dignity. I went home and faced the challenge. I was pleased with the new harmonies and musical devices which I worked out and then, with a certain element of cynicism remaining (as I remembered the advice to 'make it BIG') I chose the largest sheet of manuscript paper that I could find, saying to myself, 'I'll fill every stave of that immense orchestral score if I can possibly manage it.' Harp, organ, off-stage trumpets and a battery of percussion (for the 'great roll on the drums') accounted for a large number of those staves. Indeed I would have liked a couple more for the percussion, but by then there was only just enough room left for the rest of a full symphony orchestra. I completed the score on 6 July 1961 and awaited judgement. To my surprise, my arrangement was chosen.

At the end of October in that year a recording was made in the Phoenix Hall with the RÉSO conducted by Colonel James Doyle.[30] A considerable amount of experimentation was necessary to obtain the right effect of the distant off-stage trumpets, so that they would give the impression of sounding from over the hills in the countryside. Mr Byrne was in the control room, and when the recording was completed he was absolutely delighted. He nearly shook the arm off me in a fit of hand-shaking enthusiasm.

'Mr Boydell – you have made my visit to the Old Country well worthwhile. That great roll on the drums which I suggested will go perfectly with my film shot of the Aer Lingus jet taking off from Shannon!'

And so my arrangement of the National Anthem was broadcast every night for several decades from the opening of the television service on 31 December 1961. I duly received my fifty pounds, but I didn't earn another penny from it, even though the first three bars of introduction consist of original music. The small print in my contract stipulated that the copyright of the complete arrangement had been bought out. Even if my three original bars earned royalties of a penny or two each time, I would have done quite well. I did however stipulate that only the recorded version with the correct balance of sound for the distant trumpets could be played without express permission.

As a matter of interest, the copyright of the tune, including permission to perform any arrangement in public, was held by the Department of Finance. RÉ, being at the time a government service, was able to negotiate this permission for my arrangement. Some others have made arrangements (including, believe it or not, Sir Thomas Beecham, for a visit of the Royal Philharmonic Orchestra to the old Theatre Royal in Hawkins Street which he conducted in 1948), but strictly speaking they were breaking the law by doing so.[31]

---

30. James Doyle was director of the Army School of Music from 1947 to 1971.
31. For reports on this concert and the performance of the National Anthem by the Royal Philharmonic Orchestra under Beecham, see 'An Irishman's Diary', *The Irish Times*, 18 October 1948 and 'Cordial Welcome for Famous Conductor', *Sunday Independent*, 20 October 1948. The latter report noted: 'When the orchestra played the National Anthem, its unusual arrangement and variation of the air suggested the thought that an official orchestral arrangement should be published as soon as possible, before the danger of visiting orchestras creating a new National Anthem becomes too acute.'

After dwelling so much on humorous anecdotes and dramatic catastrophes, it would be nice to end these memoirs on a positive note by describing very briefly what has crystallised in my mind as the most rewarding and enjoyable experience in a lifetime of music.

The seed planted under Boris Ord in the Cambridge Madrigal Society grew throughout the years into a very special feeling for the vocal music of the Renaissance and the early seventeenth century. In September 1958, after discussion with a few musical friends who shared my enthusiasm for this kind of music, we realised that there was an opportunity not only to provide great enjoyment for ourselves, but to fill a gap in the Irish concert scene. Thus we formed a chamber choir of ten voices with the idea of specialising in this period of unaccompanied vocal music. Believing at the time that the Elizabethan lutenist-composer John Dowland had been born in Dalkey, outside Dublin, we assumed the title 'The Dowland Consort'. (The idea that Dowland was an Irishman was one of the many false trails laid by Grattan Flood, whose book on the history of music in Ireland has led many to false conclusions.[32] In spite of the fact that a tablet was erected to his memory in a park in Dalkey, it has since been proved convincingly by Diana Poulton and others that Dowland had no direct connection with this country.)[33]

As director, in addition to being bass singer, I was able to enjoy the best of two worlds. Alongside me as baritone was Tomás Ó Suilleabháin, who had made an important contribution to Irish music as a radio singer who had specialised in the performance of songs by Irish composers.[34] Dick Cooper and his wife Cáit Lanigan, both well-known soloists, sang tenor and soprano. My wife Mary was one of the four sopranos, the other two being Eilís O'Sullivan and Gráinne Yeats. Gráinne was well-known as an expert on Irish folksongs, performing many of them to her own accompaniment on the Irish harp.[35] In our earlier concerts she would perform a group of folksongs as a contrast to the *a capella* singing. The altos were Hazel Morris and Enid Chaloner. The second tenor was Leonard Jose from the choir of St Patrick's Cathedral. When he later transferred to a collegiate choir

---

32. W.H. Grattan Flood first claimed that John Dowland was Irish in 'New Facts about John Dowland', *The Gentleman's Magazine*, vol. 301 (1906), pp. 287–9. See also his *A History of Irish Music*, 3rd edn (Dublin: Browne & Nolan, 1913), p. 178, and 'Irish Ancestry of Garland, Dowland, Campion and Purcell', *Music and Letters*, vol. 3, no. 1 (1921), pp. 59–65. On Flood, see also *EMIR*, pp. 394–8.

33. Diana Poulton, *John Dowland*, 2nd rev. edn (London: Faber & Faber, 1982). See also *EMIR*, pp. 310–11.

34. On Tomás Ó Suilleabháin, see *EMIR*, pp. 812–13.

35. On Gráinne Yeats, see *EMIR*, pp. 1076–7.

in Oxford his place was taken by George Bannister, who also hailed from St Patrick's.

In those days, music from four hundred years ago was considered much more 'highbrow' and reserved for academic study than it is now. In order to break down these barriers and draw in a wider public, we planned an approach to concert-giving which was aimed at informal communication. Instead of standing stiffly in well-ordered ranks, we attempted to create the relaxed and intimate atmosphere of domestic music-making by sitting informally around a semi-circular table. This was specially designed so as to be taken to pieces, forming easily transportable sections that could be carried on the roof-rack of a car for touring. I sat at one end, directing the ensemble, and I introduced each item, providing translations for the pieces in Italian, French or German.

The activities of the Dowland Consort began with tentative try-out recitals in schools. I obtained funding from the Arts Council to visit two schools in Waterford in January 1959. My letter of request to the Arts Council caused considerable amusement; for without thinking about double meanings, I asked for a subvention 'to bring my new Consort to Waterford'.

Our first public recital in Dublin was given on 10 April 1959 and received 'rave' notices in the press. We worked together in the Consort over a period of eleven years, during which we gave about 110 recitals. Apart from two dozen or so Dublin recitals (including five for the Italian Cultural Institute) we sang in London (Wigmore Hall), Chester, Liverpool, Manchester, Belfast, Derry and Cork; and about fifty concerts in other Irish towns. Ten recitals were broadcast by the BBC, fourteen by RTÉ, and seventeen concerts were given in schools throughout the country. Among the most memorable occasions was the London concert at the Wigmore Hall in September 1964. On the strength of this we were awarded the Harriet Cohen International Music Award. And then there was the summer concert planned to be given on a barge moored at the Thirteenth Lock on the Grand Canal. The heavens opened, and the rain poured down, so that audience and all had to retreat to an eighteenth-century barn nearby, where we sang sitting on sacks of grain.

There were some funny incidents too. We gave a concert at a convent in Cavan around Christmas time. The stage was set up for the school pantomime, which was *Babes in the Wood*. Our table was set in a leafy grove and surrounded by cardboard tree trunks. A novice nun was put in charge of the lighting and was determined to add her special contribution to the

The Dowland Consort on the *Late Late Show*, RTÉ television, February 1968 (*l. to r.*): Richard Cooper, George Bannister (tenors); Eilís O'Sullivan, Cáit Cooper (sopranos); Gráinne Yeats, Mary Boydell (mezzo-sopranos); Enid Chaloner, Hazel Morris (altos); Tomás Ó Suilleabháin, Brian Boydell (basses).
IMAGE COURTESY OF RTÉ ARCHIVES

success of the evening. She devised the idea of dimming the lights in the sad moments and bringing them up to full brilliance to enhance the happy ones. We began to sing the complex six-part madrigal by John Ward *Out from the vale of deep despair*. In order to fit the large number of vocal lines on the page, it is printed in very small type. As soon as she heard the words 'deep despair', down went the lights. In our efforts to follow the music, down went all ten of our heads as though we were about to kiss the pages in some strange ritual of worship. Then came the refrain of 'Fa, la, la' (where she missed the mood of sad nostalgia) and up came the lights again. Up came the heads. After a couple of enactments of this ritualistic ballet we all began to get the giggles. It is difficult to sing a long-sustained line and giggle at the same time.

Another highlight in our career was the gramophone record we made for Alpha Records, consisting of French chansons and German lieder and including the remarkable *Deutsche Sprüche von Leben und Tod* by Leonhard

Lechner.[36] (There seems to be some malignant fate hanging over any gramophone recordings with which I have been concerned. Both the New Irish Recording Company, who released my *Symphonic Inscapes*, and the Alpha Record Company concerned in this case went out of business shortly after releasing these records.)[37]

Perhaps the most gratifying outcome of the career of the Dowland Consort was not a purely musical one: though it does, I think, demonstrate the benign power of music. When we came together thirty-six years ago (as I write) we were a very heterogeneous bunch of individuals as far as background was concerned: Irish-speaking nationalists, Protestant Anglo-Irish, married and single, and whatever other cultural differences you can think of. Our experience of working together in the performance of music had the effect of welding the members of the Consort into a family of life-long friends. We still meet together two or three times a year, enjoy a good meal, and follow it by singing favourite pieces from our repertoire. (Perhaps I should say that we now croak our way through them!)

By 1969, after eleven years, there were no readily available new fields to conquer. I felt that, having reached a high degree of perfection in performance, some special incentive was needed to attain higher standards. A projected tour of the United States failed to materialise; in any case, it was very difficult to arrange such ventures since our work did not comprise a full-time professional commitment, many of the members having full-time employment. I was apprehensive that if no such stimulus to further endeavour were found, a certain element of enthusiasm and aspiration might slowly leak away from our performances. The alternative was to cease our activities. We took this step with sadness: though I think it was the right decision. On 8 November 1969 we gave our Farewell Concert in the Examination Hall in TCD. To supply appropriate material to advertise the occasion I sent a letter to the newspapers from which the following is an extract, which sums up our history with some remarkable statistics:

> The programme for this 'Farewell Recital' (which I enclose) was arrived at by asking each member of the Consort to suggest items from our repertoire of over 300 Renaissance pieces which they most enjoyed singing.

---

36. *Renaissance Lieder and Chansons* (LP, Alpha PHA 3001, 1965).

37. *Symphonic Inscapes* op. 64 (1968) was recorded by the New Irish Recording Company in 1974 (LP, NIR 011) performed by the RTÉSO conducted by Albert Rosen. The New Irish Recording Company had earlier released an LP of solo piano music performed by Charles Lynch (NIR 001), which included two works by Brian: *Dance for an Ancient Ritual*, op. 39a (1959) and *Capriccio*, op. 48 (1959).

This resulted in what would amount to a five-hour 'sing-in'. On deciding that some consideration should be given to our audience, there followed a pruning session in which we had, with almost tearful reluctance, to jettison almost three-and-a-half hours of music which some individuals, or even the whole group, were wildly enthusiastic about. The result is a programme of not too unreasonable duration, including many of the items which we know our audiences have enjoyed too.

The repertoire from which this programme has been chosen has been built up during the 11 years of the Consort's activities, and includes ... a total of about 307 works by about 70 different Renaissance composers. Included in the above are 21 items of Monteverdi, 21 of Weelkes, 30 of Lassus.

Stalin was in power [*sic*] and the Iron Curtain was still drawn down when, at my suggestion, the University of Dublin decided to offer an honorary MusD degree to Shostakovich.[38] There was some doubt as to whether he would be permitted to travel to Dublin for the occasion, since he was under a certain degree of suspicion in Soviet Russia and they were also concerned for his safety, especially since he was not in the best of health, having recently suffered a heart attack. After an anxiously long time waiting, we heard that permission would indeed be granted, though he and his wife would be accompanied by the First Secretary of the Soviet embassy in London. This was Mr Filatov, who was to keep an eye on him with the assistance of several 'heavies' with very square shoulders and badly cut Iron Curtain suits. They were to be seen secretively mingling with the crowd everywhere the composer went.

After meeting the Russian party at the airport on 5 July, Shostakovich and his charming young wife Irina were driven to Dublin and installed in the Royal Hibernian Hotel in Dawson Street. On the way, they were fascinated with the advertisements and political graffiti along the streets. Such things just didn't exist in Russia. That evening the New Irish Chamber Orchestra was to play his 'Chamber Symphony' (the Eighth String Quartet transcribed by Rudolph Barshai) at St Patrick's Cathedral, with the composer as guest of honour. We offered them dinner beforehand, but Shostakovich was too tired after the journey and stayed in his room with his wife. Mary and I

---

38. Although highly anachronistic (Stalin had died in 1953), the opening comment 'Stalin was in power' has been retained here. Leonid Brezhnev was Russian leader at the time Shostakovitch visited Dublin in July 1972.

were left with Filatov to entertain. During the dinner I was called to the phone to discuss the composer's reception at the cathedral. While I was absent, Filatov opened a large volume he had on his knees and showed Mary an extensive file on me, describing everything about me, including all my known political allegiances.

At the cathedral we were met by John Bradley, the Dean's Vicar. In a state of nervous anxiety I introduced him to the composer as 'Old John Braddelum' (with the English West-Country folk song ringing in my ears). We were ushered to the front pew and the packed audience stood up in honour of the great musician. Not so far away the square-shouldered 'heavies' could be seen in the audience. After the performance of his Chamber Symphony, the composer took his bow and then mingled amongst the members of the orchestra congratulating them individually.

The next day there was the Commencements ceremony in TCD, when Dmitri Shostakovich was awarded his honorary Doctor in Music. He was clearly very frail, having some difficulty in mounting the few steps to the platform. That evening there was the special Commencement Dinner in the Dining Hall.

The next day he was busily occupied meeting Irish composers and musicians. We were anxious that he was being over-burdened with official functions and decided that on Saturday we should arrange a more relaxed day for his entertainment. And so, Mary and I asked him and his wife to an informal lunch in our home in Baily. We picked them up at their hotel in the morning and drove them out to Howth. There we bought fresh-caught fish on the pier and Mary brought Irina into the local supermarket, which absolutely fascinated her. We then drove to our house where Mary cooked a simple fish dish. The pair were delighted with our kitchen, especially with the old cottage dresser on which we keep, in traditional style, our plates and dishes.

We were unable to shake off Filatov, who insisted on joining the party. At the same time I had asked Ron Hill and his wife. Ron was a member of the academic staff in TCD, a fluent Russian speaker and with a keen and informed knowledge of music. He was to act as my interpreter, since Shostakovich had very little English, and we didn't quite trust Filatov. During the lunch party, Shostakovich expressed an interest in Irish contemporary music and wished to hear some. I also wanted to ask him about the real position of the composer in the Soviet Union, about which I felt that we in the West had been subjected to unreliable propaganda. The problem was how to get rid of Filatov, so that we could talk freely. Mary had a brilliant

Shostakovich with his wife Irina Antonovna at Brian and Mary's house, July 1972.

idea: she announced that we had arranged an international croquet match, and we expected Filatov to represent Russia.[39] He could hardly be so discourteous as to refuse, and he was happy to be given the red ball (with much laughter!). My sons Cormac and Barra had devised a special set of rules guaranteeing that the game would last at least two hours. And so, Ron Hill and I brought Shostakovich into the music room to listen to contemporary Irish works and discuss attitudes to composition.

I asked the question, 'We gather that composers in the Soviet Union are discouraged from experimenting with new techniques. How then can Russian music develop along with the evolution of its counterpart in the rest of Europe?'

'You are misinformed,' he said. 'Of course we are encouraged to experiment and explore new ideas; but not to inflict our experiments on the public. We discuss our new ideas amongst ourselves in the Union of Composers.'

39. As a family we were then quite unaware of the popularity of croquet in Russia from the late nineteenth century. Chekhov, for example, had a passion for the game, and it was enthusiastically played by Soviet citizens well into the 1930s. See Rosamund Bartlett, *Chekhov: scenes from a life* (London: The Free Press, 2005), pp. 221–3.

If I could sum up my impression from our fascinating conversation, I would say that Shostakovich had been brought up with the Soviet ideals of Lenin, just as a sincere Irish Catholic who had been nurtured with his religion as part of unquestioned faith. Then, in the Irish context, along comes a bishop whose actions and teaching seem to contradict the fundamental beliefs so strongly held for a lifetime. In Russia, the errant bishop was Stalin, whose actions didn't seem to follow the idealism of the faith in which Shostakovich had been nurtured.

An unforgettable day, with the privilege of meeting a very great composer on intimate terms. With the croquet match concluded, we all sat outside in the warm sun, taking photographs of the occasion and enjoying relaxed conversation. As they left, Mary was given a pair of traditional Russian knitted gloves, and I was presented with an autographed score and recording of the composer's Thirteenth Symphony.

Salmon fishing on the River Boyne, County Meath, c. 1950.

LEABHARLANN
CO. CHILL DARA

JANUARY

1 January 1950. Sunday

Charles [Acton] rang up early in a great state about Michael McMullin's notice convening the General Meeting of the Music Association, which baldly stated that, owing to the absence of a quorum at the last *three* council meetings, the General Meeting would be held on Jan. 10th. Michael is certainly fed up with the whole thing, since it did not turn out to his liking viz. as a society to 'down' [Fachtna] O'Hannrachain, and to publish his memorandum. This notice seems designed to wreck any future the MAI might have.

... Listened to the Hallé orchestra under Barbirolli playing Reger's *Variation and Fugue on a Theme of Mozart* (not very enthusiastic) and Delius's *A Song of Summer* (BBC Home [Service])

2 January 1950. Monday

... Sent a copy of a radio script to an admirer who missed the broadcast. Ordered orchestral parts from Boosey & Hawkes, and gathered together Music Association documents for [Anthony] Farrington to look at. Edgar Deale and I are trying to persuade him to take on the secretaryship – I hope he does – he would be the ideal man (if not the only one) to save it – since he is so detached, experienced and dignified ...

3 January 1950. Tuesday

Typed out radio script for Thursday, in the morning – a series I call 'To detonate the bomb of argument'. The first is a cynical examination of audiences and applause – put across in a very exaggerated way to annoy people, and perhaps make them think. I am particularly interested in a method of listening at concerts of which I have found myself guilty, and I'm sure many other musically educated people are – I am vigorously trying to cure myself. I find myself listing critically so as to form an opinion about the performance since I am sure to be asked what I thought of it afterwards. This isn't listening to the music! I am becoming increasingly interested in *music*, and decreasingly so in *performance*. The brilliant performance makes one jump from one's seat – it doesn't need any concentrated thought to recognise it. Even so with the really bad performance. In between there is a vast field of adequate to good performances – here it is better to reserve the energy of concentration for the music itself. The musical public as a whole would do far better to value music higher than performance, which is far from the true state of affairs.

… Edgar Deale rang up to read the letter he had written to Michael McMullin re the notice of the MAI General Meeting. A real snorter. He revealed that McMullin had apparently stated that if the MAI did not turn out to his liking he would do his best to wreck it! … Put a call through to Aloys Fleischmann to try and persuade him to come up to the meeting. Also rang Fred May.

Got down to work on the Bloch Second [String] Quartet and Beethoven op. 127 – the scores of both have disappeared. *I must stop lending music.* Listened to the records of the Bloch, and then a fascinating talk on African Music from the [BBC] Third Programme.

4 January 1950. Wednesday

One of those exasperating mornings when one spends an enormous amount of time accomplishing nothing. The hunt for the score of the Bloch quartet meant nearly an hour at the telephone. Couldn't get onto Mrs Pye – the last resort – so drove out there to see her. Traced her in the house of Mrs Justice Reddin. She hadn't got a copy – but I lectured her about the MAI. She is one of those who suspected a clique. I did my best to persuade her that it *would* be a clique unless people like her were to join. Rushed back to try to catch Betty Sullivan during the interval of the [RÉ] Orchestra rehearsal. Was too late – so had to leave a note … One good thing this morning was a letter from Farrington to say that he would do secretary for the MAI for the present anyway.

… Back in time to hear Joe Groocock's musical comedy *The Island of Dreams* from the BBC. I was expecting so much that I was a little disappointed – though I enjoyed it immensely. The tunes – with a couple of exceptions – didn't seem as fresh as some of his earlier ones – and the production was a bit slipshod. Didn't think much of Havelock Nelson's orchestrations. Betty [Sullivan] rang up to say she had got me a score of the Bloch. Rushed down to Phoenix Hall and found her with the Cirulli Quartet rehearsing my quartet.[1] Their playing of it is so far dead from the neck up and down. I hope I can make them do something about it at the rehearsal on Saturday.

After an awful rush – making a few notes and changing – went to talk to the Gramophone Society on Beethoven op. 127 and Bloch Second [String]

---

1. Brian's String Quartet no. 1, op. 31, was composed in 1949. Although he consistently refers in his diary to this ensemble as the 'Ceruli' (or 'Cerulli') quartet (or collectively as the 'Ceruli people'), it was founded by and named after the Italian violinist Zola Cirulli, who joined the RÉSO in 1948. Brian's spelling has been corrected throughout.

Quartet … Came home to find Robert McKeever. Persuaded him to help in the reconstruction of the MAI.

5 January 1950. Thursday

Bull – a BBC balance officer – is over here to try and do something about that side of RÉ. Michael Murtagh, Brendan Dunne and self are invited to 'tail' him and learn what we can. I gather the idea is to train in balance control officers for RÉ. I am not keen on that sort of job – if I got it they would consider that enough – and never give me anything decent to do. Anyway, I am 'tailing' Bull, who is a very good fellow, to learn what I can for my own personal interest. Turned up at the new studio at Portobello, where he was solving an acoustical problem with the [RÉ] Light Orchestra as rabbits. Most interesting. Had coffee with Brendan Dunne and Bull. He confirms my intuitive suspicions about quality from RÉ. Most of the top is lost on the loud lines which have no periodic boosts ['repeaters' added above. *Ed.*]. Equipment itself is out of date. The Phoenix Hall is over damped, and the back of the stage reflects frequencies around 500 Hz, and kills the rest.

With great glee I picked up the recording machine at Douglas Radio. Two resisters had gone high. It is now working perfectly. Played about with it for an hour or so after lunch – experimenting with recording direct from radio. Mary recorded a song. Then off to a radio rehearsal. Had a chat with Larry Morrow and Arthur Duff[2] – I'm very fond of them both. What a pity Arthur has no enthusiasm. Left in my nominations for the MAI council – nearly forgot John Beckett who is home again, and should be of great use.

… DOP rehearsal in the evening – a late start (7.45) – but did good work on [Beethoven's] Battle Symphony (which we are doing for academic interest and amusement). Had to rush off for a broadcast at 8.30 – my tirade on the concert audience. Returned and rehearsed the slow movement of the Haydn 'Farewell' [Symphony]. Short committee meeting afterwards.

6 January 1950. Friday

Edgar [Deale] sent me a copy of his correspondence with Michael [McMullin] about the MAI. Michael's attitude is quite extraordinary – he clearly reveals himself as a would-be dictator. Edgar's replies to his letters should be strong enough to disturb even a lizard like M[ichael].

Returned to work on the first Intermezzo of *The Buried Moon*,[3] and spent much of the morning at that. Aloys Fleischmann wired to say he will come

---

2. Arthur Duff (1899–1956), composer, conductor and radio producer (see *EMIR*, p. 334).
3. The ballet suite *The Buried Moon*, op. 32a, would receive its first performance given by the DOP in Drogheda on 25 February 1950 (see below), conducted by the composer.

up for the weekend to discuss the MAI. We are all going to meet at Joe Groocock's tomorrow night (Edgar, Joe, Aloys, Fred May, Olive Smith and self). Charles [Acton] also rang up to hear of developments.

… I walked home to continue [composing]. Ran into Bobs Figgis at Ballsbridge and had a short chat about the Music Club, which has been wound up. I told him I would be keen for some Chamber Music Club to arise provided the social atmosphere could be kept out. Returned home and finished the Intermezzo. Tackled the problem of the final dance as it should appear in the concert suite. I am rather uncertain about the quality of some of the ballet music: I will probably have to make changes.

… Lunch with Aunt Edie.[4] Good eats. She produced a pile of old music from which I picked some wonderful Victorian period pieces. We must have a Victorian party with appropriate music some time.

… Rosen came in after supper. He [Hans Waldemar Rosen] seems to like my music, and is going to do what he can to arrange performances in Germany. Played him the records of *The Feather of Death* and [*In Memoriam Mahatma*] *Gandhi*.[5] Also played Bloch [String Quartet] no. 2 and some Guillaume de Machaut and Monteverdi. About the singing of this old music he produced an interesting idea – comparing its finesse and delicacy with that of the Burgundian painting, Rosen suggested that voice-production was quite different then to now – more like choir-boy tone – through the top of the head. Heaviness must be avoided. He may perform my early *Mary Moder* with the RÉ Choir.[6] He also wants to interest a singer in *The Feather of Death*. Lent me records of a Bruckner symphony – hopes to convert me I imagine – also the incredible *Japanese Festival Music* of [Richard] Strauss written for 5,000 marks, a gold medal and a chest of tea.[7]

7 January 1950. Saturday

To the Radio[8] to pick up the score of [my] String Quartet. Message from O'Hannrachain that RÉ will not be getting a harpsichord this year. We hope to persuade McCullough's [music shop] to import one, and are relying on RÉ to hire it. The price of a good concert harpsichord is very high

---

4. Brian's aunt Edith Boydell, who lived in Raglan Road, Ballsbridge.
5. *The Feather of Death*, op. 22, song cycle (1943, to texts by Thurloe Conolly) for baritone, flute, violin, viola, cello; *In Memoriam Mahatma Gandhi*, op. 30, for orchestra (1948). A private 78rpm recording had been made of *The Feather of Death*.
6. *Mary Moder (An Easter Carol)*, op. 12 (1940).
7. *Japanische Festmusik*, op. 84 (1940).
8. Recurring references in the diary to 'the Radio' are to the RÉ studios located in the GPO building in O'Connell Street.

though. Was introduced to Mander – the visiting Italian conductor.[9] On to the Phoenix Hall to supervise a rehearsal of my quartet, I took complete charge, and the results are much more encouraging today. They must do a great deal more work though. The trouble about rehearsing one's own work is that the imagination supplies much that is not actually there …

… Aloys Fleischmann arrived shortly after 8 p.m. Then Edgar and Olive Smith came, and we all went off to Joe [Groocock]'s, picking up Fred May on the way … Thoroughly thrashed out the whole MAI situation, and planned for most eventualities – I hope! It is grand to have Aloys, who is so thoroughly trustworthy, wise and level-headed. It appears that [Michael] Bowles is mixed up in the formation of some body or other which may get access to public funds. This complicates the issue.

Was glad to see Fred again – and he seemed quite normal again after time has mellowed the shock of his losing the Abbey job.[10]

8 January 1950. Sunday

… Aloys was off seeing Michael McMullin, and came back to lunch with the welcome news that he will not cause unpleasantness at the General Meeting as long as Edgar is not in the chair.

… Aloys and I shut ourselves in the music room. I put the recorder through its paces, and he was duly amazed. Then played the ballet music. He seemed very impressed with the music itself, but was a little doubtful about its choreographic possibilities.

… Gramophone evening – Hentschels, Betty [Sullivan] and Tom [Kelly], the Maguires, Hans Rosen, Robert McDowell, Yvonne and Thurloe,[11] and Aloys. Listened to the Strauss *Japanese Festival Music* – incredibly pompous and awful, except for one passable section in the style of *Don Juan*. Then Prokofiev *Scythian Suite*, which gets more and more disappointing every time I hear it. Then Bartok Sixth [String] Quartet – magnificent. We discussed the humour of the Burletta – is it grim humour? Or does the dissonance of Bartok's language make us think grimly? Then we had the Berg *Wozzek* fragments – what a shame there is not a more complete recording … Finished up with Warlock's *Curlew*. Wolfram Hentschel is a grand fellow – I like him more and more. He is most anxious about the performance of

---

9. Francesco Mander first visited Dublin to conduct four concerts with the RÉSO in 1948, returning a number of times thereafter.

10. Frederick May had held the position of director of music at the Abbey Theatre since 1936. He was succeeded by Éamonn Ó Gallchobhair.

11. Brian's sister Yvonne, with whom he remained close throughout their lives, and her husband Thurloe Conolly.

my quartet, and hopes I will be able to coax a good performance from the Cirulli people. He is himself forming a new quartet.

9 January 1950. Monday

Aloys left early to pay many calls, and smooth out the path of the MAI with F.J. Kelly, who is to be chairman tomorrow night. His help, trustworthiness and tact have been invaluable in averting a catastrophe (I hope!).

... A cup of tea, and off to the Academy [RIAM] – term starts there today. Interviewed a new pupil, and gave lessons to most of the old lot.

Quintette de l'Atelier at RDS. César Franck and Florent Schmitt piano quintets. Was very tired after many late nights, and fell fast asleep in the Franck. Was looking forward to the Schmitt after the *Tragedy of Salomé* but was most disappointed. An interminable work (fully an hour) – sort of mixture of Franck, Debussy and Wagner. Thought it must be a very early work, but find it only just predates *Salomé*.[12] Had a few words with Ó Broin sen., who seemed to enjoy it.[13] Met Charles [Acton], who came back for tea and cake ... a good deal of talk about the MAI (getting pretty tired of talking about it after all the fuss!). Sent wire to John Beckett to tell him about the meeting. Late to bed again blast it!

10 January 1950. Tuesday

... I went to [RÉ] to see about the copying of the quartet parts and borrow a recording of the Haydn 'Farewell' Symphony. Short amusing chat with Larry Morrow. Called in to see Martin McCullough about the harpsichord ... Denis Donoghue came in after lunch for a lesson, and we spent the time finding the right position for the microphone in recording. I also recorded a song with my own accompaniment. I then got to work at the scoring of the first ballet Intermezzo [from *The Buried Moon*] ... Gave a lesson to Mabel Peat, then a quick supper and off to the council meeting of the MAI.

Edgar [Deale], Olive Smith, Mrs Larchet, Joe [Groocock], Tony Hughes and Michael O'Higgins present. Looked as if there would be a row after all – for we had an abusive letter from Michael McM[ullin] refusing to attend. We discussed procedure, and drew up a report. I was terribly upset by it all – I hate these rows.

12. Florent Schmitt (1870–1958), Quintet for piano and strings in B major, op. 51 (1908).
13. As Secretary of the Department of Posts and Telegraphs and with a keen interest in music, León Ó Broin was enormously influential in the development of the RÉ Orchestra. His son Éimear (1927–2013) was a staff conductor with RÉ/RTÉ over many years. See further Pine, *Music and Broadcasting, passim.*

Went up for the General Meeting, and had to wait over half an hour for a quorum. F.J. Kelly in the chair – he managed things superbly. The council were also very well-behaved, and in spite of evil omens, a major row was averted, thank goodness. I made an urgent speech as one of the founders appealing for the universal aspect of the MAI as representative of music opinion in Ireland *in toto* – we must urge *all* factions to join. Charles [Acton] made a good speech on constructive policy – though quibbled about some minor points too. John Miley is now on the council – also ['Joe' crossed out] Malone of the Music Federation.[14] I only hope that Tony Farrington and Robert McKeever will not regret having taken on the jobs of secretary and assistant secretary. Told Michael McM. about the quartet performance – I just had to say something to him – felt so awful sitting there and looking at the floor. Joe [Groocock] and Robert McK. came back with us for a cup of tea and some amusement with the recording machine. I feel a great sense of relief that this trouble is over – at least for the present. First council meeting to be on February 1st.

11 January 1950. Wednesday

… Took a look at *The Irish Times* review of the year, and saw that although a page is given to painting, and one to drama, there is no mention of music. If *The Irish Times* had an editor who had an interest in music, it could do a great deal.

Continued the scoring of the Intermezzo … After a cup of tea I studied the score of the Haydn 'Farewell' Symphony. There are very few expression marks, and dynamics must be worked out. Listened to Henry Wood's recording. Then edited a part to keep the clarinets happy without letting them be too obtrusive. While Mary practised singing after supper I read Mícheál Mac Liammóir's diary of making the *Othello* film published in *The Irish Times*.[15]

Charles Lynch recital. John [Miley] and Charles [Acton] resplendent in tails to receive at the door. A small, but good audience. *Four Excursions* by Samuel Barber were rather empty – perhaps if played with more 'swing' they would be more effective. No. 3 is the best.[16] Then the Bax 1934 Sonata (dedicated to C[harles] L[ynch]). I found this a most stimulating work – unlike most of Bax's music, which fails to keep my attention. Its form is

---

14. John Miley played clarinet in the DOP. See Chapter 3 (above), p. 44.
15. Mícheál Mac Liammóir played the role of Iago in Orson Welles' film of *Othello* released in 1952.
16. Samuel Barber's *[Four] Excursions*, op. 20 were premiered (excluding no. 3 which was initially omitted from the set by the publisher) by Horowitz in January 1945.

more taut, and the rhythmical movement has more drive than in many other works. Then Brahms op. 10 *Ballades*. Early Brahms – and rather muddy, but warm and again enjoyable. Encores included Chopin F major Nocturne and John Ireland *[The] Island Spell* (was reminded of Dorothy Stokes's remark about C.L. and 'cascades of notes').[17] I wish C.L. wouldn't play Chopin (or Mozart either) – he is far too heavy-handed and heavy-minded.

Tea at the [Royal] Hibernian Hotel afterwards. John, Charles, C.L., Violet (plastered with makeup as usual), Carol Little[18] and Joan McElroy. Tried to pin down C.L. for our concert on March 2nd – a hopeless fellow to arrange things with. His decision is still vague. Amusing chat about awful performances in which we had taken part. C.L. has never forgotten the Tchaikovsky concerto with the DOP under Havelock Nelson![19]

12 January 1950. Thursday

Very loath to get up this morning – so many late and energetic nights: but Cormac had to be at school, so I got an early start with completing my arrangement of the wind parts for the Haydn symphony. (Parts had to be written for clarinets and flutes.) Hard at this all morning – finished just after lunch …. Music for Handel's *Water Music* arrived by post in time for tonight.

To the Phoenix Hall at 2.30 to meet Bull, the BBC engineer. He is going to help me record my quartet on my machine next Tuesday. Arranged for him to come in on Sunday evening to see it and have a chat. He gave us a 'lecture' on microphones. O'Hannrachain and B[rendan] Dunne there too. Interesting to see them taking notes – every word went down. I was glad of my experience of taking notes at Cambridge. Most interesting information.

Rushed off at 4.00 to teach at the Academy [i.e. RIAM]. Another new pupil. [Jaroslav] Vaneček came in to ask me to take on the conductorship of the new Academy Orchestra – which sounds a promising combination. I am very keen on this – though how I am going to find the time I don't know. It *may* mean getting rid of some pupils – or anyway a bit of juggling. If I am well paid it will be worth it – though in any case I would enjoy the work if the orchestra is to be a good one. Good position too.

---

17. 'The Island Spell' is the first of John Ireland's *Decorations* (or *Three Pieces for Piano*), composed in 1912/13.

18. Charles Acton's future wife (see reference to engagement, 30 March below).

19. Charles Lynch played Tchaikovsky's Piano Concerto in B flat minor with the DOP conducted by Havelock Nelson on 6 October 1942 at the Mansion House, Dublin. Commenting on the concerto being 'a difficult work to conduct', the *Irish Independent* (7 October 1942) noted that 'it was no wonder, then, that the wind groups occasionally went awry'. Neither the *Irish Times* nor the *Irish Press* reviews (same date) noted any particular issues.

… Good hard work at DOP rehearsal – all on the Haydn. New clarinet called Gilbert comes all the way from Mullingar. He seems good, and his keenness in coming promises great things. Charles Lynch called in to say he would play Beethoven [Piano Concerto] no. 3 with us – so we are delighted. Committee meeting afterwards – nothing of vital importance.

13 January 1950. Friday

Bright sunny day – but rather cold. Saxifrage 'His Majesty' has two flowers full out. The slugs have been rather active in the mild weather …

On with the score [of the Intermezzo from *The Buried Moon Suite*] in the afternoon – interrupted by a few pupils for lessons. Made a recording with Betty Colclough, and found with dismay that something is wrong again with the machine – terrific background noise when playing back. Such a nuisance with the important recording of my quartet next Tuesday …

[Listened to] the second of the series of broadcasts on African music. Fascinating description of the complexities of the rhythm. Made some recordings of the examples – but being [BBC] Third Programme it was not coming over well. I was wondering about the possibilities of using some of these rhythms in our music – but I think we could only succeed in using the superficial qualities – just like the bad arranger of folksongs; and besides, this rhythmical type is purely African and therefore alien to the spirit and traditions of European music.

… Have now practically finished the score [of the Intermezzo] – only six or seven more bars. Must try and get parts ready for next Thursday. I am rather anxious about the difficulty of the brass parts in the other Intermezzo (written for the ECA[20] programme). I have yet to write a finale to round off the suite. It will be a matter of using some of the final dance of the ballet, and perhaps the procession music.

14 January 1950. Saturday

… The plants arrived from Donard today.[21] Azaleas 'Orange Beauty' and 'Satsuki', and rhododendrons hanceanum and incana. Ericas Springwood white, Mrs Maxwell and H.E. Beale. Clemati jackmanii superba and sieboldii, and acer palmatum dissectum autopurpureum. Unpacked them before lunch and just had time to plant a couple. Heeled in the rest.

---

20. ECA most probably refers to the European Consultative Assembly, established in 1949 with Ireland as a founding member.
21. The Slieve Donard Nursery in Newcastle, Co. Down, established in 1904, was one of Ireland's leading plant nurseries. It closed in 1975.

… A lesson to Mabel Peat first, then into town … Left the recorder in with Rogers. (It turned out that there seems to be something wrong with the head – not so simple. Why should this happen just before one of its most important jobs? I have brought it back hoping Bull will be able to suggest something tomorrow) … I went to the Phoenix Hall to rehearse the quartet. Very much better today – in fact it may be quite a good performance after all …

15 January 1950. Sunday

John Miley [clarinet] and Chris Haughey [bassoon] turned up for the wind trio rehearsal at 11.00.[22] We worked pretty thoroughly at the first two movements of the Ibert trio. The recording machine was a great help (even though not working well) – extraordinary how noticeable messy fingering, untidy attacks after breathing and bad ensemble show up on a recording. We were disgusted with the first recording, though improved a lot as a result of it. Got John to check over some of the clarinet shakes in the Intermezzo score.

Finished planting the shrubs after lunch, and then went to see about the starting trouble in the car … Left the car with Grattan [Norman] … Funny how everything goes wrong at once. The metronome broke this morning. Puncture yesterday – and the recording machine! Norman Bull, the BBC man, came in to supper. Most interesting chat … He tells me that I will be offered the job of Balance and Control at RÉ. The question is do I want it? He thinks that as long as I treat it not as an end in itself, but as a means of livelihood I should take it – and try it anyway. It should give me enough time for composition. I could then give up teaching, which would be a great relief, since the responsibility is such a weight on the mind. Discussed the Belfast job too. It is so hard to make a decision. He assures me that I am held in high regard by the RÉ officials, and that they would not just give me the job to keep me quiet. This is encouraging.

16 January 1950. Monday

Dropped … the recorder at Douglas Radio and then met Norman Bull at the Phoenix Hall. Practical demonstration of microphone placing – and out-of-phase effects. Equipment explained, and was told how to broadcast an orchestral performance by following the music in the score so as to anticipate overloading etc. Brendan Dunne came in later … went off with B[rendan] D[unne] and N[orman] B[ull] for coffee. Rather a pointless

---

22. Brian played oboe.

argument about what I described as the Catholic Church's *fear* of communism and intellectuals, showing a sign of weakness. Norman Bull has no faith, which was a bait for B[rendan] D[unne]. I think this business of balancing a musical performance could be quite fascinating. It would be rather a waster though if RÉ don't do more to improve their transmitting equipment ... [After lunch at home] ... drove ... into town and called for the recorder ... [It] is now ... working perfectly again – just a resister gone again.

Teaching at the Academy. New pupil to interview – hard to know what to do about new pupils with everything hanging in the air. Have also agreed to take over the Academy Orchestra. This will mean a lot of changing round of pupils, which may eventually be of no avail.

Pasquier Trio at RDS[23] ... Interesting programme – Four preludes and fugues taken from Mozart, W.F. Bach, J.S. B[ach], Schubert – delightful. Jean Martinon (saw the [manuscript] two years ago) an interesting work, which I think has a good deal to say, though would like to hear it again. Some of it a bit too clever. Finally Jean Françaix, during which I had a most violent revulsion against this damned *slickness* of much of modern French music. This work is a bundle of clever tricks saying absolutely nothing. Got very angry indeed ... Robert McKeever, Charles and John Miley came in afterwards to discuss the DOP's visit to Drogheda. Also discussed this RÉ job. I am now determined to take the job – anyway on trial, *provided that* (1) I can continue the DOP; (2) I am not forbidden by civil service red tape from expressing my musical opinions in public – and can continue the MAI work; (3) The hours are reasonable enough to allow time for composition; (4) I can still have concerts with the RÉ Orchestra; (5) I can still do broadcast talks. In fact I value my personal freedom and the cause of music in Ireland more than Balance and Control and £700.

17 January 1950. Tuesday
Brought the recorder down to Portobello studio ready for the recording of [my string] quartet. Stayed for some time hoping to meet Norman Bull. Chatted with the engineer, and watched Dermot O'Hara rehearse the Light Orchestra. N[orman] B[ull] didn't turn up, so I came home and finished the score of the Intermezzo.

... Then [afternoon] to Portobello studio for the balance test for the

---

23. French string trio comprising brothers Jean (violin), Pierre (viola) and Etienne Pasquier (cello), founded in 1927.

recording of the quartet. Took a lead off from the speaker and fed into 'Radio' on my machine. Norman Bull took a lot of trouble balancing. Joe Groocock and Brendan Dunne turned up to hear the work, and Arthur Duff was there – Arthur looking very broken – had a pleasant chat with him. The performance went pretty well, though Betty [Sullivan, cello] missed a turnover in the last movement, and was a beat or two out for a few bars. Got a very good recording, though the tape was crooked at the very opening, and distorted a few bars. Played the recording through to the Cirulli people, which helped them a lot, I think. Both Joe and Brendan seem genuinely enthusiastic about the work. I don't believe poor Arthur could be enthusiastic about anything! – anyway he passed no remarks!

Came home to teach M[abel] Peat and Dorothy Graham. Felt very worn out and depressed – must be the coming together of so many things – the run of bad luck with material things going wrong, the strain of the quartet performance, and the uncertainty of my future with the possibility of this new job in RÉ … I have decided by the way to dedicate the quartet to Betty [Sullivan] and Tom [Kelly] together – I hope their alliance is a permanent one, for they are so good for one another. Loathed the idea of lecturing to the People's College on Beethoven [Symphony] no. 7 (second and third movements) – but the audience stimulated me – particularly the general questions afterwards, and I finished the day in better form – though very tired.

18 January 1950. Wednesday
… I spent most of the morning and afternoon doing a radio script – enjoying myself at the expense of 'The Platform Manner'. Lessons to Rosemary and Denis [Donoghue] …

To Portobello at 6.30. Tested the recording machine to make sure the tape would run smoothly. Felt very keyed up for the first performance of [my string] quartet – the culmination of three years' work. Only Tom [Kelly] and Mary in the studio. Arthur Duff and the pianist of the [RÉ] Light Orchestra in the control room, with that incredibly stupid engineer (fortunately, perhaps, I don't know his name). Arthur remarked that it was all very well to *look* stupid, or to *be* stupid – but both together is too much. Performance much better than yesterday – though poor Betty [Sullivan] got a fit of nerves in the same place which went wrong yesterday, and made a false entry at that same place in the last movement. She got over it very well though. Arthur followed the score, and made comic remarks – 'Ah – Coleridge Taylor', etc. We were terrified the silly engineer would turn up the wrong mike or something. Got an excellent recording. The Cirulli people seem genuinely enthusiastic about the work – and I think they did their very best with it. The performance was far better than I had expected – though the Griller [Quartet] is what I really want.

I was most touched by a wire from Fred May wishing the work a good send-off. Thanked the Cirulli people profusely, and went off with Mary having arranged to meet Betty and Tom at the Unicorn [restaurant] at 8.20. Mary and I had a few drinks to celebrate, and then went to hear Charles Lynch play the Berg Sonata op. 1 – which was at my request. I was interested in the work – though I feel it should not have been written for the piano. The audience didn't like it, I'm afraid. We wanted to celebrate, so made our escape. Had to run the gauntlet of Charles Acton, who was very serious, efficient, and fussed running the concert. 'Go and have a strong cup of coffee and come back to hear the Brahms.' Mary had had enough to drink to burst into laughter! Met Betty and Tom as arranged, and over an excellent meal with wine, we had a great talk. I officially told them of my decision to dedicate the quartet to the pair of them … Wolfram Hentschel was in the Unicorn with Mander, the Italian conductor, and their wives. Had a short and amusing chat with Wolfram, and a word or two with Mander.

19 January 1950. Thursday
Spent the first half of the morning cutting up logs. Then worked out the Prelude for *The Buried Moon Suite*. Have decided to start with the priest summoning the procession which then disappears into the distance (as at the end of Scene 2). Then Intermezzo no. 1 – 'The Lament of the Buried Moon', and as a finale, the second Intermezzo, symbolising the determination of the villagers to release and save the moon. This is the Intermezzo I wrote for the ECA programme as *Intermezzo from Ireland*. Started scoring the March this morning. Recorded the script on the 'Platform Manner' for 'Music Stand' at RÉ in the afternoon. O'Hannrachain suggests that the Cirulli people should play my quartet at the Phoenix Hall recital in February. Ralph [Cusack] rang up, and I was delighted to hear that he was most moved by the work. Had a word with Hans Rosen, and gave him a lift to Westland Row.[24] Taught the Academy pupils, with a break for a cup of tea with Denis [Donoghue]. Had an amusing chat with Dorothy Stokes in the street. She coined a new phrase: 'the penny-a-quaver mentality' of the

---

24. Location of the RIAM.

RÉ Orchestra! DOP rehearsal: worked on the Beethoven Concerto no. 3. Then Fred O'Callaghan, the student conductor for this session, took over for the Haydn 'Farewell'.[25] He has a very good beat – but is at present uninspiring. He was of course very nervous. Charles [Acton] and Carol Little came back to hear the recording of the quartet. Charles seems most impressed. It was the first time I really had the opportunity of listening properly myself. At the moment, I do think it is my most significant work to date.

20 January 1950. Friday

[M]ost of the day was spent in solid work at the score of the March for the [*Buried Moon*] ballet suite. I find it very hard to decide whether this March comes off or not. The problem was to write a fairly straightforward diatonic march to represent the simple reactions of the country people as opposed to the evil things of the marsh [*sic*]. Either it will sound like a parody of Walton's parody of Elgar, or it will come off. Performance (perhaps even only in the right context of the Ballet) must be the eventual arbiter....

... Lessons to Olwen Roe, Rosemary and Dorothy Graham. The recording machine was amazingly useful with Olwen, and convinced Dorothy that a big hollow throat does not necessarily produce a dark sound. Joe [Groocock] rang up to say how much he enjoyed the quartet, and seemed genuinely enthusiastic ... A winter aconite is coming up – in spite of the fact that Boris [the cat] dug it up during the summer. Crocus laevigatus is nearly over, and the 'His Majesty' saxifrage is still flowering well. The jasmine is not as good as it was a week ago. Yvonne called in at supper, and gave a lovely description of the family listening to the quartet at Ballybride.[26]

Went down town to go to [the cinema]. On finding that we could not get in till 8.30, we called in at the Phoenix Hall to hear Michael Bowles conducting for the first time since his 'fall'.[27] Wolfram Hentschel described him as most arrogant, and having no feeling for music. [Wagner's] *Meistersinger* overture was very dull ...

---

25. Fred O'Callaghan (b. Dublin, 1927) would become conductor of the DOP from 1967 to 1971, thereafter frequently conducting individual concerts until 1995. He enlisted in the Army School of Music, was commissioned in 1951, in which year he graduated from UCD with a BMus, and was appointed conductor of the Army No. 1 Band in 1971 (*EMIR*, p. 746).
26. Brian's parents' house in Shankill, near Bray, County Wicklow.
27. Michael Bowles, who had previously been chief conductor of the radio orchestra, had resigned from RÉ in 1948 when, following the establishment of the expanded RÉSO, he was not appointed conductor of the new orchestra. See Pine, *Music and Broadcasting*, pp. 118f.

21 January 1950. Saturday

... I worked on the March [of the *Buried Moon Suite*] ... After lunch we went off to see Ralph [Cusack] and Nancy ... Went round the garden first – most impressed by iris bakeriana – reticulate type – though very early, and seems most hardy. Also crocus chrysanthus var. bronze [second part of name not recorded],[28] a completely bronze outside with golden yellow within. Crocus imperati susiamus and laevigatus were out also, and some lovely cyclamen corms ... [29]

There is always lots to talk about there – too much really. Discussed the radio job, the quartet, Betty and Tom, music of all kinds, living in Ireland and so on ... We listened to the recent Prokofiev violin sonata (as recorded by Menuhin) and both agree that it is well up to the standard of the best of his works like the Second Violin Concerto.[30] I must hear it again soon – since I found the first movement a bit puzzling (not knowing how long it was going to be, and therefore missing the proportions) ...

22 January 1950. Sunday

... [Fetched] Chris Haughey for the wind trio rehearsal. We worked hard at the third and fourth movements of the Ibert, finally making a recording to check our work. There is still something wrong with the machine – if only there was someone in Dublin who really knew all about them – apart from Peter Hunt, whom I don't like to ask since he is so busy. Oboe tone is particularly badly distorted. I spent the afternoon on the March score, and very nearly finished it ...

... Gramophone evening[:] the Hentschels, Betty and Tom, the Rosens, Thurloe and Yvonne, and Robert McDowell came: an ideal gathering with no one to spoil the listening atmosphere. (Extraordinary how even one unmusical person, or a bad listener, can ruin listening for everyone else – even though he may not make a sound!) Started off with some early music. De Machault, de la Barre, Montéclaire, etc. Then a number of madrigals – Monteverdi, Gesualdo, Byrd, Weelkes, Wilbye, Ward. Then the quintet for flute, oboe and string trio of J.C. Bach – the sort of good-humoured music which puts everyone in good form. Then we listened to my quartet – the recording made at the recording session on Tuesday first, then after tea, the

---

28. Written as 'var. Bronze ... ', indicating that Brian could not recall the full name of the variety. Possibly crocus chrysanthus 'Zwanenburg bronze'?
29. Ralph Cusack operated a specialist nursery garden from his house in Annamoe, Co. Wicklow, issuing catalogues each year of available bulbs and other plants.
30. Yehudi Menuhin's recording of Prokofiev's Violin Sonata no. 1, op. 80 (1946), was issued by EMI in 1949. The Violin Concerto no. 2 dates from 1935.

recording of the performance. An improvement in the later performance was very obvious. Everyone seems genuinely enthusiastic – especially Wolfram and Hans Rosen. Hans is obviously a very acute listener – spotting all the details of its construction. Wolfram has formed a new quartet – the 'Dublin Quartet' consisting of [François] D'Albert, Billy Shanahan, Maire Larchet and himself.[31] He is very keen to play [my] quartet – and may play it in London. It is obvious that the Cirulli people (apart from Betty) could never really play it as I wish. The particular idea they miss is the nervous excitement of the rests – which they treat merely as breaks, rather than 'silent music'. I think some of my metronome marks are a bit on the slow side. Wolfram also suggested one or two technical emendations to help the effect by bowing …

23 January 1950. Monday

… I set to work and finished the score of the March. Almost exactly as I put the last note down, John Beckett turned up unexpectedly. Was delighted to see him, since he is always such a chance bird of passage. He had listened to the quartet broadcast, but wanted to hear it again – so I put on the recording for him … John seems very impressed, which means a great deal to me. He paid me the compliment of believing that I had found a suitable language of expression through which I was concerned with saying things of artistic importance. He feels that he is still very much searching for his means, and that his work has therefore no significance yet. I think he underrates his work, but he is obviously going through a period of experiment, and also a period of harsh self-criticism amounting at times almost to doubt. I will be very surprised indeed if my original prediction that he will become the most significant Irish composer of all of us does not turn out to be true. In many ways he has grown and developed so alarmingly quickly – there will have to be a time for this rapid development and sea of collected impressions to settle down and crystallise. We talked about fugal developments – he quoted the one in the Walton symphony as a fiasco, since a fugue suggests a *beginning*, and therefore cancels out all that has gone before.[32] He was quite sure however that the fugue in the Scherzo of my quartet does *not* suffer from this fault, but does in fact *grow out* of the preceding music, which is what I intended. John is going to start a choir for the study of sixteenth-century music, and I recommended some voices to him – I hope he gets it going, for

31. On Francois D'Albert, see Chapter 5 (above). William ('Billy') Shanahan (violin) and Maire Larchet (viola) had been members of the RÉSO since its foundation.
32. William Walton's First Symphony dates from 1931–5 (his Second Symphony (1957–60) postdates this diary).

there is a great need for such a thing. He hopes that he *might* get the job of conducting the Radio [Éireann] choir. If we can get a harpsichord, he will play the Bach E major [Concerto] with the DOP in June.

Had a very nice letter from Aloys [Fleischmann] about the quartet. He is a most reliable and quick-minded critic. He immediately saw the problem of performance which the Cirulli people didn't master – that of overcoming the sectional construction of the first and last movements and knitting them into a whole. Teaching all afternoon …

24 January 1950. Tuesday

[W]ent to Portobello Studio to get the parts that had been copied by Donnelly & Co. … Came back and spent the greater part of the day correcting all the mistakes in the copied parts. It infuriates me to think that you can't rely on anyone to do things properly. It would almost have been quicker to do them myself. In transposing the clarinet parts up a semitone for clarinet in A, he succeeded in writing the scale of E flat as D#, F natural, G, G#, A, C, D, D#! How they will read it I don't know … First rehearsal of the Academy Orchestra 5.30–7.30. Very mixed bag led by Fanny Feehan.[33] At the moment all the good players are in the [first violins], and the seconds are bad. This must be changed. Rehearsed Handel Minuet from *Berenice*, Purcell Chaconne in G min, and Boyce Symphony no. 3. Rushed home for a quick meal – then to lecture at the People's College at 8.15 – last movement of Beethoven [Symphony] no. 7. Tried to explain significance of key centres – succeeded I think …

25 January 1950. Wednesday

… I slept late in an attempt to recover some energy. Longing for the Boyne to open,[34] and then I can be sure of one day in the week to relax. Did some more work on the parts of the suite … and then went off … for a rehearsal of [Mendelssohn's] *Elijah*. Was not singing well – too tired. I must be very bad company for Mary at the moment – silly little things irritate me. Must be the result of a big rush of work, the indecision about the future (the RÉ job) and so many material things going wrong (about seven different things with the car). Rehearsed again after lunch … [then] I went on with the work, and also started the programme notes for the DOP concert.

---

33. Fanny Feehan (d. 1996) would later write as a theatre and music critic for a number of Dublin newspapers including the *Evening Press*, *Sunday Tribune*, *Sunday Press*, *Irish Times* and the fortnightly review *Hibernia*. She married Mervyn Wall (novelist, playwright and secretary of the Arts Council from 1957 to 1975).

34. The salmon fishing season on the River Boyne in County Meath opened annually in February (see 15 February below).

Charles Lynch recital in the evening. Started with the Berg op. 1 Sonata which was repeated (from last week) to give the audience a chance of hearing it a second time. The harmonic idiom becomes very tiring, since there is not enough rhythmical vitality to relieve it. The harmonic tension seems rather indiscriminately planned, and one gets the impression that Berg was striving after *noises*, and losing sight of the movement of the music. Then some Beethoven Bagatelles – amusing, but played too heavily. Chatted with Rhona Marshall,[35] Tony Farrington and Edgar [Deale] and others in the interval. Honegger *Toccata and Variations*, Bax *Winter Water* (repeated as encore) and Holst's amusing *On Chrissemas Day in the Morning* completed the programme, with a Holst Toccata on a Scottish tune to finish with.[36] Was impressed by the atmosphere of the Bax, and simply delighted with the humour of the Holst pieces (might arrange *Chrissemas Day* for orchestra?) …

26 January 1950. Thursday

Gradually getting rather warmer again, some things in the garden look a bit sorry after the frosty days. Crocus laevigatus, which has been out since about Christmas, is over now. Sieberi, etruscus and chrysanthus are ready to follow very soon … [F]etched the parts of the March which had been copied. Spent the morning doing special flute parts so that Yvonne can take part … . [W]ent to see Grattan [Norman] in Cope Street about the carburettor. When I reached home, the off-side rear brake drum was red hot – the rear wheel bearing had packed up. This somehow brings the series of troubles to a climax. I hope the end of them. [37]

… [After supper] the DOP rehearsal – one of those very bad ones. Tried to get something out of my ballet suite, but there were no good cellos there,

---

35. Rhona Marshall (1903–94) taught at the RIAM from 1920 and was one of the leading piano teachers of her time in Ireland (*EMIR*, pp. 628–9).

36. Holst's spelling of 'Chrissemas' is given here, although written in the diary as 'Christmas'.

37. At this time Brian owned a 1935 Lancia Augusta saloon, which he had bought for £25 and which had been causing considerable trouble over the previous weeks, although he really appreciated the qualities of the car. A review of this model in the British motoring magazine *Motorsport* in 1934 (September issue, p. 519) expressed precisely those same qualities in this car which Brian would continue throughout his life to regard as paramount when choosing a new car: 'The Lancia "Augusta", then, is a car which will appeal strongly to those who take a keen interest in their motors and motoring. It is beautifully designed and constructed … On the performance side, it is a joy to drive and will get the better of faster cars on an ordinary give-and-take road. When motor-car manufacturers are turning more and more to mass-production methods, and the cars themselves are consequently losing the separate personalities which were so noticeable to enthusiastic motorists a few years ago, it is satisfying to be reminded that a few manufacturers, at least, are not giving up the careful design and manufacture on which their reputations have been based.' Brian might have written those same words himself.

and intonation in the wind was appalling. Then some work on the Handel *Water Music*. John Benson did well with his first attempt at fourth horn. [Fred] O'Callaghan worked on the symphony while I rushed home to get the last number of the [*Buried Moon*] suite which I had left behind. Betty and Tom came – and they nearly put me in reasonable form again – but I didn't see them for long enough. Usual committee meeting afterwards but was too tired to take anything in …

27 January 1950. Friday

A very slack day – an attempt to take things easy and regain some vitality!

… Terry Beckett came to supper, and we talked about the MAI. I persuaded him of its ultimate value, and he is joining enthusiastically, and going to do what he can to dispel the suspicions regarding it, and get more members. Also talked about music criticism – he is keen to try and get a column in the [*Irish*] *Times* for the preview of forthcoming musical events. The MAI should back this. Discussed the position of [León] Ó Broin as the man who wrongly has more power over musical matters in Ireland than anyone …

28 January 1950. Saturday

… Lessons to M. Peat and Elizabeth Harben. Funny the way all these English girls in Trinity have the same complaint of 'white' singing with a closed throat – I have three of them as pupils. Made a vigorous attempt, with some success, to get E.H.'s throat more open!

… Went to Ballybride in the afternoon … Eileen[38] has got hold of some rumour that I may be offered a job assisting Hewson[39] in Trinity. Another uncertainty for the already muddled future!

Quiet evening at home – except for a visit to RÉ to meet Terry O'Sullivan,[40] who gave me the £40 for the ECA commission.

29 January 1950. Sunday

Usual Sunday morning rehearsal of the wind trio. John Miley arrived with Chris Haughey at about 11, and we worked at the last movement of the Ibert, finally recording the whole work. We are beginning to play quite well together, though my trouble is that I don't get enough time to practise, and

---

38. Brian's mother.
39. George Hewson (1881–1972), professor of Music at TCD since 1935 and organist of St Patrick's Cathedral in Dublin from 1920 to 1960 (*EMIR*, p. 485). Brian succeeded him as professor of music in 1962.
40. Journalist and author of the regular social column 'Diary' in the *Evening Press*.

the fingering is messy. Chris is not very hot on the high register either. We are going to start on a Milhaud trio next week. Left Chris down at [Nelson's] Pillar to catch a bus … Called in at Wynne's Hotel to see if Norman Bull was about – haven't seen him for some time – but failed to contact him.

The predicted snow came as rain today, in spite of the bitter cold wind. I hope we have lots of it to fill up the Boyne for the beginning of the salmon season …

… Finished the programme notes of the DOP concert before going to bed (including a note on the ballet suite from *The Buried Moon*).

30 January 1950. Monday

… Left the clarinet part of the Intermezzo to be recopied at Portobello studio. Then to the Phoenix Hall in search of Norman Bull. Had a chat with Billy Shanahan about the new Dublin Quartet. Also spoke to Wolfram and Betty, and told Maire Larchet that if and when I get another concert with the RÉ Orchestra, I want to do the Hindemith *Trauermusik*. Norman Bull had been in Belfast over the weekend, and was not back yet. Called at May's music shop, and picked out records from a French [*sic*] collection – Hindemith Violin Concerto, and Honegger Symphony for Strings – to be kept aside for when I can afford to buy them. Bought a new [conducting] baton. Pat Lavery, the cellist, is working there now. Paid another visit to Portobello – no sign of Norman Bull yet, so went home and copied special flute parts for the suite so that [my sister] Yvonne may take part in the performance

… Lessons to Rosemary and Olwen after lunch (using the recording machine) – then to the Academy … Teaching unmusical singers is most soul-destroying, and wears me out. One pupil has been trying to learn *Who is Sylvia?* for a whole month, and sings it out of tune with $4\frac{1}{4}$ beats in most of the bars. So dreadful that I am left speechless. I enjoy teaching a really promising pupil but singing attracts all the worst dabblers because they think it is an easy accomplishment to attain. If I were able to take teaching less seriously it would be less of a strain – as it is I feel such a responsibility for each pupil which continually weighs on my conscience. Peter Gibbs [String] Quartet at the RDS. A young group trained by the Grillers (very obviously so). They didn't seem to have the fire and enthusiasm one would expect from a group so young. The playing of soft passages on the fingerboard is most effective – avoiding wiry tone – but it can be overdone. I have only heard the Grillers use this technique to perfection. Beautiful performance of Purcell Chaconne, followed by Mozart in G [K.387], a mirror of the Griller's interpretation. Then Bloch no. 2, for the first time in Ireland as a live performance. Magnificent work, though their performance just missed something – there seemed to be a lack of 'body' in the energetic driving passages. Met Charles [Acton], John Miley, Robert McDowell, Betty and Tom, Billy Shanahan and the Hentschels. The last asked us back for coffee … drove to Harold's Cross where they have their house. We are getting very fond of them, and agree on so many points … Wolfram again asserts his confident faith in my quartet and bewails the fact that there is so little opportunity for its recognition here. Also discussed conducting, and my problem with the RÉSO who regard me as a student. Wolfram suggests losing my temper at rehearsal and *making* them realise that I know a great deal more about the music than such a collection of café musicians and 'penny-a-quaverites'. Easier said than done – but I may try it yet …

31 January 1950. Tuesday
Started a radio script for Thursday in the morning – discussing controversial musical topics such as the relationship between colour and music – particularly the vexed question of the association of colours with keys. Spent the greater part of the morning working on the *Elijah*. I shouldn't really sing in public at all, since I haven't time to practise regularly, which is essential – but I can't bear letting unmusical idiots take my place! Lovely sunny day after a keen frost – Crocus sieberis is just out – a glorious shade of blue …

Lessons to Elizabeth Harben and Denis Donoghue after lunch. Denis has to sing his scholarship songs tomorrow evening. He is not in good health at all. Then more work on the script. Academy Orchestra at 6.00. Fanny Feehan is not as good a leader as she should be with all the experience she has – unpleasantly pleased with herself. Came home just in time to have a quick supper before lecturing at the People's College and spent most of the time answering the phone [from] Norman Bull and Brendan Dunne. Last of the series of lectures on Beethoven [Symphony] no. 7. An enthusiastic crowd who should form a good nucleus of enthusiasm. They were very grateful for the lectures … The rush of things on Tuesday evening leaves me dead beat! Michael Morrow [41] and friend called in about the production of a masque he has dug out. Most remarkable appearance – hasn't cut his hair for a year!

41. Although born in London, Michael Morrow (1929–94) came from a Belfast family of illustrators and cartoonists and was studying at this time at the Dublin College of Art. He played recorder and lute in the Dublin Society of Renaissance Music before moving to London in 1953, where he would later co-found the pioneering early-music ensemble Musica Reservata with John Beckett (*EMIR*, p. 686). As an art student, he designed a book plate for Brian and Mary ('Ex libris Brian and Mary Boydell'), which featured a figure blowing a wind instrument.

Brian receiving the RÉ Chamber Music Prize for his String Quartet no. 1 in December 1949 from Charles Kelly, Deputy Director of Broadcasting, with Fachtna Ó hAnnracháin, Music Director of RÉ, in attendance.

COURTESY OF *THE IRISH TIMES* AND THE BOARD OF TRINITY COLLEGE DUBLIN

FEBRUARY

1 February 1950. Wednesday

… Went to Portobello to fetch the corrected clarinet part. Had an amusing chat with the engineer whose voice came over the air when the transmission of the RÉ Waterford concert broke down, saying, 'That's the second bloody speaker gone now!' Also short chat with Val Keogh.[1] Worked till 12.00 on the radio script – complicated subject this question of colour and music – took a good deal of thought to clarify the issue. Lesson to Rosemary at 12.00 …

… Cold and rainy today. Should fill up the Boyne![2] … Then after supper to the first meeting of the new MAI Council. I was in the chair. An impression of enthusiasm, and we got through a great deal of work quite efficiently. Michael McMullin … refused to vote on any issue, and did his best to withhold information of which there was no record from his time of secretaryship! … [We] elected panels of foreign and Irish panels to judge Irish compositions worthy of recommendation. Plans for a Bach Festival, and many other points.

2 February 1950. Thursday

Called at Phoenix Hall to have a word with [Harry] Thwaites the trombone player [of the RÉSO] to ask him to play for the DOP Concert – also his colleague [Paddy Feeney] on the bass trombone. I was anxious to have good trombones owing to the difficulty of my suite. They will both play, so all is well … Left the script in at the Radio, and came home to do a report on the proposed Composers' Group of the MAI for the Bulletin.

Rehearsal and recording of my script for 'Music Stand' at RÉ in the afternoon. Joe [Groocock] was there rehearsing his talk on the Bach family, playing illustrations on the piano. Even though Joe doesn't actually practise as a pianist, he is an excellent player of eighteenth-century music. He has got that lightness which Charles Lynch never has – though Charles is the one pianist in Ireland who can produce real *tone* from his instrument.

Teaching at the Academy from 3.45 to 6.45. Quick supper at home, then the DOP rehearsal. A good rehearsal this week. My suite is beginning to come into shape. Gilbert, the clarinet from Mullingar, has brought along

1. Val Keogh would later become orchestral manager of the RÉ/RTÉ Symphony Orchestra.
2. In anticipation of the opening of the salmon fishing season on the River Boyne. See 12 and 15 February below.

his brother as fourth horn (or second) – wonderful to have four horns of our own. We all thoroughly enjoyed playing the Handel *Water Music*. I played oboe and [Fred] O'Callaghan conducted …

3 February 1950. Friday

… [H]ad to get the Lancia out to Grattan's for its overhaul. Certain amount of trouble starting – the battery was dead so that the petrol pump wouldn't work (it needed priming anyway) … Eventually decided to tow her with the Alvis[3] … Lessons to Rosemary and Olwen after lunch. Rosemary is going to London for 10 days, having some lessons with Louise Trenton,[4] and then to the Portadown Feis full of confidence that she will win the cups! … After tea … I set off for Tullamore, calling at May's [music shop] on the way for a slushy recording of the *Monastery Garden* to illustrate bogus sentimentality.[5] Alvis ran very well – steady 50 [mph] most of the way. Other people's lights – unable to dim properly – are the bogey on this road. Met a drunk lorry – or perhaps asleep – which forced me onto the grass verge … Good audience for 'The Art of the Listener'. A Mr Rogers in the chair, and usual front row of priests … Good discussion afterwards in which I was very strong about Ireland being *potentially* though not actually a musical country, the fault lying in the complete lack of musical education in the schools. Went down very well. Lecture seemed a great success … To a pub afterwards as usual … had to avoid drinking too much in view of my tummy and driving home. Left at midnight. Bright moon and clear roads. Stopped on the open road [for a break] and had that very strange feeling of being quite alone with the overpowering immensity of the night sky – miles from anywhere. Gave a lift to a commercial traveller who had broken down, and got back shortly before 2.

4 February 1950. Saturday

Lessons to M. Peat and E. Harben in the morning … and then to the Gresham [Hotel] for lunch with Norman Bull. We were both late – so all was well … Chatted about music in Ireland, motor cars, broadcasting, the

---

3. In addition to the 1935 Lancia Augusta, Brian had for some years already owned a second-hand, pre-war Alvis (model not known). Alvis cars were made in Coventry, England, between 1920 and 1967.
4. Brian had taken singing lessons with Louise Trenton in London in 1938/9. See Memoir (Part I) above, p. 17 and also Part II: Diary (below), 27 May to 4 June 1950.
5. Albert Ketèlbey's *In a Monastery Garden* was composed for orchestra in 1914 and published the following year in an arrangement for piano.

ISCM,[6] the BBC and everything. He tells me that the Belfast job should get one in on the conducting racket – I am beginning to think that I should try for it after all – though I can't stand the idea of living in Belfast. I shall feel most disturbed until this uncertainty sorts itself out. Nothing more definite about the RÉ job yet, which we discussed at some length. O'Hannrachain was lunching behind us with Dr Alexander, who is responsible for the ribbon microphone. Didn't know he was there, but Norman tells me I didn't say anything unwise. We like Norman. I hope he will come and stay next time he is over.

... a marvellous evening with Ralph and Nancy [Cusack] to dinner ... Listened to Prokofiev *Scythian Suite*, my quartet, and the Bartok Violin Concerto [no. 2]. Conversation and arguments on every subject under the sun, as usual with Ralph. Very violent argument about the possibility of a musician who agreed to stay in Nazi Germany ever being really great – e.g. Furtwängler ... A memorable evening which is impossible to describe briefly.

5 February 1950. Sunday
... Brought [Cormac and Barra] off to fetch Chris Haughey, and we rehearsed the Milhaud trio. If we can get the notes played really 'slickly' it should 'play itself'. Worked with the help of the recorder as usual which showed up all our technical imperfections. A very enjoyable rehearsal – though I wish I could find more time to practise the oboe.

... Gave a lesson to Leslie Packham at 8 – an interesting lesson. Since singing must be essentially natural, and therefore relaxed, the anxiety to sing well can cause muscular tightness. This business of *trying* to sing well, rather than just *singing* well is one of the great problems of teaching; and it becomes accentuated as soon as one goes thoroughly into the question of voice production. It is a problem which hardly touches the 'hack' teacher who spends lessons just running though songs!

When I can get L.P. to sing a phrase without thinking – as he is walking across the room – out it comes with clear frontal tone (since the fundamentals are by now reasonably automatic). Get him to try and improve on this and feel its sensation, and the jaw tightens, drawing back the tone so that it becomes dark and wooden.

Getting increasingly interested in the Belfast conducting job again – if only it weren't in Belfast!

---

6. International Society for Contemporary Music, founded in 1922. The most recent annual ISCM World Music Day hosted in London had been in 1946.

6 February 1950. Monday

Decided to take things fairly easy this week so as not to be tired for Thursday's performance of [Mendelssohn's] *Elijah* ... The DOP are getting great free publicity since Charles [Acton] wrote to the papers asking for the loan of cannons, for an unspecified purpose.[7] Amusing letter in the [*Irish*] *Times* this morning, and we hope to get something in the 'Irishman's Diary'.[8] Prepared an *ad lib* part for third and fourth horns for the ballet suite, so as to keep our new horn players amused. Then teaching at the Academy. [One of the cellists] called in with some fuss about the seating of the cellos in the Academy orchestra. These small-minded players are always much more interested in where they sit than in the music. The amusing thing is that I put it in such a way to her that she couldn't very well refuse the suggestion that she sit at the back by herself in order to encourage the bad players at the second desk!! All this delayed the teaching so that I got half an hour behind schedule ... returned home for supper ... Went off to hear Pierre Fournier at the RDS. Unaccompanied Bach [Cello Suite] in C minor (no. 5), Beethoven [Cello Sonata] op. 102 no. 1 in C major – a most interesting work which I would like to hear again several times (and better played, incidentally).[9] Then a sonata by Locatelli in which the fungus of virtuosity did much to spoil the early eighteenth-century charm. I imagine it was an arrangement, since I can find no mention of any cello works of his in Grove.

Pendulum has swung again – I now am determined to have a shot at the Belfast job – it should lead somewhere, and would anyway be an experience. It would be good to go away, get a good reputation outside, and then come back again.

7 February 1950. Tuesday

... finished the ad lib horn parts of the ballet suite. Also did a good deal of singing practice. Such a lovely mild sunny morning that we all went out and did some gardening just before lunch. The group of crocus sieberi was full out, so I photographed it.

Academy orchestra rehearsal from 5.45–7.15. Worked on the Purcell chaconne most of the time trying to get the changes of mood between the variations (as well as some more right notes and less clumsy bowing!). Had ordered a meal at Jurys Hotel for exactly 7.25, so as not to be too late for

---

7. The cannons were for the upcoming performance of Beethoven's 'Battle' Symphony at the concert on 2 March (see below). See also Memoir (Part I) above, p. 48.
8. A regular and ongoing opinion column in *The Irish Times*.
9. Pierre Fournier (1906–86) was one of the foremost cellists of his generation. His recordings of Bach's six suites for solo cello (1960) are still highly regarded.

the DOP rehearsal (changed from Thursday) … of course my meal was not ready – had to wait 15 minutes.

Worked on the third number of my suite at the DOP rehearsal, which was in a sort of lecture theatre at the Friends' Meeting House. Not a very suitable room with very queer sound. The trouble caused by the mistakes in the parts is terrible. It will take a lot more work yet to bring it into shape. Then worked on the Beethoven concerto. Four hours almost continual rehearsing is a bit too much, and I was made a little irritable by trying vainly to save my voice. The low hum of odd noises from an orchestra is most wearing. I must insist on more quietness – they get slack about this from time to time …

8 February 1950. Wednesday

It really isn't worth getting orchestral parts copied, unless the copyist is first rate – in the time spent on these parts of the ballet suite both at home and in rehearsal, I could have done most of them myself without all the annoying mistakes. Spent the morning doing a complete new part for the horns of the third number (Intermezzo) and timps – also a new trumpet part for the second number. Very cold again today, with bright sun …

… the final rehearsal for *Elijah* … My part didn't give me any real trouble. Dorothy [Graham] is a most promising conductor, I think – she has real verve and musicianship. Technically she is rather stiff in the beat, and funnily enough has many of my own faults – she admitted to copying my style! One of these faults is too much body movement. However, she managed to produce a wonderful result from the Clontarf Choral Society.

9 February 1950. Thursday

Took things very easy today – to be well rested for the performance tonight. Any kind of tiredness seems to affect singing more than any other musical activity …

… Went to tea with Charles [Acton] and [his mother] Mrs La Touche. Charles and I went into the history of Beethoven's 'Battle' Symphony, and found out all we could about Maelzel, the inventor of the panharmonicon for which the work was originally written. This was so as to be able to answer with authority a letter in *The* [*Irish*] *Times* on the subject. A good deal of chat about the DOP and so forth. Charles is really becoming quite monstrous in his role of sacrificing all principles to avoid causing offence or misunderstanding. He is now afraid of the performance of the 'Battle' with 'Rule Britannia' in conjunction with the Protestant surrounding (text on the wall) in the Metropolitan Hall.[10] Suggests hanging a tricolour over the text. Then suggested we invite Our Lady's Choral Society to join with us in a concert to explode the idea that we are a Protestant orchestra. We'll be off to give a concert in Rome next in aid of the suppression of communism!! A bath and shave, a glass of sherry and a sniff of Benzedrine inhaler and off to the *Elijah* performance. Packed hall with most appreciative audience. Have rarely sung better – curious how I can do things vocally when stimulated by an audience which I can't possibly accomplish in practice! Was able to sing all the high passages pianissimo, and sang throughout with great ease. We all enjoyed ourselves, and so did the audience, I gather …

Very tired after all this – slept like a log.

(Afterthought) – I remember one thing during the *Elijah* performance which nearly put me off my stride – that was the sight of Dorothy Stokes with some friend in the gallery. She was reclining over the space of three seats, whispering apparently critically all the time, and referring to the score. I wonder does she ever allow herself to *enjoy* a performance!

10 February 1950. Friday

… Then went to the Radio to see about the copying of the new parts of [my string] quartet … to Peter Hunt, where we chatted about the recording machine. He is having mysterious trouble with his Magnetophone [*sic*].[11] Gave him a lift down to the Metropole [cinema], and find that he thinks as I do about the quality of real motor cars!

… Thurloe [Conolly] dropped in and had lunch with us. A number of his pictures are off to America for exhibition, and he expects very good returns in sales. I am sure he will be doing very well for himself quite soon.

11 February 1950. Saturday

… Wrote to the Town Clerk of Belfast asking to be notified of any developments in the Belfast appointment … ordered the Albinoni oboe concerto from Boosey [& Hawkes] for the Drogheda concert … After tea

---

10. Beethoven was persuaded to write his so-called 'Battle' Symphony, or 'Wellington's Victory', following the Duke of Wellington's victory over the French at the Battle of Vitoria in 1813. It quotes the tunes 'God Save the King' and 'Rule Britannia' to represent the British army. The Metropolitan Hall in Lower Abbey Street, a late nineteenth-century evangelical hall, was regularly used by the DOP as a concert venue. It was demolished in the 1970s to make way for the Irish Life Centre.

11. The Magnetophon, a pioneering type of magnetic tape recorder, was developed in Germany before and during the Second World War. Examples seized by the Allies in 1944/5 formed the basis for significant advances in tape-recording technologies after the war.

we went to Grattan's. The Lancia is nearly ready, and all the faults are in hand. Now waiting for new fabric couplings of the suspension. We should have her again in a week's time.

… Charles rang up … all about how to behave towards John O'Donovan the … music critic. It appears that J.O'D. was under the illusion that I am a man of means who broadcasts, teaches and conducts as a hobby. Since he has learned the truth, he regrets his various personal insults and is offering the olive branch. Good – but I don't need Charles's advice on how to receive him when he asks for an interview about the forthcoming DOP concert …

12 February 1950. Sunday

… [wind trio rehearsal in the morning] …

Charles Pyke called after lunch, and we all set off for Slane to see the river [Boyne] and find out about our beats.[12] Was pleased to find him a good driver, especially since we were in one of these spongy modern Hillmans. He has done trials driving in the past, and is interested in motor cars. The Boyne was right over the banks – far too much rain for any hope of fish for the unfortunates who open the season today … The river looks lovely at this point – in a deep gorge with wooded banks, overlooked by Slane Castle, which must be an immense house inside. Looking forward greatly to getting to know this part of the river from every point of view … drove home just in time for the gramophone evening … Hentschels, Robert McDowell and John Benson with his girl Muriel Nolan. Pleasant evening – Sibelius [Symphony] no. 4 and *Tapiola* (strange meat for Wolfram's German upbringing – he didn't really get these), and the Hindemith Second String Trio which excited us all immensely – I hadn't played it for a couple of years – goodness knows why, for it is magnificent.

13 February 1950. Monday

We all went off together in the Alvis … then on to May's [music shop] where I changed the metronome they had sold me for a more satisfactory one …

Teaching at the Academy from 3.30 to 6.15 … then home to give Dorothy Graham a lesson.

… NB Mary thinks I make myself too vulnerable to people! I give too much of myself away to those who don't respect confidence.

---

12. Each year Brian would lease the fishing with a number of his colleagues for one day a week during the salmon and trout seasons on a specified 'beat' or stretch of the Boyne river.

14 February 1950. Tuesday

... Two lessons in the afternoon to E. Harben and Denis Donoghue. Denis sings at a prizewinners concert at the RIAM tonight – he should sing well (two Britten folk songs – the *Sally Gardens* and *O Come You Not from Newcastle*).

A rehearsal of the quartet at 5.15 for tomorrow's performance – first one in public. The playing of it is much improved, and some further improvements were made at this rehearsal – mostly a matter of speeds and accents. There seems to be more drive now.

The rehearsal of the Academy orchestra from 6.00–7.30. More work on the Purcell Chaconne, and then we tried to make something of the opera Viani is doing at the RIAM[13] – trying to take a rehearsal from a vocal score with no letters is a hopeless business.

Then a quick meal at the Grosvenor Hotel [on Westland Row] ... and then took over the DOP rehearsal from Hazel Lewis [née de Courcy] who had started for me. Worked on Haydn's 'Farewell', and then on my [*Buried Moon*] suite. Depressingly bad rehearsal – intonation in cellos was *appalling* – feel almost like cancelling the performance of my work, it is so bad. Perhaps the brass when they arrive will pull it together. John O'Donovan turned up at the end of the rehearsal wanting an interview. He is definitely feeling rather bad about some of the things he has said about me in his rag *Radio Review*, and seems genuinely keen on making amends. He came home with me and I gave him 'the dope' on myself and the orchestra. Was rather too tired for this sort of thing after four hours rehearsing – but he wants it in a hurry. Left him home, and then got to bed. Very excited about tomorrow – salmon and the quartet!!

15 February 1950. Wednesday

The regular day in the country once a week, which is such a rest and relief, and for which I have been longing through the winter, is here at last ... Started fishing [at Slane] at 11.00 – having been shown the best lies[14] by Jimmy the gillie. Was into something within ten minutes, which proved to be a pike – 9¾ lbs. The river was high, and began to rise (4'10" to 5'0" from 11.00 to 1.00). The water was very dirty. Saw a number of travelling fish, but none of them would look at me. Steady drizzle, with some heavy rain in the morning. Water 42° F, air 48° ... Had lunch by the river. In spite of the

13. Adelio Viani (b. Milan, 1882, d. Dublin, 1965) was Professor of Singing at the RIAM from 1917 to 1964. In 1928 he founded the Dublin Operatic Society, the forerunner of the Dublin Grand Opera Society (*EMIR*, pp. 1027–8; see also Pine and Acton, *To Talent Alone*, *passim*).
14. i.e. where the salmon gather in the river.

gale, it was completely sheltered in the deep cut by the river, and very mild, the bird song was wonderful – and a group of wagtails flitted round at lunch time … got back in nice time to change for supper at 7.00. Ralph [Cusack] to supper in a most congenial mood – so often is when quite sober! Went off to the Phoenix Hall for the chamber concert in which my quartet was to have its first public performance. Evelyn Rothwell opened the programme with a Sammartini oboe sonata – beautiful oboe playing – she is nearly as good as Goossens.[15] Her perfect phrasing showed up Rhoda Coghill's rather wooden accompaniment. Then the Cirulli people playing the Tchaikovsky *Andante Cantabile* – they made it sound even longer than it is. What a choice![16] Then some more oboe pieces, by which time there was only 20 minutes left, so I was sure the broadcast of my quartet would be cut off in the middle, as indeed it was – extraordinary how often this happens to me; they might almost be doing this on purpose! Was most anxious during the performance, and could not really relax as I can with the recording where I *know* that no catastrophe is imminent! I thought the first two movements were rather dull, though they woke up and put much more life into the last movement than before. Got a great ovation from the very small audience that were there – recalled three times for a bow.

Critics and radio staff were noticeably absent. [My mother] Eileen there with Thurloe and Yvonne, the Hentschels of course – Tom, John Benson, Mrs Larchet and the daughters,[17] Billy Shanahan, [François] D'Albert and Jack [E.J.] Moeran, who sat with us.[18] We liked him enormously this evening – having got a rather bad impression when we first met him. A generous-minded fellow, and very friendly. He seemed glad to be asked for a drink afterwards, so … we went to the Stag's Head. Talked with Moeran about music in general, and found many points of agreement. He seemed to like the quartet, and wants to hear it again. Billy Shanahan paid me the nicest compliment which I felt was very sincere – he said that as the first significant quartet written in Dublin, it was an epoch-making work for Irish music.

15. Evelyn Rothwell (1911–2008), a noted English oboist and wife of the conductor Sir John Barbirolli, was a pupil of the English oboist Léon Goossens.
16. The slow movement of Tchaikovsky's String Quartet no. 1. Brian would never lose his at best lukewarm opinion of Tchaikovsky's music.
17. Madeline, wife of John F. Larchet, and their daughters Maire (who joined the RÉ Orchestra as a viola player in 1946, later becoming principal violist in the RTÉSO) and Sheila (a noted concert and Irish harpist, at that time principal harpist with the RÉ Orchestra and subsequently in England with the Hallé Orchestra).
18. The English-born composer E.J. Moeran (1894–1950) was of part-Irish ancestry and increasingly identified with Ireland, where he spent much of the latter part of his life. He was living in Kenmare, Co. Kerry when he died in December 1950 (*EMIR*, pp. 673–5).

(He does not like Fred May's [string quartet].) .... As usual the performance of my quartet had absolutely no publicity at all.

16 February 1950. Thursday

… I had to go to McCullough's and try and cancel the piano we had hired for this evening's rehearsal.[19] Charlie Lynch was supposed to come – but has disappeared to Cork – blast him. He rang up at 7.00 very apologetic. It is quite impossible to be angry with him! Usual teaching at the Academy – then after a quick supper, the DOP rehearsal. Polishing on the Haydn and Handel. Carol Little was a great help with the Beethoven concerto, reading the piano part to give us the leads. Worked till 9.10 on the ballet suite which is still very bad. Long committee meeting … mostly arrangements for the Drogheda concert.

17 February 1950. Friday

Incredibly mild yesterday and today – lovely feeling that spring is here .... Things are bursting out in the garden .... Spent much of the morning cataloguing and arranging a new batch of records which Ralph [Cusack] got for me from Douglas at about ⅓rd price. Fascinating stuff, mostly unobtainable now. Mahler Symphony no. 9, Walton Viola Concerto, Strauss *Sinfonia domestica*, Ferguson Octet, Bach Sonata in C for 2 violins, cello and harpsichord, Stravinsky Violin Concerto, quarter-tone music of Hába, Indonesian music and Dvořák Symphony no. 4.[20] Played the Hába which is fascinatingly queer, and a bit of the Stravinsky which is of the very dry neo-classical period.[21] Before this we went out to fetch the Lancia from Grattan Norman's – grand to have her again, going beautifully, and so smoothly with the new transmission couplings and the clutch in order again. Mary drove the Lancia back, and I had quite a job to keep up with her in the Alvis.

… Have started copying really good parts for the leading desks of violas and cellos for *The Buried Moon Suite* so as to be finished with any possibilities of mistakes in the parts. Did the viola part of the March tonight.

---

19. McCullough's music shop amalgamated in 1967/8 with its principal rival Pigott & Co. to become McCullough Pigott.

20. First published in 1892 as his Symphony no. 4 and still known by that number in 1950, Dvořák's Symphony in G major, op. 88, is now listed as no. 8. Composer Howard Ferguson (1908–99) was born in Belfast and lived in England. His Octet (for clarinet, bassoon, horn, string quartet and double-bass) dates from 1933.

21. Brian believed that music should reflect and engage the emotions. When applied to music, the adjective 'dry' represented the antithesis of what he believed in.

18 February 1950. Saturday

… [At Ralph Cusack's] Ralph had to go to Bray to fetch Betty and Tom, so as soon as we had tried to listen to part of the Kodály Unaccompanied Cello Sonata with the children distracting us, we left in time to be home for tea. This Kodály work is really remarkable – I am longing to hear it properly without distraction for this taste suggests tremendous power.

The Lancia is going beautifully – so smoothly – it seemed no effort to tour at any speed up to the 60s [mph].

… Listened to the new Bach Sonata in C for 2 violins, cello and harpsichord – it is grand, with a wonderful fugue on a descending chromatic subject. Also Strauss's *Sinfonia Domestica* which I heard for the first time. Must listen soon to it again, for it seems most interesting.

Continued copying the parts for the [*Buried Moon*]suite.

19 February 1950. Sunday

My turn to fetch Chris [Haughey] for the rehearsal. We read through two Mozart divertimenti this morning. I was playing incredibly badly – bad fingering and my lip giving out all the time! However, we enjoyed ourselves.

… Finished the parts for the cellos and violas in the suite; and then listened to *La Tragédie de Salomé* by Florent Schmitt.[22] Didn't seem quite so excited by it this evening as I have been before – but perhaps I am not in good listening form.

… Rather a lazy day.

20 February 1950. Monday

… went to buy clothes pegs and screws for making candle-stands for the Haydn 'Farewell' Symphony. Spent much of the morning at this. Then had to go out to meet Croly [*sic*], the contractor at the Metropolitan Hall, to arrange for alterations to the platform for the concert. Then to the Academy, where I had a talk with [John F.] Larchet about the Belfast job, and the Academy orchestra. He is going to give me a testimonial for Belfast. Difficult to decide who the best people would be – pity no *English Protestant* knows about my conducting activity! – They are so bigoted up there. Bax and Thirkill of Cambridge should fill that bill, however.[23] Have decided to

22. Ballet music composed by Florent Schmitt in 1907.
23. Brian knew Arnold Bax through the latter's frequent visits to Ireland when he usually stayed with Aloys Fleischmann in Cork. Brian would have considered him suitable to 'fill that bill' owing not only to his being a prominent English composer but also Master of the King's Musick since 1942. Sir Henry Thirkill was Master of Clare College, Cambridge at the time Brian was a student there.

get testimonials from Larchet, [Jean] Martinon and O'Hannrachain, and give Bax and Thirkill with some Mason friend of [my father's] as referees.

Lesson to Olwen after lunch, then continued the candle-holders [for the Haydn symphony] until I had to go out to the Academy ...

... Sisyrinchium grandiflorum is just coming out – an incredible plant with such a huge flower for such a flimsy support, almost unbelievable. And such a wonderful rich colour, more what you would expect in midsummer.

21 February 1950. Tuesday

It turned out to be quite a big job preparing the candles for the Haydn symphony – spent the greater part of the morning at it ... At 4.30 yesterday the army rang up Charles to inform him that no instruments would be available for the DOP concerts – after three weeks' notice! So I had to rush down to the Phoenix Hall to collar two trumpets, an oboe and timpani player. It was like trying to catch kittens – for when the rehearsal finished they all made for the door at once; however I managed to book them – so that there is a great weight off my mind as regards the brass section of *The Buried Moon Suite*.

... [lessons to singing pupils in the afternoon] ... Wind rehearsal at the Academy at 7.30. Unfortunately a number of the section could not attend, so that it was not as useful as it might have been. We worked hard until 10.00.

22 February 1950. Wednesday

... reached Slane at about 10.15. Dull drizzly sort of day, rather cold ... One of those rather dead days on which the fish don't seem to move ... With my usual superstition I left the gaff a couple of hundred yards up the bank, and then got into a big fish ... I yelled to Martin,[24] who was fishing the opposite bank, and he came over in the boat in time to gaff the fish. It was an enormous lock fish – fresh run, of 29¼ lbs. My best fish ever. That was a great tonic! Very difficult casting on this beat with the cliff and bushes so close behind.

After my meal at the hotel [in Slane], I drove back pretty fast for the DOP rehearsal ... The full orchestra made a great difference to my suite, which began to come into shape. Still having trouble with the parts – had to take back the percussion and trumpet parts to correct. The effect of the candles in the Haydn was wonderful. It was 10.15 before we could try the

---

24. The identity of 'Martin', with whom Brian fished, is unclear.

Beethoven concerto … Charlie Lynch paid me the compliment of saying that it was bliss after playing the same work under Mosco Carner[25] some time ago! Rehearsal went on to 10.50 …

23 February 1950. Thursday

Left the salmon in at Dolan's [fishmonger] for sale – hope to pay off a good deal of the expense of the fishing with this monster … Spent most of the morning dealing with correspondence. Filled out the application form for the Belfast appointment.

Had to go to the Academy to teach at 12.30. Then, after lunch, I started correcting the trumpet and percussion parts of the suite. First lessons then to the two new [singing] pupils. Then off to the Academy to teach. Very difficult problem with the new pupil who can produce two entirely different voices – both of them wrong! It is either pushed with the throat, or wide, back and breathy. Spent a great deal of time trying to extract the good qualities from both and produce a third voice which would be according to the rules!!

This left very little time for supper, and I was a little late for the DOP extra rehearsal. Was feeling very tired – but it was one of those rehearsals which have a stimulating rather than a tiring effect. Got a tremendous amount of detailed work done both on the Haydn symphony and my suite. I am definitely feeling much happier about things now.

Had to take stern measures with Pat L., the cellist, who has failed to turn up to a large number of rehearsals and never bothers to tell anyone. She will not be allowed to play in the concert – and will probably be so peeved that she will leave the orchestra. But we don't want people like that who are not keen. Pity we haven't more good cellos though! Good news via Mrs Ticher[26] that the Martin Quartet are almost certain of a performance of my quartet from the BBC

In the paper today that [Michael] Bowles has been appointed conductor of the New Zealand National Orchestra!![27]

---

25. Mosco Carner (born Mosco Cohen, 1904–85) was born in Vienna but settled in London in 1933. He conducted the RÉ Orchestra and the RÉSO on a number of occasions in 1947–8, and he was also a guest conductor with the Royal Philharmonic Orchestra, the BBC Symphony Orchestra and the London Symphony Orchestra. He subsequently established a career as a musicologist and music critic.

26. Mrs Ticher, who with her husband Kurt had fled to Ireland from Nazi Germany, played viola in the DOP, of which they became lifelong supporters and patrons.

27. Michael Bowles was the first conductor of the newly established New Zealand Symphony Orchestra, a position he held from 1950 to 1954 (*EMIR*, p. 112).

24 February 1950. Friday

… Mary had a cold, and this would be the sort of day when everything becomes a fuss. The telephone rang no less than nine times in one hour, Barra was rather cranky, and the door bell seemed to ring all the time with pupils and messengers! Neither of us had a chance to relax all day. When all the lessons were done at 7.15 I left for an evening with Ralph [Cusack] and Nancy. Mary didn't come because of her cold … Owing probably to general tiredness the wine affected my tummy, and I began to feel very miserable – hoping it would pass off. Tried to listen to a Bach sonata for 2 flutes and harpsichord, but felt wretched – suggested I should go home. However, the conversation began to develop on such interesting lines that I recovered completely, and we talked solidly until 5.30 am. It is a very long time since I talked the night through, and this was a most memorable occasion … We discussed cosmology in relation to universal ideas, and argued about religious beliefs … Also talked of music in general, of painting, liberalism and so on … Quite impossible to give any idea of the enormously wide field [covered] by our conversation, or of the immensely stimulating effect it had on us both. Ralph … is certainly one of the really valuable people in this country, in that he has that very rare and essential quality of being thoroughly alive – not only in intellect, but emotionally and sensuously. It doesn't matter that the latter often runs away with his intellect!

25 February 1950. Saturday

… [en route to the DOP concert in Drogheda] picked up the two trumpets and Joe Murphy at the GPO, and Chris Haughey in Drumcondra. We just arrived in Drogheda at 6.00. Most of the orchestra were late, so the rehearsal didn't stop till nearly 7.00. A small but enthusiastic audience. The orchestra seemed to enjoy themselves, and after I had given a short lecture on the instruments, they gave quite a good performance. The 1st [violins] were rather unsteady. My work [*The Buried Moon Suite*] went very well really – most encouraging for next Thursday. The Haydn 'Farewell' went without any technical hitch over the candles, and brought the house down. Usual speeches of thanks, and then a very good supper in Drogheda Grammar School … This was the first time that the DOP played outside the environs of Dublin. A great success. David Lane[28] played the Albinoni Oboe Concerto excellently – and we both enjoyed doing it!

---

28. David Lane, a surgeon by profession, was a gifted oboe player who remained with the DOP for many years. He became a close friend of Brian's through their shared love of fly-fishing (see further below, 7 May 1950).

26 February 1950. Sunday

… Charles Lynch was to come at 12.00 – but arrived according to expectations just after 1.30 – for lunch. Very cold, with frost last night, lovely clear day with brilliant sun. Tulipa turkestanica opened today, and the crocuses were wide open like stars … Charles L. and I spent all the afternoon working on the Beethoven C minor Concerto – there are one or two very tricky bits of ensemble work. I think I know what he is going to do now.

Talked about various musicians over a cup of tea. We both agree that Tony Hughes has promise *only* if he can learn to be alive and less academic. He is dangerously pleased with himself – also, like all Irish pianists with the exception of Charles, he is unable to produce real *tone* from a piano. The fundamental principle of weight and line seems little understood by performers here …

Gramophone evening … Listened to Bach Sonata for 2 violins, cello and harpsichord (*grand* work – one of the church sonatas). French fifteenth-century songs, unaccompanied. Should be heard out of doors – preferably over water. Then Stravinsky Violin Concerto. Very dry, but amusing: rather like a mixture of Bach, Mozart and – say – Chausson, seen through a paranoiac mirror! Then the Hába quarter tone pieces – from a string quartet, and a vocal quartet from *Matka*.[29] His music sounds very sick – like an athlete whose muscles have collapsed. Then we enjoyed the Walton Viola Concerto …

27 February 1950. Monday

As far as I can remember, I seem to have spent most of the morning on the phone – all sorts of arrangements about the final rehearsal, the cannons for [Beethoven's] 'Battle' Symphony, seating, etc., etc. A suggestion has come in that the orchestra should visit Clonmel – if it is feasible it should be great fun.

From 2.00 till 7.30 I was teaching all the time. First at home, and then at the Academy.

28 February 1950. Tuesday

Went off to Dockrells[30] in the morning to bang things and find how to make a noise like a cannon for the 'Battle' Symphony. Introduced myself to Mr

---

29. Czech composer Alois Hába (1893–1973) composed his opera *Matka* ('Mother') in 1929. It was premiered in Munich in 1931.
30. Dublin builders' suppliers and hardware store.

Jackson … who promised to lend me the necessary. Tried sheets of plywood in the timber store, then went to the sheet metal place, and finally chose a large sheet of 24 gauge steel, which, when beaten with an iron hammer, seemed to make the best noise.

Gorgeous morning. Iris reticulata var. Hercules is nearly out – most exciting … Lessons to Terence Carter, Rosemary and Denis [Donoghue] before lunch …

… Got to work on the tension of the tape in the recorder, and cured the trouble of the tape twisting. Then the Academy orchestra. Great waste of time again over Viani's opera …

MARCH

1 March 1950. Wednesday

Had to be sure not to forget to put all the necessary things into the car, since I was to go direct to the final rehearsal from Slane. Left in a plan of the orchestra seating with John Miley before breakfast … [salmon fishing at Slane, nothing caught]. Left at 6.00 and drove back pretty fast. [Charles] Pyke's Hillman Minx can certainly shift – though I am not sure it would make such speed on a twisty road. Arrived at the Metropolitan Hall at 6.50, and helped with the arrangement of the stage.

Long and tiring final rehearsal. Handel went well enough. Then a terrible muddle over the different parts in the Beethoven 'Battle' – eventually sorted out somehow. Mary came to the rehearsal with the recording machine to record my work – and of course everyone made awful mistakes, which made me rather annoyed. It was very cold in the hall so that the wind were badly out of tune. The concerto went quite well, and Charles Lynch seemed happy about it. [The two violinists] are not making such an excruciating noise at the end of the Haydn 'Farewell' as at Drogheda. Finished, in every sense of the word, at about 10.45 …

2 March 1950. Thursday

… Wonderfully warm day. It is amazing how quickly flowers grow and burst into flower as soon as it gets warm. The ordinary crocuses under the pear tree are a wonderful sight … Gave two lessons after lunch – to the two new pupils. Then we went off to fix curtains in the Metro[politan] Hall for the disappearing trick in the Haydn 'Farewell' … At home again, I listened to the recording Mary made of the rehearsal of the Beethoven concerto – just to refresh my memory of what Charles Lynch did with it – very useful. Was very surprised how different the balance is between the rostrum and the back of the hall.

Then a bath and change … Dinner at the Unicorn with a glass of wine and a cigar which was rather damp – disappointing. We brought the recording machine to get a complete record of my work, and had some trouble finding a convenient source of current in the hall. However, that was eventually fixed. Full house for the concert – which is a great thing for the DOP – and they really rose to the occasion. The concerto went well – no terrible moments! … The audience seemed to enjoy my work [*The Buried Moon Suite*], which went rather better than previously. The 'Farewell' and the

'Battle' brought the house down of course. Pleasant tea party afterwards. Talked with all sorts of people. Some German friends of the Tichers had never heard the 'Battle', and were most amazed to hear it in Dublin for the first time …

3 March 1950. Friday

Walter Beckett rather unkind to our poor horn players in his criticism [in *The Irish Times*].[1] He doesn't realise that three of them are playing in an orchestra for the first time! Listened to the recording Mary made of *The Buried Moon Suite*: it really is rather difficult for the DOP – and doesn't quite come off with playing that is not first-rate. A good recording which I shall keep. Hope to do it with the Radio Orchestra when I get a chance – will get a better recording then. Now that the concert is over there are hundreds of things to be done that have been put aside – letters galore to be answered …

Long afternoon's teaching – was at it all the time from 2.00 till 7.30 …

4 March 1950. Saturday

… Quiet evening at home – made corrections in the scores of the quartet – mainly metronome marks. Listened to a bit of a new symphony by Sauget [*sic*] coming over badly from the Third Programme.[2] Sounded most interesting, and pleasantly free from French trickery.

5 March 1950. Sunday

No rehearsal of the wind trio this morning … A dream day – not a cloud in the sky, and really warm. Crocuses all out like stars … Tried to listen to Britten's *Let's Make an Opera* – but … too much distraction. However, I recorded Part II – the actual opera part, and listened to it in the evening. I am not particularly impressed by the music, though I like the whole idea.

… [in the evening] we listened to the recording of my suite made at the DOP concert – and the 'Battle' Symphony as recorded at the final rehearsal. Managed to get all papers sorted today, and an enormous number of bills and letters dealt with. Many of the letters were concerned with the Belfast job …

---

1. The Dublin-born composer Walter Beckett (1914–96), a cousin of Samuel Beckett, wrote for *The Irish Times* between 1946 and 1952. See further *EMIR*, pp. 73–4.
2. Henri Sauguet (1901–89), French composer. The 'new symphony' referred to was most probably Sauguet's Symphony no. 2 'Allégorique' (*Les Saisons*), composed in 1949 and scored for solo soprano, chorus, children's chorus, and orchestra.

6 March 1950. Monday

... to the Radio, to give back the corrected score of my quartet – I revised the metronome marks yesterday. Saw O'Hannrachain about a testimonial for Belfast, and had a general chat with him. Also suggested that I do a regular weekly preview of the forthcoming music. It should serve to focus attention on performances of interesting music. As it is, the publicity for music is shocking – the press gives little or no help ... Called at Crawfords for petrol on the way home, and met Henry Wheeler ... He is on the council of this new Arts Association onto which I have been invited. I tried to get information about it, but he is not a very active member. I can't see myself working with Michael McMullin and the other musical member from the Operatic Society!

... [Lessons at home] and then had to go off to the Academy. Usual full list of pupils ...

DOP committee meeting due [at home] at 8.00, but owing to the fog they were late. Let them hear the recording of the ballet suite, and then we committeed in the dining room till 11.00. Hate these long committee meetings! Decided on the following programme for the summer concert: Bach Suite no. 3 in D (with clarinets for trumpets), Bach Concerto for Harpsichord (if we can get one) or else Violin Concerto in A min., Schubert Unfinished Symphony, some Irish work (which I must find) and finish with [Beethoven] *Egmont* overture.

7 March 1950. Tuesday

[At home, teaching and working in the garden]

8 March 1950. Wednesday

... lecture in Navan [Co. Meath]. Met Byron (who spells his name in some queer Gaelic way)[3] at the technical schools, and was faced with the shock of a portable gramophone for the illustrations. He managed at the last moment to procure a decent electric gramophone – though the audience were kept waiting ¾ hour. Dr Dunne, the local high priest, was in the chair. A rather sinister-looking priest who hunted and drank (he was pretty tight). The sight of the small audience confirmed my suspicions that Navan should not have asked for such an advanced lecture as 'Music of our time'. I cut chunks out of it, and kept it on as low a level as possible – no easy task with a lecture which must presume a reasonable knowledge of ordinary music. However,

3. 'Byron' appears to be Brian's transcription of an Irish name unfamiliar to him.

in spite of the fact that very few could have understood much, the audience seemed to enjoy it, and behaved most attentively. They seem keen to have me back again, and are also keen on the idea of the DOP visiting Navan. A few drinks with Byron afterwards. A very decent sort really. Talking of the North of Ireland he made the extraordinary remark that as soon as you cross the border it matters what religion you are, whereas here no one cares a damn! Just shows that if you are among the majority, you don't notice it. Enjoyed the drive home on the Navan road, which is so much more interesting to drive than the long straight Slane road ...

9 March 1950. Thursday

Everything rather confused this morning ... I find I can't get anything done when [Cormac and Barra] are about asking questions!

... After supper we went to Trinity [Choral Society concert]. Mary singing in the chorus – I was listening for once. I enjoyed their performance of the Byrd Mass – even though there were some wrong notes, and other minor mistakes – it was obvious that Joe Groocock really knows how to do Elizabethan music, unlike Alice Yoakley with the Culwick [Choral Society].[4] Their Byrd was atrocious. The Mozart Requiem was not actually so enjoyable, though the performance was a great credit to the choir considering the difficulty of the work and the short time available for rehearsal. Dorothy Graham as soprano solo sang very well really – most musical. With bare shoulders I could see very clearly her unfortunate habit of trying to help high notes with her shoulder muscles. She has however improved immensely ...

Forgot to mention a rehearsal at the Academy in the afternoon with Sydney Bryans and Denis [Donoghue] for the Bach *Es ist vollbracht* and the final aria from *Elijah* which Denis is to perform on Saturday at the Students' Musical Union [at the RIAM]. I was playing oboe.

The bass and tenor [soloists] in the Requiem at Trinity were unbelievably awful! The bass was Ballard from St Patrick's [Cathedral] – never heard such an unpleasant noise.

10 March 1950. Friday

Not feeling too good today – must have caught a touch of this 'flu ... I decided to put off pupils and take it easy. Nuisance having to speak at the UCD Architectural Association tonight. Tonight is the inaugural meeting

---

4. Joseph Groocock was conductor of the University of Dublin Choral Society ('Trinity Choral') from 1945 to 1981.

of the Arts Association – can't go owing to the other engagement. Tried to get some member of the MAI council to go along and see what develops. I have been asked to go on the council, and have been waiting for word from Liam O'Laoghaire (the Hon. Sec.), since I want to discuss the whole thing with him … It is important that the Arts Assoc. should recognise the authority of the Music Association in musical matters.

… [After supper] went off to the UCD Architectural Association. Was feeling rather dreadful, so took a nip of whiskey to bolster me up. Seán Keating and Desmond FitzGerald were the other speakers.[5] The subject was 'The Same Approach'. None of us could gather what exactly this meant – and even after we had all spoken we were not much wiser as to the purpose of the discussion, which turned out to be a general argument on aesthetics. Critics were discussed – Romantic and Classical ideas – definitions of art and the usual perennial ideas. Had to disagree violently with FitzGerald when he said that music was different from the other arts in being less disciplined. Had a battle of words with a rather silly jester who claimed that 'the music of modern America' (e.g. Woody Herman)[6] was the great artistic expression of the day. Tore him to shreds …

11 March 1950. Saturday

… both of us had a heavy dose of 'flu, and had to stay in bed …

14 March 1950. Tuesday

Still in bed – though our temperatures are down today … Got a few letters written … Just as we were getting ready for sleep, John Beckett turned up. He always turns up at the most unexpected moments. He had been lecturing to the People's College. We had a chat about all sorts of musical matters. He is not [composing] at present – rather depressed about it I think – but I'm sure he will get going again soon. He was at the DOP concert and enjoyed

---

5. Seán Keating (1889–1977) was one of the most prominent Irish artists of the mid-twentieth century, working in a romantic-realist style; he became president of the Royal Hibernian Academy in 1950. The architect Desmond FitzGerald (1911–87) designed the new Dublin airport terminal, completed in 1940 and widely regarded as a key work in the introduction of the international modernist style of architecture to Ireland.

6. Despite Brian's dismissal of the music represented by Woody Herman (1913–87), already one of the most popular American jazz clarinetists, saxophonists and big band leaders by the later 1940s, he did later express a certain respect for jazz, especially Louis Armstrong. Perhaps ironically in the present context, it was Woody Herman who had commissioned Igor Stravinsky's *Ebony Concerto* (1945). The recording made by Stravinsky and Herman in 1946 was not issued until 1951 (Columbia ML 4398) and Brian would probably not have known this work in 1950.

my suite except for the March. When I explained about the context in the ballet he thought that in the right context it should come off – but doesn't when isolated as it is in the suite – 'too polished and unpretentious'!

15 March 1950. Wednesday

Convalescing today … Spent some time working out the positions on the dial of the various broadcasting stations which have new wavelengths from today … Great excitement – the new wavelength for the [BBC] Third Programme gives us good reception! – At least at 6.00 this evening it was good enough to make a recording of some lovely thirteenth-century music. What possibilities this opens up!!

Spent the evening listening to the wireless … Bach's *Magnificat* and then 'Scrapbook for 1929'.

16 March 1950. Thursday

… Still feeling very wobbly – both of us, and are furious this illness is taking so long … Wrote letters to Patrick Egan, Redmond Friel,[7] [Thomas C.] Kelly[8] and Aloys Fleischmann asking them if they had a work suitable for the DOP …

17 March 1950. Friday[9]

Definitely better today … John Miley called in in the morning, and we thrashed out the problem of the programme for the DOP concert. We had to abandon the Schubert 'Unfinished' [Symphony], because I had forgotten there were trombones. Have now provisionally fixed on Bach Suite no. 3 and Brandenburg [Concerto] no. 3 and *Wachet auf* – Schubert [Symphony] no. 3 in D, an Irish work, and [Beethoven] *Egmont* [overture]. No real concerto in fact. …

… [In the evening] I tried to get a recording of Hindemith's Fifth String Quartet, but [radio reception from] the Third [Programme] is very disappointing this evening …

7. Redmond Friel (1907–79) was a prolific if conservative Northern Irish composer whose output focused on arrangements of traditional melodies for orchestra and for choirs (*EMIR*, pp. 410–11).

8. T.C. Kelly (1917–85) was an exact contemporary of Brian. His prolific output (like that of Redmond Friel, above) focused on arrangements of traditional melodies, many commissioned and performed by the RÉ Light Orchestra (*EMIR*, p. 562).

9. Brian's thirty-third birthday.

18 March 1950. Saturday

… Mary went into town in the bus, and brought me back a present of the score of *Le Sacre du Printemps* of Stravinsky. Had a fascinating time perusing this. Also typed out copies of some of my testimonials for the Belfast job …

19 March 1950. Sunday

… Pottered about the garden for most of the morning. Tulipa praestans will soon be out – showing its brilliant red bud already. Great promise on t[ulipa] hageri splendens. Planted a linum arboreum and some convolvulus mauritanica on the wall. The lewisias are putting on a great growth, including the little baby which I detached in the autumn (l. cotyledon). Came in and wrote a long letter to Louise Trenton …

20 March 1950. Monday

… Teaching again in the afternoon – not at all keen on the idea! Quite a number of pupils failed to turn up at the Academy, so I had time to get out the Bach Brandenburg no. 3 from the library for the DOP, and discuss the arrangement of the orchestra with Carol Little …

21 March 1950. Tuesday

Spent all the available time between teaching, arranging and editing the parts of the Bach Brandenburg no. 3. I am arranging for all the nine-part writing to be played by pairs of violins and single violas and cellos – certain passages to be played by soloists, and the rest join in in the tuttis. This will be a difficult undertaking, which I hope the orchestra will manage adequately. Denis [Donoghue] helped me, after his lesson in the afternoon. I just managed to get the job done before leaving for the Academy orchestra rehearsal at 6.00. Rather a bad attendance, but got some good work done on the Boyce Symphony no. 3. Had a hurried meal at the Grosvenor Hotel, and then on to the DOP rehearsal, on Tuesday this week owing to the Culwick [Choral Society] concert on Thursday. A rather poor attendance here too, though we enjoyed ourselves playing through [Beethoven's] *Egmont* [overture] and the Bach Suite no. 3. We had an informal orchestra meeting for the airing of views. It appears we may be invited to Maynooth, which would be rather fun. …

… [Added later at top of page:] Had lunch at the Unicorn with Liam O'Laoghaire – discussing the Arts Association. I have decided to accept their invitation onto the council. Discussed the position of the MAI and general topics concerning the arts in Ireland. Liam is a most likeable fellow: full of enthusiasm, and with a very intelligent and liberal outlook … [10]

22 March 1950. Wednesday

[Fishing at Slane]

23 March 1950. Thursday

… [Went] to the Phoenix Hall to ask Martinon for a testimonial for the Belfast job. Had a word with Wolfram Hentschel, and Arthur Nachstern, who was in his only too frequent mood of thinking I had come to dislike him, since I had not been talking to him enough recently! Nancie Lord was telling me how Martinon appears to be in a queer mood – on the defensive, expecting non-cooperation from the orchestra all the time. Knowing the orchestra to be such a pack of children, and Martinon to be unduly sensitive, the fault probably lies on both sides. I found Martinon in very good form – definitely pleased to see me, and willing to help – which is a change from his off-hand manner of last year.

When I got home, I looked through the *Suite for String Orchestra* sent for performance with the DOP by Thomas Kelly of Newry.[11] Although of the folksy type, it is definitely above the average of this kind of thing. I think we should give it a performance. …

… Felt I had better go to the Culwick [Choral Society] concert in the evening – rather to put in an official appearance. I never really enjoy their concerts which seem to lack the vitality and enthusiasm which one finds in most amateur societies … They certainly should avoid doing sixteenth-century stuff – their Morley was appallingly bad and stiff. The folksong arrangements were well done, though Larchet's *Castle of Dromore* showed up as a bad arrangement next to two Vaughan Williams settings. The Sanctus from the Bach Mass [in B minor] lacked weight, and the accompaniment on piano (Dorothy Stokes) and American organ (Joe Groocock) was quite inadequate. Francis Engel was the soloist.[12] I had not heard him before, and was most disappointed. His Brahms was as flabby as himself, though his Bach Italian Concerto was better – though rhythmically unsteady …

---

10. The qualifications 'full of enthusiasm', 'very intelligent' and 'liberal' reflect the highest praise in Brian's opinion of other people.
11. Although referred to here as *Suite for String Orchestra*, this would be T.C. Kelly's *Three Pieces for Strings* composed in 1949.
12. The Swiss pianist Francis Engel taught at the RIAM.

24 March 1950. Friday

... [Went] to fetch the testimonial from Martinon. I hope they know who he is up North![13] ... Then to [John F.] Larchet's house, where I saw Mrs L., and asked about his testimonial (I shan't actually use it). Saw Mrs Montgomery,[14] who lives in the next house, and asked her to play one of the solo violas in the Bach Brandenburg with the DOP.

A gorgeous sunny morning, so I spent most of the time in the garden ... Typed out copies of Martinon's testimonial before lunch ... Spent the rest of the afternoon teaching, and getting my application for the Belfast job ready in between lessons ...

We had tried to get seats for the Dublin Marionette Group's show at the Peacock [Theatre], but failed. At 7.30, Victor Keys rang up to say he had two seats for us, so we rushed our supper and arrived just in time. First a short play for puppets by G.B. Shaw – not a good puppet play – too much dialogue, and it doesn't exploit the medium.[15] Then a melodrama based on a story by E[dgar] A[llan] Poe, and an Irish ballad (*The Leather Breeches*). These were well done, though the voices always give rather an amateur effect. The big piece of the evening was Ravel's *L'enfant et les sortilèges* – which I had originally suggested to them. It is definitely the best thing they have done – but it is a pity they did not attempt the magical transformation from the nursery to the garden ... Saw Victor Keys for a few moments after the show, and congratulated many of the others.

25 March 1950. Saturday

... Ralph and Nancy [Cusack] came to lunch ... Ralph has been asked to act on the Cultural Board of [the Department of] External Affairs. If he does not fly off the handle and get put off, he will be an excellent influence there – being the only one who knows anything at all about music. He is suggesting that recordings should be made of Irish works ...

26 March 1950. Sunday

... After lunch, we put the hood down on the car for the first time this year, and went off to Blessington. I spent the afternoon spinning for trout with the new threadline outfit, which I am beginning to master ...

Wolfram and Ingrid Hentschel and Rory Childers came for the gramophone evening. We played Bach Suite no. 3, and had a great deal of

13. This comment is an interesting reflection on the relative lack of contact and communication at the time between the Republic and Northern Ireland.
14. Not identified more closely.
15. Probably George Bernard Shaw's *Shakes versus Shav*, a short puppet play written in 1949 and his last completed dramatic work.

argument about speeds and appoggiaturas. Then Prokofiev Violin Concerto no. 2 – which didn't impress Wolfram very much on first hearing. We then talked a good deal about romanticism, conductors, theosophy, etc., etc. After tea we played my *Feather of Death* and *In Memoriam M. Gandhi* – they were particularly impressed by the latter. We finished up with Bloch's Second [String] Quartet – which I enjoyed better than ever before. Every-one was very excited by it. I am becoming increasingly convinced that it is one of the masterpieces of our time.

27 March 1950. Monday

Decided I must get on with extending the ballet suite from *The Buried Moon*. I am very keen to include the 'Death Dance of the Evil Tree', which should be exciting.[16] The problem is to arrange the various sections in the right order. Then there is the RÉ prize for an orchestral piece, so I want to withhold some of the ballet music for that. Decided that the first scene complete should make an orchestral piece on its own. Spent much of the morning thinking about this, and trying out various sections. Also did some work in the garden … Usual teaching in the afternoon …

We went to Aleck Crichton's in the evening, bringing a pile of music.[17] A queer pair were there – rather likeable. A Mr J.H.P. Campbell and Jim Wilson, who appears to be his boyfriend. The latter is a composer, whom I have never come across.[18] He played some of his songs – all to French texts – and the music itself is permeated by the Fauré atmosphere. The accompaniment figures are independent and interesting – though the music as a whole lacks any personality – rather like Wilson himself. This is all on a first impression of course. As a man, Wilson is very pleasant – obviously very interested in music, and seems to share many of my opinions – except that he enjoys Rossini immensely!

Mary sang a couple of arias from Handel's *Susanna* and the *Vier Ernste Gesänge* of Brahms, with Aleck Crichton. I also sang one or two other songs, and played a Handel oboe sonata and the slow movement from my Oboe Quintet.[19]

---

16. This movement from the incomplete ballet *The Buried Moon*, op. 32 (1949) was not in-cluded in the ballet suite (op. 32a).
17. Aleck (a gifted amateur pianist) and Joan Crichton were family friends.
18. James ('Jim') Wilson (1922–2005) was born in London but settled in Dublin at this time. He became a key figure in the MAI, taught composition at the RIAM, and was one of Ireland's leading composers of the later twentieth century. He would soon become a good friend of Brian and Mary. See further Mark Fitzgerald, *The Life and Music of James Wilson* (Cork: Cork University Press, 2015).
19. Oboe Quintet, op. 11 (1940).

28 March 1950. Tuesday

Wrote a report for Poole of the RDS on my last two lectures in Tullamore and Navan.[20] Also suggested that the RDS should supply me with a portable means of playing the records, since it is too chancy depending on what is provided locally – and besides, my records are being rapidly worn out by heavy pick-ups. I also did some more work on certain details of *The Buried Moon* – filling in some gaps in the Dance of the Moon.

… Felt very lazy in the afternoon – sat in front of my manuscripts and accomplished very little! … Lesson to Betty Colclough, and then off to the Academy to take the orchestra rehearsal. A rather small attendance – but we had a most enjoyable rehearsal. After tidying passages in the Boyce Symphony and the Handel Minuet, we had great fun with the old chestnut – the *Marche Militaire* of Schubert. I pulled the time all over the place so as to teach them to follow the stick. We then read a Brahms Hungarian dance, also with violent changes of tempo! The Academy orchestra is not a very satisfactory business – it is too junior [for] the seniors, and too senior for the less good players, and falls between two stools. Talked with Vaneček about this, and suggested *one* orchestra mainly of juniors, and let the seniors devote their time to chamber music, since they mostly get their orchestral training outside with the DOP and other bodies.

Spent the evening with Edgar and Ruth [Deale] – the Farringtons were there … discussed the MAI and many other topics, including the position of Larchet at the Academy. The Board is after his blood. Connery, the new secretary, seems to be a good man.[21]

29 March 1950. Wednesday

… set off for Slane with the car open. The warm sun of early morning soon disappeared, and it became rather cold. I had the whole top of the river to myself in the morning … When I stopped at 6.30, I was dead tired. Drove straight back to the council meeting of the MAI. A good meeting. We decided to go ahead with two Bach commemoration concerts with the RÉ Orchestra; Joe [Groocock] and I are to decide on the programmes. Also discussed directives for the Cultural Relations Committee, which Ralph [Cusack] will try to persuade them to bring into effect …

20. Dr Horace Hewitt Poole (1886–1962) was Registrar of the RDS from 1929 to 1962. On the lectures in Tullamore and Navan, see 3 February and 8 March above.
21. Matthew Connery was Secretary of the RIAM from 1949 to 1953 (Pine and Acton, *To Talent Alone*, p. 367).

30 March 1950. Thursday

... I went to the Academy in the Alvis (the tax expires at the end of the month). Spent all the time between lessons looking through Bach cantatas for the Bach concert sponsored by the MAI.

A good DOP rehearsal in the evening, Worked very thoroughly on [Beethoven's] *Egmont*, and got it good enough to lay aside until nearer the concert. Played through Bach *Wachet auf* which will not give much trouble. Then worked on the first movement of the Bach Suite no. 3. Finished the rehearsal by trying out Thomas Kelly's *Suite for Strings*, which we will do at this concert.

After a short committee meeting, Charles [Acton] and Carol [Little] (who have announced their engagement) came back for tea ... Charles is looking ten years younger as a result of all this – though Carol is looking a wreck! [Charles's mother] has apparently been causing a good deal of trouble, but is now resigned. I do hope the thing comes off – we are rather worried about their plan for a long engagement to allow Carol to study at the RCM ...

31 March 1950. Friday

Spent much of the morning trying to sort out the long waves on the dial of the wireless, since [Radio] Luxembourg is to broadcast 'This is Ireland' on Sunday, with my music – and naturally I want to be able to hear it! ...

I wish I weren't feeling so unsettled and disinclined to work. I am longing to get down to some thorough work at composition again, but don't seem to have the inclination at present. It will come, I suppose, soon. Teaching was rather exasperating today. Pupils who were coming on well seem to have forgotten how to sing ...

Drove out to Ralph and Nancy [Cusack] as soon as I had finished the last pupil ... Had a long chat with Ralph about the Cultural Board [*sic* Cultural Relations Committee], and advised him on several musical points ... Listened first to the Kodály Sonata for Unaccompanied Cello. Definitely a very inspired work, but it brings up many controversial problems. Is the solo cello a medium which imposes *too many* limitations! Instruments were made by musicians in the first place to perform the music they conceived – composers are now inclined to be dominated by the instruments they have developed – the particular case being the keyboard instruments, without which Schönbergian atonality would probably not have arisen. In enjoying a work for solo cello, how much of our enjoyment comes from a sense of amazement that such a noise could be produced by such limited means? A work of this nature is also apt to contain many passages of the instrumental exercise type – again dictated by the technique of the cello. That these limitations can be overcome is, I think, shown in the Bartok Sonata for Unaccompanied Violin. After listening then to a short thirteenth-century piece for mediaeval harp, we listened to the recent Prokofiev Violin Sonata – which seems to have the best qualities of the Second Violin Concerto – amazing to think that such a fine work could arise under the conditions dictated to Prokofiev in Russia.[22] We drove back at 1.30 a.m.

---

22. Cf. similar comments made when listening to the same work on 21 January (above).

Under starter's orders at the Enniskerry hillclimb in his 1926 Type 13 'Brescia' Bugatti, April 1947. The absence of a crash helmet or any other safety equipment (let alone the cigarette!) was not unusual at the time.

COURTESY OF *THE IRISH TIMES* AND THE BOARD OF TRINITY COLLEGE DUBLIN

LEABHARLANN CO. CHILL DARA

APRIL

1 April 1950. Saturday

… Apart from a lesson to M[abel] Peat, I spent most of the morning overhauling the recording machine. Borrowed a spring balance from Lennox Chemicals to adjust the tension on the tape, which seems to be rather critical. Also cleaned the recording head with acetone ….

… Spent the evening at home – the first quiet evening for a long time. Tried to listen to Hindemith's Piano Concerto on the [BBC] Third Programme, but the reception was impossibly bad. The wireless is hopeless now – can't hear anything well except RÉ and the [BBC] Light Programme, which is rather limiting to say the least of it! …

2 April 1950. Sunday

… Had planned to go fishing at Blessington with Cyril Dugdale,[1] bringing the family to play by the lake – but it turned out such a horrible day – cold and showery …. [Cyril] spent the evening with us, and overhauled the wireless and amplifier. He promises to make us an extension to the wireless equipment which should get good reception from the Third Programme. We then experimented with the best way to record from the wireless, using the various output leads from the output transformer. We talked a great deal as usual – Cyril did most of it of course ….

It cleared up unexpectedly without our knowing it this evening, and we missed the lunar eclipse, which was very annoying.

3 April 1950. Monday

Got a bit of correspondence done this morning. Very cold working without a fire. I did a few moments gardening to warm up, but was driven in by a heavy shower …. Spent the rest of the morning making out a schedule of work for the DOP rehearsals, so as to save the wind hanging about with nothing to do while we work at the string pieces – and also to have the work for Wolfram Hentschel and Capt. Brennock cut and dried (they are acting as 'student conductors' this session).[2]

---

1. Cyril Dugdale had qualified as a dentist from TCD alongside Mary's brother Dudley. As well as being the family's dentist until he moved to Dungannon *c.* 1970, he was one of Brian's regular fishing companions.
2. Captain (later Colonel) J.P. Brennock would subsequently succeed Colonel J.M. Doyle as Director of the Army School of Music.

… [In the afternoon] I went on to teach at the Academy, and also continue my research into the Bach cantatas. Saw Vaneček for a few moments to try and clarify the future position of the Academy orchestra.

… I cooked the supper. We then listened to … some of a piano quintet by Shostakovich, which sounded quite interesting in parts.[3]

4 April 1950. Tuesday

… I had a lunch date with John Ryan – the editor of *Envoy*. He has asked me to do a series of musical articles for his magazine. An excellent lunch at the Bailey, which is under [his] new management and vastly improved. We talked generally about the state of music in Ireland. The short-story editor was also there – a name I didn't catch. The two of them are full of youthful enthusiasm, but struck me as not having any real depth of knowledge. Got back in time to meet a Chinese soprano – Miss Yang – who has been doing a CEMA tour in the North with Havelock Nelson.[4] Havelock sent her to me to see what could be done about arranging recitals or concerts here – but I was not able to be of much help. She told me that the BBC are looking for a conductor for their new Western Region Orchestra – so I wrote off immediately just in case there was any chance of getting it. After a lesson to Denis, Charles and Carol came to tea. So odd to see Charles indulging in romantic horse-play! …

Academy orchestra rehearsal was enjoyable – reading through new music, and rehearsing Brahms Hungarian Dance no. 6.

Joe Groocock came to supper. We decided (as musical advisers) on the programme of cantatas for the second MAI Bach concert in the autumn. The problem was to find a pair of cantatas which between them don't use more than two soloists. *Thou guide of Israel* (must look up the number and German title),[5] *Sie werden aus Saba kommen*,[6] Brandenburg 3 or 6, and Suite no. 1 should make a good programme. Joe in great form. Listened to the recording of *The Buried Moon Suite*, which he admired. Played about with the machine recording Joe reading mediaeval verse (!) and a couple of my Joyce songs.[7] Then Olive Smith rang up to get the result of our meeting.[8]

---

3. Shostakovich's Piano Quintet op. 57 dates from 1940.
4. CEMA (Committee for the Encouragement of Music and the Arts), founded in 1940, was the forerunner of the Arts Council of Great Britain. Although the latter was formally established by charter in 1946, Brian is here referring to it under its earlier name.
5. *Du Hirte Israel, höre*, BWV 104.
6. BWV 65.
7. The first performance of *Five Joyce Songs* op. 28 had been given by Brian, accompanied by Joseph Groocock, on 28 October 1946.
8. Olive Smith was honorary secretary of the MAI.

5 April 1950. Wednesday

Not very pleasant weather for fishing – though not so bad as yesterday … Plenty of fish jumping round, but couldn't interest them in prawns, baits or fly. The only excitement was poaching His Lordship's[9] water, either Martin or I keeping watch in case he came up! …

6 April 1950. Thursday

Went to the RDS to see [Horace] Poole about next year's lectures for the RDS vocational scheme. Also suggested the possibility of the Society providing amplifying equipment – since I have so much trouble in this direction in the country centres. After seeing him, I went to the library to look for books by Rudolf Steiner – I want to find out more about his philosophy …

Usual teaching before lunch, and in the afternoon, at the Academy … I took the bus. I had to give advice on a piano at Pigott's to a friend of Frank Kieran's at 3.00 …

7 April 1950. Friday [Good Friday]

… Our new [baby]sitter came for the first time this evening, so Mary and I went off after supper to see Joe [Groocock] and Rhoda … Discussed technical matters of orchestration with Joe – the problem of orchestrating a contrapuntal piece like a passacaglia, expanding it, and yet not clouding the clarity. Joe also pointed out to me one or two fascinating things about the Bach '48', including what seems to be a very weak passage in Fugue 8 from Book 1 …

8 April 1950. Saturday

A miserably cold day again, with heavy showers and very strong winds … In the afternoon we went to the Botanic Gardens, where we had to spend most of the time in the greenhouses avoiding the heavy rain … In the evening we … tried to listen to Frank Martin's new oratorio *Golgotha* – but it wasn't coming over well from the [BBC] Third Programme. By mistake I got a rather interesting work for wind instruments from Prague – don't know who it was by.

9 April 1950. Sunday

… Havelock Nelson is in Dublin, and we had a long conversation on the phone. He tells me that the Belfast job [i.e. the position of conductor] is a

---

9. Lord Mountcharles, owner of Slane Castle on the River Boyne.

most vague affair. A very chancy business. I may have a chance of getting it. I wonder do I really want it? – I think any change would be a good thing. He was very pleasant on the phone.

10 April 1950. Monday

Still the same miserable weather. I thought I should get out for a bit, so I went off to Blessington to fish, without much hope of catching anything. I have seldom fished under such miserable conditions. Nearly blown into the lake once, and the hail cut my ears … I was in the most unusual state this afternoon of being actually bored. The children [Cormac and Barra] tied us to the house, and their presence prevented me from doing anything on my own – like some work for instance …

11 April 1950. Tuesday

… Worked a bit more in the garden … and when [the babysitter] arrived, we went off to [the cinema] … Micheál Mac Liammóir and Hilton Edwards were sitting in front, and seemed very glad to see us. We chatted as we went out afterwards.

The cinema organist treated us to a programme 'inspired' by the idea of a pilgrimage to Rome. Most of the music used was very Protestant[!].

12 April 1950. Wednesday

The same old weather, so I didn't think the Boyne would be much good. Left rather late, and got down … at about 12.00 in a heavy shower … Just at the end of the beat in the Island Run, I got into a fish I hadn't seen. Terrific fun on the little threadline rod. The fish insisted on hugging the bank all the time. I got him in after about 15 minutes, and had difficulty gaffing him with the high bank. Fresh run 8½ lbs … After lunch … I was into another fish – a very game fellow, very fresh – 9½ lbs …

13 April 1950. Thursday

Dorothy Jobling Purser rang up to say that there was a lot of music at Rathmines Castle which she wanted to get rid of, so I went off there in the car. On the way I disposed of the larger salmon for £2-2s … I brought back a colossal collection of music – most of the standard oratorios and operas, and a few hundred songs. This will make a most useful reference library …

DOP rehearsal … A bad attendance of 1st violins, which rather spoilt the rehearsal. Capt. Brennock conducted in a read-through of the Schubert

Symphony no. 3 and also [Beethoven's] *Egmont* (I played oboe). He is definitely good. I then rehearsed the Bach suite and Brandenburg. There are so many details to be considered in these works that I must do a great deal more work on the scores – I felt rather unsure of myself, which is a worrying symptom of the queer state I seem to be in …

14 April 1950. Friday

… We went down town in the morning to get a card-index file for cataloguing my music. We also went out to Glenmaroon, the Guinness's place outside Chapelizod, where there is to be an auction.[10] I had heard there was a harpsichord up for sale, and arranged to see it – unfortunately it turned out to be nothing of the kind – though a rather interesting upright grand of the 1840 period – finely worked, with the harp-like frame standing up behind the keyboard. An amazing Edwardian-Tudor-Baronial mansion which we must explore at the official view of the auction …

Except for a couple of lessons, I spent the rest of the day sorting and rearranging all my books and music – a terrific job, but one I enjoy. Cataloguing will be another business!

Listened to a new orchestral work by Walter Beckett on RÉ conducted by Martinon – he calls it *Triple Fantasy*.[11] I made a recording of it. First impression was favourable, though not very exciting – I must listen to it properly – for I find it hard to listen intently when working the recording machine. …

Have been thinking a great deal about this curious state of mind I seem to be in – no real enthusiasm for the normal jobs on hand. Definitely bored by teaching, and have no inclination to get down to anything like composition or writing radio scripts for the coming series. I feel I just want to be free of everything and get right away from the petty round of Dublin music. I also seem to be acutely conscious of my lack of knowledge on so many important things – e.g. the Beethoven sonatas, Wolf songs, [Bach's] 48 etc: and yet I have no energy to do anything about it. These crises pass in time, generally dispelled by some excitement. This crisis is rather worse than the usual run. If I get the Belfast job, there would be new fields of

---

10. Glenmaroon House, adjoining Phoenix Park, was built in the Tudor style by the Hon. (Arthur) Ernest Guinness *c.*1905. Following Guinness's death in 1949 it passed to the Irish government as part settlement of his death duties, in connection with which the auction referred to here would have been held. It was subsequently bought by the Daughters of Charity for use as a convent.

11. 'Triple Fantasy' is the third movement of Beckett's *Suite for Orchestra* composed in 1945.

activity to master – the change would be good, even though the job may not be of much value. One thing is certain in my mind – I must have a change. All this mental turmoil makes me moody, and at times irritable …

15 April 1950. Saturday

… Found that [the] Enniskerry Hill Climb was on, so [we] went down in the Lancia to watch a bit of it. Was amazed how cautious most of the cars were on the top bend[12] – though one Allard took it fast and slid round the place. Was disappointed in the performance of Kelly in his Maserati. A Mercury Special did the best time …

16 April 1950. Sunday

… A good selection of people came for our annual playing of the records of [Bach's] *St Matthew Passion* … We had an interesting discussion about the interpretation of the chorales. There is no doubt that when performed with a certain dramatic feeling – with crescendos, pianissimo, slowly and so on – that they have a great effect on the present-day audience – though this is not what was intended. The traditional rendering makes them appear as solid rocks about which the drama hangs – and the dramatic content of the rest is shown up by their restrained solidity. I think I prefer the traditional rendering – though I am not convinced that the more dramatic presentation is not possible …

17 April 1950. Monday

… The Academy opened again today. Arrived in time to ascertain the orchestration of the cantatas we have chosen for the Bach centenary [*sic*, bicentenary] concert promoted by the MAI. I also looked through a score sent to me by Gerard Victory for performance with the DOP – it seems interesting enough – though his music never seems convincing – I am afraid his technique is very deficient.[13]

After supper … I had to go off to my first attendance at the Council of the Arts Association of Ireland. Seems a very vague affair, and I am rather

12. Brian had taken part in the competitive motorsport of hillclimbing in his 'Brescia' Bugatti and knew the course at Enniskerry, Co. Wicklow, from first-hand experience (see illustration, pp. 176–7). For a Pathé news film report of this 1950 event see http://www.youtube.com/watch?v=jdgyYa0MQas

13. Gerard Victory (1921–95) would go on to establish himself as one of the most prolific Irish composers of the twentieth century. It is unclear which work of Victory's is referred to here: one possibility is one or more movements from his ballet music *The Enchanted Garden* which dates from 1950 (see Bernard Harrison (ed.), *Catalogue of Contemporary Irish Music* (Dublin: Irish Composers' Centre, 1982), p. 150); see further *EMIR*, pp. 1028–31.

doubtful about whether it will come to anything. Liam O'Laoghaire seems a good man with plenty of drive.[14] I didn't like Scholfield, the chairman, who seems a rather pugnacious type. Anne Yeats[15] was there, also Desmond Clarke, Edward Toner,[16] Brendan Nielan and Gorman.[17] They are to have a public meeting on Wednesday to inaugurate the Dublin branch, at which I cannot be present until late perhaps. …

18 April 1950. Tuesday

Miserably cold and wet today … This was just as well, since I had a great deal of work to get done, bills to be paid, etc., etc. Made out a new syllabus for my RDS Extension lectures, including one on instruments and one on 'Music before the time of Bach' …

Academy orchestra at 6.00 – final rehearsal for the concert next Monday at which we play Handel Minuet from *Berenice*, Boyce Symphony no. 5 and Brahms Hungarian Dance no. 6. Was most insistent that only those who attended this rehearsal should be allowed to play at the concert – in spite of Vaneček's suggestion that a very good second violin should join for the concert.

After supper there was a meeting of the Bach Centenary sub-committee of the MAI: Tony Farrington, Joe Groocock, Dorothy Stokes and Olive Smith. We got the programme and soloists fixed, and most other arrangements. Dorothy Stokes in great form, with a lovely description of O'Hannrachain being slippery in Sligo – he will never commit himself!

Joe came back afterwards, and we had a good talk – he was in one of his mysterious moods when you never know whether he is being serious or pulling your leg!

20 April 1950. Thursday

… Interviewed a new pupil – a Trimble (vague relation of Joan)[18] who seems keen. Gave her the usual lecture, trying to make her realise what she is taking on. I think she will start next Monday. Spent free moments during

---

14. Liam O'Laoghaire founded the Irish Film Society with Edward Toner in 1936.
15. Anne Yeats (1919–2001), artist and daughter of W.B. Yeats. In 1950 Cormac (then aged four) was attending regular art lessons with her on Saturday mornings.
16. See note 14 above.
17. 'Gorman', possibly a misspelling for [Maurice] Gorham, Director of Broadcasting at RÉ?
18. The Enniskillen-born pianist and composer Joan Trimble (1915–2000). See further *EMIR*, pp. 1008–9; Alasdair Jamieson, *Music in Northern Ireland – Two Major Figures: Havelock Nelson (1917–1996) and Joan Trimble (1915–2000)* (Tolworth: Grosvenor House Publishing, 2017).

teaching at the Academy working on the Bach scores for the DOP. The bowing is rather a problem.

Very good DOP rehearsal. We got the first two movements of the Schubert symphony into quite good shape, and played through the Bach *Wachet auf*. Then I let the wind go, and we worked hard at the first movement of the Brandenburg. We worked till nearly 10, and then had a short committee meeting …

21 April 1950. Friday

… got started with my script for next Wednesday's broadcast on Beethoven [Symphony] no. 7 – but found the work very heavy going. Sometimes I can write a script straight off without much trouble – and at other times each sentence needs many minutes of thought.

In honour of Mary's birthday we went to Jammet's in the evening[19] … Always see an interesting collection of people at Jammets: hunty-shooty country aristocracy, fat businessmen with their very confidential secretaries …

23 April 1950. Sunday

… I got a little more work done on the radio script for next Wednesday – but still seem to be in sticky form for writing. I spent the afternoon giving the Lancia a routine check-over … We had a supper party in the evening [guests included Charles Acton and Carol, and John Beckett] … We started by discussing techniques in jazz, and played some examples of slick trumpet-playing on the gramophone. Afterwards, we played some of my own recordings: the thirteenth-century music, my quartet, *The Buried Moon Suite* as played by the DOP, and the *Intermezzo from Ireland* as played on the [Radio] Luxembourg ECA programme.[20]

It was a very pleasant evening, though Charles was rather professorial and long-winded – inclined to be embarrassingly patronising with John Beckett. John stayed the night, since he had no car. The others departed at about 1.00.

---

19. Jammet's restaurant in Nassau Street was opened by two French brothers, Michel and François Jammet, in 1901 and remained in business until 1967. It was renowned as one of Dublin's finest restaurants. Brian's brother-in-law Thurloe Conolly painted murals for the restaurant in the 1940s. See further Alison Maxwell, *Jammet's of Dublin: 1901 to 1967* (Dublin: The Lilliput Press, 2012).
20. See above, 31 March.

24 April 1950. Monday

… I had a long chat with John Beckett about the interpretation of the Bach pieces we are doing with the DOP – and about all sorts of things. When he went, I got down to the radio script, and worked between pupils at it until I had to go to the Academy …

… After a quick supper I had to go down to the Academy again for the performance by the Academy orchestra … I gave the orchestra a run-through rehearsal at 7.30, and then listened to the solo items of the concert by the string pupils … Great promise is shown by a very young violinist – Mary Gallagher – about nine years old, who played the Kuchler concertino.[21] The orchestra played well really – and everyone enjoyed the Brahms Hungarian Dance, which we played with great gusto.

Was talking to Mrs Vaneček, and have at last arranged for them to come round to supper with us on Sunday week …

25 April 1950. Tuesday

So cold today that it actually *snowed* – I believe Punchestown Races[22] had to be postponed because of three inches of snow on the course! Even with a fire in the music room, it was hard to keep warm at a sitting job – for I finished the radio script for Wednesday … Went to deliver the script at the Radio …

Immediately after lunch Carol Little arrived to work with me on the bowing of the Bach Suite no. 3. It really *is* a problem deciding on the bowing of Bach. It took us the whole afternoon, but we did a pretty thorough job especially on the air. Denis [Donoghue] arrived for his lesson, and we had a cup of tea, during which an argument arose about the question of taking advice from one teacher when studying with another. Carol and I, and Betty Colclough (who had arrived by this time) think that any *positive* advice is of value – though destructive criticism from another teacher is a bad thing. Denis has the typical Irish Catholic attitude of unquestioning faith in one teacher alone, and denies the possibility of good coming from outside advice. The result of this argument was that Denis couldn't have a lesson, for I had to get on with [the next pupil] …

---

21. Mary Gallagher would go on to become a noted violinist appearing on a number of occasions as soloist with the RÉSO performing works including the Khachaturian and Prokofiev 2nd concertos. She was leader of the New Irish Chamber Orchestra (see 'Irish Chamber Orchestra', *EMIR*, pp. 527–8) from 1970 to 1980. The German violinist, composer and pedagogue Ferdinand Küchler (1867–1937) composed a number of student violin concertinos in the baroque style, published in the 1930s.
22. The annual Irish National Hunt Festival, a major event in the Irish equestrian calendar, has been held at Punchestown racecourse in County Kildare annually in April since 1861.

26 April 1950. Wednesday

Got up early so as to be down at the Boyne in good time … After a few casts … I was into a fish – to my intense surprise! … A fine fresh fish of 13 lbs … Nothing more doing, so I drove back in time for lunch … Thurloe [Conolly] called in, having just bought a curious kind of oboe – about 18" long, pitched in G (I think). He thinks it is a 'pastoral oboe'. We tried to play it with an oboe reed, but it obviously needs a smaller one. I took photos of it, and measured it, so as to ask Philip Bate about it.[23] I then timed my radio script, and after a cup of tea went off to broadcast it. Made a mistake in the timing, and had to cut the final section – but I think it went well.[24] After supper, I went out to Grattan Norman's, for a queer ticking noise has developed in the Lancia which is not a loose tappet. After a good look round we found it was a broken internal valve spring. We were very pleased with ourselves when we replaced it without removing the head. I supported the valve from underneath and picked out the cotters, while Grattan depressed the spring. Very cold working outside! I think the front coil springs have gone again – but I will carry on with them as they are for the time being.

27 April 1950. Thursday

… Arriving home [from a morning fishing on the Boyne] I found Ralph [Cusack] had called in for lunch. Having renounced the Devil in the form of society and its accoutrements of dress suits etc. he has been asked to attend the Hamburg Opera with McBride [sic].[25] With the ticket was a note, so typical of the Irish civil service, which baldly said, 'You're to wear evening dress' – so after recovering from his fury at this note, Ralph has now to go and hire the Devil! …

Hard work at the DOP rehearsal. First of all the Thomas Kelly suite, which should not present much difficulty – then the Bach suite till 9.00 – then Brennock rehearsed the Schubert symphony. I enjoyed myself playing oboe with David Lane …

---

23. Brian appears first to have met Philip Bate when he lived in London in 1938–9. Bate (1909–99), a leading English collector and authority on woodwind and brass instruments, gave his important collection of historic wind instruments to Oxford University in 1968. He and his wife were lifelong friends of Brian and Mary. See further *NGroveD2*, vol. 2, p. 901.
24. Radio programmes at the time were broadcast live.
25. The Hamburg State Opera was invited by the Dublin Grand Opera Society to bring its productions of *Don Giovanni* and *Cosi fan tutte* to Dublin in 1950. Seán MacBride was Minister for External Affairs between 1948 and 1951.

28 April 1950. Friday

… ['The usual teaching'] … Mary went off to meet Marcus Dods[26] at 7.00 – he wired to say he would spend a night with us, since he was called to an audition for the Belfast job – by which I can assume that there is no question of my getting it: in a way I am rather relieved! We brought Marcus to the Dolphin [restaurant] and had an excellent tornedos chasseur …

… Joe [Groocock] is writing a sonatina for piano which sounds most interesting …

29 April 1950. Saturday

… [in the evening] we had to go off to the Irish Housewives concert.[27] Charles and Carol came with us. Mary had gathered that it was to be a concert of genuine folksongs from Wales and Brittany – it turned out to be a real 'parish concert' – piano out of tune, amazing lack of taste and practically nothing genuine! We were bored stiff until a budding John McCormack got up and reduced us to helplessness with the most wonderful slush I have heard for ages – *Home Sweet Home* and all! We left after the interval …

30 April 1950. Sunday

… Marcus is a grand person to have with us – for he takes an interest in everything, and one feels that he is happy doing the things we normally do, which is rare for a visitor … Mary brought Marcus to catch the boat at Dún Laoghaire, and I tidied up the room for the gramophone evening … We listened to Bach Suite no. 3, Bach Concerto in C for 2 harpsichords, the Mozart Clarinet Concerto, Arkhangelsky 'Credo',[28] Casella's *Tarantella*,[29] and then the Bartok [2nd] Violin Concerto – which stands the supreme test of being far more exciting than one ever expects! It really is one of the *great* works of our age. A very enjoyable evening, though we were very tired when they had all gone.

---

26. Marcus Dods (1918–84) was a close contemporary of Brian's both at Rugby School and at Cambridge. At this time he was assistant music director in the Rank Organisation. He would later become conductor and chorus master at Sadler's Wells Opera Company and principal conductor of the BBC Concert Orchestra.
27. The Irish Housewives Association, established in 1942, pursued a progressive and often radical agenda for the status of women in Irish society and for the protection of consumers' rights.
28. Alexander Arkhangelsky (1846–1924) was a noted composer in the development of Russian sacred music.
29. The Italian Alfredo Casella (1883–1947) composed his *Tarantella* for cello and piano in 1934.

MAY, JUNE

1 May 1950. Monday

… Still warm today – though the amount of intermittent rain is worrying me because I don't want a flood on the Boyne! The usual teaching here and at the Academy. Merle Hanna[1] has got hold of some wonderful Purcell songs, realised by Britten – I must get a copy … There is a performance of *Dido and Aeneas* in the air – I hope it comes to something – I may be asked to conduct it; which I will do as long as the standard promises to be reasonably high …

… *Envoy* was published today, with an article by me.[2] They never let me see a proof as promised, and there are several inaccuracies. I am very annoyed about this.

Saw Neville Johnson's exhibition today with Thurloe [Conolly] – very interesting, including one magnificent 'Objet trouvé'.[3]

2 May 1950. Tuesday

Hard work all day putting the bowing of the Bach suite into the orchestral parts. Carol Little came to help me at the job. It would have been easy enough if I had not started thinking as we copied the bowing from my score – but thinking about it made me change what I had decided on, several times! … I continued the work, apart from lessons, in the afternoon, and Carol came back to help later. Then had to go off and rehearse the Academy orchestra – reading through a large selection of things to see what they liked. I was absolutely dead at the end of all this …

3 May 1950. Wednesday

[Fishing most of the day] … I had to leave at 4.00 to be back in time for my broadcast, and had a fast run back tailing a new Sunbeam Talbot, which seemed to hold the road very well. After the broadcast I was handed a note

---

1. A singing pupil at the RIAM.
2. The periodical *Envoy: A Review of Literature and Art* was founded by artist John Ryan to provide an outlet for Irish writers and artists. It ran from December 1949 to July 1951. Brian's article 'Culture and Chauvinism' appeared in *Envoy*, vol. 2, no. 6 (May 1950), pp. 75–9.
3. Born in England, Neville Johnson (1911–99) came to Belfast in 1934 and lived in Dublin from 1947 to 1958. He was one of a group of Northern Irish artists (including George Campbell, Gerard Dillon, Daniel O'Neill and Colin Middleton) who exhibited at the Victor Waddington Galleries in South Anne Street, Dublin. His paintings of this period show the influence of both surrealism and cubism. See further Dickon Hall and Eoin O'Brien, *Neville Johnson: paint the smell of grass*, exhibition catalogue (Bangor: Ava Gallery, 2008).

asking me to delete a certain sentence in the script!! … I am ashamed to say I clean forgot about the council meeting of the MAI! …

4 May 1950. Thursday

Finished putting the bow-marks in the parts of the Bach suite in the morning, and went as usual to the Academy to give a lesson to Merle Hanna. We had the trout for lunch …

… Very late starting the DOP rehearsal, but it was a good one. Thorough work on the Kelly suite, and the Brandenburg and the Bach suite. My bowing of the Bach seems to work out all right …

5 May 1950. Friday

… Spent the afternoon teaching – until supper time, using the recording machine with Rosemary and Betty Colclough. The adjustment of the tape-tension is most critical, and seems to go out of adjustment very easily. I readjusted it at tea-time, and made a marked improvement …

… The *Motor* this week has a description of the new Lancia Aurelia, which seems to be a really first-rate car.[4] Lovely to be able to afford one! On economy and performance alone it leaves all the English cars miles behind.

6 May 1950. Saturday

Lessons to M. Peat and Andrew L. in the morning. The latter is a most exasperating fellow to teach, since he could sing so well, and yet I can't stop him forcing tone with his throat. I can even get him to sing an odd isolated phrase quite correctly, but he doesn't seem able to apply this to other situations. He is one of those nervous people who have no facilities for practice at home without feeling that he is being overheard and criticised – this has a lot to do with it I think. He is very interested in gardening, so we had to look round, and also gave him some pieces for his garden.

… We were bemoaning the fact that we had not been able to get tickets for the Hamburg Opera, who are performing *Don Giovanni* and *Cosi fan tutte* at the Gaiety, until Aleck Crichton rang up and offered us tickets for this evening – very good seats in the dress circle. We changed and went off in great excitement. The performance was superb – such wonderful teamwork and hitch-less production. The singers were also such brilliant actors. The Radio [Éireann] Orchestra played really well too – especially Laurent's

---

4. Brian indulged his interest in motoring by subscribing to the weekly car magazine *Motor* up at least to the 1970s.

horn playing.[5] The opera was like champagne to us – a most unforgettably stimulating evening …hent

7 May 1950. Sunday

… I left the car for Mary, and went off [to go fishing] on the pillion of David [Lane]'s motor-bike – an experience which was new for me, and which I regarded with nervous apprehension. However, I soon got used to it, and ended by enjoying the experience – though by the time we had covered the 35 miles to Barnatten reservoir [Co. Louth] I was pretty sore, had to walk with my legs wide apart, and had melted a good deal of my fishing boot on the exhaust pipe! … We came back at great speed – but I was rather late for the Vanečeks, who came to supper. I was very glad to have the evening to talk to them, for they are charming people, and very sincere. They told me what a relief it was for them to come to a house where they felt they could say what they liked without fear of disapproval. Yvonne came to supper too. We discussed Steiner, music of all kinds, and the religious stranglehold in this country. Vaneček finds the behaviour and capacity for work of his pupils most interesting from the point of view of the religious background. The Catholics not only can't think for themselves, but they are also incapable of real work. I played them my quartet and the *In Memoriam Mahatma Gandhi*.

8 May 1950. Monday

Barra had poured about ½ gallon of water into the petrol tank yesterday, so I had to drain out a great deal of the petrol and clean out the system before Cormac could be left at school. Even then Mary got stuck down town, but was able to clear out the water from the carburettor on my phone instructions. I did most of the script for next Wednesday['s radio broadcast]. Wolfram Hentschel turned up in the morning, and we had some tea in the garden sitting in the beautiful warm sun. I was very glad to have a long talk with Wolfram, whom I have not had much opportunity of speaking to at length alone. My German got really quite good at the end of the morning's conversation … We take it as a great compliment that both the Hentschels and the Vanečeks (amongst others) seem to regard our house as a haven of liberalism where they can say what they like. Coming from outside, they find the narrowness of outlook in Ireland most oppressive … After the usual afternoon's teaching … we had a supper party for Joe and Rhoda [Groocock]. We also had a surprise guest in the person of

---

5. Leopold Laurent had joined the orchestra from Belgium as principal horn in 1948.

Charles Hamburg, who is visiting Dublin on a cargo boat! I hadn't seen him since Music Camp in 1939.[6] He is terrific fun – a most vivacious and argumentative fellow, not without some quite forgivable codology. He is a Jew of course, and we discussed the position of his race in music, and the possibilities of a nationalistic school of Jewish music. He claims that Bloch's music is not really Jewish in flavour, as I had expected – I wonder? We played some Monteverdi, and discussed the interesting question of the tempo of this music in view of the limited string techniques of the time with the bow held underneath.[7] He doesn't like modern music.

After Charles had gone, we played the Bach Concerto for two Harpsichords … Joe then played me the first movement of his new Sonatina for piano. Most interesting music, and quite unexpected from him. Delightfully humorous, with the same kind of flavour as Poulenc. I think it comes off very well – though has a little too much whole-tone scale which clouds the clarity of the tonality, which is so important in Joe's kind of music. I hope Joe doesn't become *too* clever; it would spoil the real charm of his music.

9 May 1950. Tuesday

… I finished my script for tomorrow, and timed it. For once I think I have a script which will not run over time.

Teaching in the afternoon, until I went down to the Radio to deliver the script and get information about the programmes which I am to preview in this new 'Music of the Week' series, which starts at the end of the month.

Then on to the Academy for the orchestra rehearsal. We started work on Britten's *Simple Symphony*, which ought to be good fun. …

11 May 1950. Thursday

… The afternoon was taken up with teaching – though there were several absentees at the Academy, so I was able to take things easy … There was a poor attendance at the DOP rehearsal … I rehearsed the Schubert thoroughly, then Brennock did the Bach *Wachet auf*. His main trouble is that he takes a long time making up his mind what comments he is going to make – he also seems to have very little backbone. Wolfram Hentschel then took us through the Bach suite. I enjoyed myself playing the oboe with David [Lane]. Wolfram was conducting for his first time, and did it remarkably well …

---

6. On the music camp, see Memoir (Part I) above, pp. 14–15.
7. A misunderstanding: the violin bow was always held with the hand above.

12 May 1950. Friday

… [In the evening] I went off to meet Mrs Maloney at the Pearl Bar –
the head of the [BBC] Third Programme whom I was to have met last
Wednesday.[8] She has the same rather overbearing manner of most high-up
BBC officials – but charming at the same time. She was however rather
tactless about Irish music, assuming it to be entirely provincial. It appears
that I may get a talk on some general musical subject if the authorities
approve of my script. Paddy Kavanagh and Cecil Salkeld were there,[9]
Paddy rather tight and talking a great deal of rubbish … Also saw John
Ryan of *Envoy*, and was able to row him [*sic*] about not seeing a proof
of my article.[10] Afterwards my car was jammed between two saloons with
their brakes on. In the presence of a guard [policeman], I did a neat bit of
burglary, opening one Austin through a 3 inch window opening, using my
starting handle to release the catch on the door!

14 May 1950. Sunday

[Following a visit by Paul Hirsch, a former acquaintance from Cambridge,
with his wife:] Curious the way so many people who visit Ireland and only
meet intelligent people go away with the idea that it is a country of such
outspokenness and freedom – an interesting contrast to what the Hentschels
and Vaněčeks feel having come to *live* here! We also talked a good deal of
music, and things in Cambridge.

… After lunch we set off in the Lancia, and drove over the Featherbed,
Lough Bray, Sally Gap, Loch Tay, and then on to Ralph [Cusack]'s …
After seeing round the garden and drinking beer, we went in to listen to
the Kodály Sonata for Unaccompanied Cello, and some early music. I am
even more convinced that this is not a really great work – in spite of Ralph's
enthusiasm – though the playing on the recording is miraculous …[11]

[Gramophone evening:] We played the Brahms F minor Piano Quartet,
Tubby the Tuba,[12] *The Foggy Dew*, Maytuss *Dnieper Power Station*,[13] Shostakovich
Age of Gold, and then Walton's *Belshazzar's Feast* – which made us all most
excited …

8. Brian had been delayed returning from fishing on the Wednesday.
9. Cecil ffrench Salkeld (1903–69) was an artist whose work was influenced by German
Expressionism.
10. For more on this meeting at the Pearl Bar, see Memoir (Part I) above, pp. 63–4.
11. This is likely to be the 1948 recording on 78 rpm discs by János Starker, which won the
Grand Prix du Disque.
12. A song dating from 1945 and made popular through Danny Kaye's recording for Decca.
13. Brian owned a copy of the Columbia 78 rpm recording (P-17121) of Alexander Mosolov's
'Mechanical Ballet' *The Iron Foundry* and Yuli (Julius) Meytus's *The Dnieper Water Power Station*
(1932), two classics of Soviet socialist musical realism.

15 May 1950. Monday

… to the Vanečeks for supper. [Kveta] was in great form … We were most interested in her paintings which are really remarkable considering the short time she has been at it. She is able to get real warmth and sunlight into her colour schemes … Jaroslav came in after teaching, and we had a most interesting supper of various Czech delicatessen.

We talked a great deal about the Academy – conditions in this country, Steiner, Norwegian culture and so on. A most enjoyable evening. She wants to paint my portrait! … It will take some time to get to know the Vanečeks well – for they are so much more 'foreign' to us than the French or Germans. Their English is not yet good enough to carry on conversation on the high level we would wish. We do feel very drawn to them.

17 May 1950. Wednesday

… Met Desmond Hickey[14] at the *Independent* [newspaper office] – I get very fed up with people like him who are always talking about themselves and their woes – the theme of the unrecognised budding genius is too overworked …

… [In the afternoon] I went off to the Radio. Kept an appointment with P.P. Maguire, who has asked me to do the incidental music for his feature programme on the Dept. of Posts and Telegraphs. Sounds an attractive idea, for which I should be quite well paid – though like most of these things it has to be ready in a hurry. I shall be very busy for the next three weeks. After the broadcast, which was perfectly timed, I rushed off to the Boyne [fishing] …

18 May 1950. Thursday

Worked on the programme notes for the DOP concert programme all morning … Studied the script of the feature broadcast about the Dept. of Posts and Telegraphs for which I am to do the music. It will be amusing work … [15]

DOP rehearsal in the evening … we did very good work on the Thomas Kelly suite, and then the Brandenburg. All soloists were present for the first time. Then Wolfram Hentschel rehearsed us in *Egmont* and the Schubert symphony – I played the oboe. We all enjoyed ourselves so well that we went on playing till after 10.00 …

---

14. Artist (1927–98).
15. This incidental music does not appear in any of Brian's lists of his works, suggesting that it was never completed.

19 May 1950. Friday

… Charles [Acton] then rang up with some most disturbing news – with all our arrangements for the DOP concert on 31 May nobody had booked the hall, and it wasn't available! Charles, being ultimately responsible for these things, was feeling in a dreadful state! After furious phoning in all directions throughout the day, we decided to postpone to 14 June – even though it means that Hazel de Courcy will not be here to lead – Carol will have to do it. I then went down town … to May's [music shop] to get gramophone needles. I couldn't resist buying the new recording of the Bach G minor Harpsichord Concerto … In the forthcoming production of *Dido and Aeneas* (November) by TCD students most of the leads are being taken by my pupils … went on to the Radio to discuss the music for the feature programme with P.P. Maguire – a nice fellow. There is very little I can get on with until the verse is written, which will mean a rush. I spent a long time attempting to get information on coming musical programmes for the series of broadcasts about the 'Music of the Week'. The difficulty of getting details is most exasperating.

… Came [into the house] in time to take a recording of Wolfram [Hentschel]'s performance of the Dvořak Cello Concerto – a most musical and moving performance … I [then] worked on next Wednesday's script on the finale of Beethoven [Symphony] no. 7 until nearly midnight.

Sold the Alvis this afternoon to an old clergyman for £55. Hurray!

20 May 1950. Saturday

The morning was taken up with timing next Wednesday's script, gathering material for the Sunday broadcast on the music of the week, and teaching.

… In the evening, the Henschsels, Alex (Wolfram's father), Betty and Tom came in to hear the recording I made of W[olfram]'s performance of the Dvořak Cello Concerto. We started off with the Bach Concerto for Harpsichord in F minor (I presume it is his *own* arrangement of the A minor fiddle Concerto)[16] – then the tape recording of the concerto, which was rather uneven in quality, but was a great help to Wolfram. After some tea, I played the recording Mary had made of my *In Memoriam* [*Mahatma Gandhi*] last Saturday …

16. Bach arranged his Violin Concerto in A minor (BWV 1041) as a harpsichord concerto in G minor (BWV 1058), which implies that this is the work which Brian is in fact citing here (not the Harpsichord Concerto in F minor (BWV 1056), the outer movements of which are thought to be arranged from a lost oboe concerto in G minor). See *NGroveD2*, vol. 2, p. 374.

21 May 1950. Sunday

… Cyril [Dugdale] called for me after lunch, and we went off in his Riley to the Boyne. I drove the car part of the way down, and was impressed by its power and cornering possibilities – though the steering control is not nearly so precise as the Lancia …

22 May 1950. Monday

With teaching and doing the script for next Sunday, I didn't have a moment at all today – just a few minutes in the garden after lunch. Finished teaching at a quarter past seven …

23 May 1950. Tuesday

Still working on the script. Went down town at 11.15 to the Metropole for the showing of the new Yeats film – and found that it was p.m. and not a.m.[17] Went on to the A[utomobile] A[ssociation] to see about the triptyque for going to the North in July,[18] and make further arrangements for our trip [to France] in August … Finished the script when I got home (working also in the afternoon).

… Academy orchestra at 6.00 – worked thoroughly on the Britten *Simple Symphony*. The seconds [violins] were very stupid and exasperating, calling for a good deal of sarcasm and mild fury. The importance of 'taking a breath' in imagination when starting a fast passage on the off beat is never realised or comprehended by bad players.

A lovely evening – I worked in the garden, weeding the rock garden, until 9.00 …

I then came in and completed one of the pieces of incidental music for the Dept. of P[osts] & T[elegraphs] feature. I enjoy writing this amusing and satirical music.

Left at 11.15 for the Yeats film. Marvellous opening address by Lennox Robinson,[19] who gesticulated as if he were plucking flowers from the air and wiping breath off a window pane. The film was really good – marvellous photography. The verse was excellently spoken by Micheál Mac Liammóir

---

17. The documentary *W.B. Yeats: a tribute* (1950) was sponsored by the Department of Foreign Affairs and directed by George Fleischmann and John D. Sheridan. It was later awarded a Certificate of Merit at the 1950 Venice Film Festival and screened at the Edinburgh Film Festival.

18. A triptyque, or customs permit for the temporary importation of a motor vehicle, was required at the time when driving a car from the Republic into Northern Ireland.

19. The dramatist and poet Lennox Robinson (1886–1958) had been closely involved with W.B. Yeats as director of the Abbey Theatre from 1909 to 1914, and later as a board member, a position he held until his death.

and Siobhán McKenna. Eamonn O'Gallagher [Ó Gallchobhair]'s music was restrained and very suitable, though never really inspired. There are many who will criticise this film because it is not quite what *they* would have done with the subject; but it remains something for this country to be proud of.

There was a sort of reception afterwards which I did not expect. Everyone there, including [the Taoiseach] Costello, [Seán] MacBride and other ministers. The Yeats family and all the *right* people … met Rory Childers and his father [Erskine], with whom I had a long chat about music … [20]

24 May 1950. Wednesday

… To the Phoenix Hall, where I wanted to find out about this composer Wismer [*sic*], whose piano concerto is to be done next Tuesday.[21] The RÉ[S]O had gone to Limerick and I found the Light Orchestra there. Chatted with some of them. Hugh Doherty has proposed that I be made an honorary member of the Musicians' Federation.[22] We then went and bought cinema reels for the recording machine.

Finished the scoring of the incidental music I wrote last night, when I got home, and tidied up some points in the scripts I had written.

… Broadcast on the finale of Beethoven no. 7 at 5.30. When giving a final review of the whole symphony, I had an incredibly difficult bit of disc-jockeying to do. It is incredible that I am expected to read my script, *and* work the records at the same time: though in actual fact there is no one available whom I could trust to do the records properly.[23] Met Eamonn O'Gallagher in the Radio, and congratulated him on his music for the Yeats film. He told me that it is now common knowledge that I am off to the BBC to study balance and control!! Extraordinary the way these rumours develop without my knowing anything about them myself! …

25 May 1950. Thursday

Horribly cold today – almost like winter again. Spent much of the odd moments getting this diary up to date. Usual Academy lesson at 12.30, and teaching in the afternoon …

20. Erskine Childers (1905–74), who had been a TD since 1938, served as a minister in various governments between 1951 and 1973, and was elected President of Ireland in 1973. His level of interest in music and the arts was unusual for a politician.
21. Pierre Wissmer (1915–92), a Swiss composer who was also active in France. He composed two piano concertos, the first in 1937, the second in 1947.
22. The musicians' trade union.
23. Bearing in mind that 78 rpm recordings of Beethoven's Symphony no. 7 typically comprised 5 discs (10 sides). For the script of this radio broadcast, see illustration p. 62 above.

A good DOP rehearsal in the evening – spent the time on *Egmont* and the Schubert symphony. Had to change round the strings a bit, since some of them … can't play on the new date for the concert …

26 May 1950. Friday

A very busy day teaching and getting radio scripts in hand – nothing much to report from it all …

I went down to the Radio at 4.30 to try and find out some of the items in the forthcoming musical programmes for the talks on the 'Music of the Week'. Most infuriating waste of time. Mrs O'Higgins is so busy, with a whole train of people coming in to ask her questions, that she had very little time to help me. I spent a whole hour getting the items for three programmes, and went away with a lot of important information still unsupplied …

P.P. Maguire rang up today with the news that the man who was to write the verse for the Dept. of P[osts] & T[elegraphs] feature had failed to produce it – making further delays and complications with the music which I am to write.

27 May 1950. Saturday

Worked on the script for next Wednesday (Haydn 'Surprise' Symphony) in the morning, and gave a few lessons … We then set out for Dublin airport to meet Louise Trenton, leaving plenty of time to have tea in the restaurant and let the boys [Cormac and Barra] see the aeroplanes. The plane was rather late, owing to the high wind, and Louise arrived having had a very bumpy crossing. We drove back and after supper spent a quiet evening chatting by the fire. I fixed up all about the pupils who want lessons from Louise, and she is very kindly going to hear the impecunious ones without a fee. Louise seems just the same as ever – full of fun. We were rather anxious about her stay, since she is really quite an old woman now, and is obviously used to comforts – but she is being very cooperative and makes things as easy as possible for Mary. It is comforting that she also has terrible worries over pupils whom she just cannot manage to teach!

28 May 1950. Sunday

Listened to the records of Rubbra's Sonata no. 2 for violin and piano in preparation for tonight's broadcast.[24] It seems a most genial and tuneful work, so unlike my rather vague memories of other works of his. Alan Dyas then arrived for a lesson with Louise. He was very nervous! As usual, Louise

---

24. Edmund Rubbra (1901–86), English composer.

managed to work wonders, and made him open his throat and send the tone out. Pinching the cheeks between the teeth with the fingers is a trick which worked very well with him. I think he enjoyed his lesson.

… In the afternoon, we sat outside in the garden [at Brian's aunt's house] doing absolutely nothing – a pleasure which we so very seldom experience – the trouble is that I keep feeling guilty about it, as though I should be getting on with something. That is the trouble with freelance work – there is always something to be done, and no time is specially set aside as *spare* time …

[In the evening] I worked on the 'Music of the Week' broadcast, gathering material for the next script … no one came this evening [for the gramophone evening] (probably because of Whit Weekend). After showing Louise the recording machine, I went off to do my broadcast on the music of the week. Louise and Mary listened, and seemed to enjoy the broadcast. Louise most amused by the way I keep changing from English to Irish accent during a broadcast!

29 May 1950. Monday
Worked all morning on the script for next Sunday's 'Music of the Week'. I quite enjoyed myself writing about Poulenc and Milhaud, and was rather pleased with some of the witticisms! …

… We went [in the car to] Howth Demesne to see the rhododendrons … [then] for a further long walk, climbing up to the top of the rock … On the way up, I met F.C. Swanton, the organist, and asked him about the organ composer Duruflé.[25] I wish I hadn't, for he is the most difficult person to escape I have ever come across. I had retreated ten yards up the path with him following me, and had repeatedly tried to get in a word to say that I must look after the family, before I finally succeeded in getting away from his involved and extraordinary conversation!

I worked all evening on the script, and managed to get it finished.

30 May 1950. Tuesday
Today Louise [Trenton] gave lessons in my presence to the first batch of my pupils. This was of the greatest benefit to me   for she was able to put her finger on the most important aspects of each pupil's problem – coming fresh to them … After lunch … we had Denis Donoghue, whom she spotted as the best of the bunch. After tea … a lesson to myself in which L. tried out a number of her new ideas on me … I then had to go off to the Academy

---

25. Maurice Duruflé (1902–86), French organist and composer.

Orchestra rehearsal – working again on the Britten *Simple Symphony*. The seconds were much better this time.

In the evening, I worked on the incidental music, and enjoyed writing an imitation of people travelling by car (three gears with a bad change) and going up steps! It is great fun having the opportunity to write light satirical music and to be able to experiment in technical effects.

31 May 1950. Wednesday

… I spent the morning working at the incidental music (scoring) and getting material for the next 'Music of the Week' broadcast. Continued the incidental music after lunch until I had to go off to the Radio to mark the records of the Haydn 'Surprise' Symphony for this evening's broadcast.[26] After this, I went to the Academy to give a lesson … Then back to the Radio for the broadcast – misjudged the timing, and had to cut some of the symphony …

… I rushed off to the Boyne, eating my supper as I went … When stalking one fish, I walked straight over the bank into the river, and was completely soaked – cigarettes and all in a mush!! However I went on fishing – dripping wet … A gorgeous evening – great fun … I took off all my clothes and drove home in a mackintosh and a rug! Good thing I didn't get a puncture or something!

1 June 1950. Thursday

All morning on the incidental music until I had to go and teach at the Academy … and after that return for lessons with Andrew Leahy and Mabel Peat with Louise. Louise seems very impressed with the results I have got from the rather limited material at my disposal.

DOP rehearsal in the evening. Louise came along and seemed most interested … We got some good work done on the Bach suite and Brandenburg, also on the Kelly pieces. Arthur Shortt, the leader of Our Lady's Choral Society, has come along to help us out in the 1st violins. It only occurred to me later that he was invited along by John Miley without consulting me at all – actually I am delighted, but this sort of thing is just what John Miley and Co. are always objecting to!

---

26. 'Marking the records' refers to the practice of preparing slips of carefully measured paper or card to identify how far in on a given side of a 78 rpm record (or, later, a 33 rpm LP) the needle should be put down in order to locate the beginning of a particular passage or excerpt to be played.

Had to hurry home to hear 'Take it from Here', from which I want to quote their theme song in this incidental music.[27] We found it an extremely funny programme – I wish we had listened to it before.

2 June 1950. Friday

… A very busy day, with another batch of pupils for Louise – and a great deal of time spent on the script for next Wednesday's broadcast … Charles [Acton] rang up with some rubbish about my slighting Carol Little as leader of the orchestra by cow-towing [*sic*] to Mrs Vince – was very curt with him – but these things make me annoyed, and upset me. I must train myself not to get so worked up about such things …

… After some tea in the garden, I went off to the Radio to get some of the programmes for the week after next for the 'Music of the Week' series. Incidentally, Cecil Salkeld rang up having immensely enjoyed the first of these broadcasts, and wants me to contribute to his weekly series (starting at the end of the month), which will include notes and criticism on all major artistic happenings … [In the evening] we then listened to the performance of the Bach [B minor] Mass from RÉ.[28] Was utterly shocked by the vast cuts, which were even worse than I had expected. I then became infuriated by Edward Lindenberg's interpretation – full of 'concertina' swellings in and out – terrible *rallentandos* everywhere, and slow, heavy, dragging tempi that ruined the flow of the music. To crown all this decapitated and decimated version, they faded out the performance exactly *nine seconds* before the final chord. I was so furious that I rang up RÉ and told Miss O'Brien what I thought of her. I was trembling with rage. Went into the garden, and watered it to try and recover from all the things that have upset me too much.

3 June 1950. Saturday[29]

Teaching in morning …
Dinner at Bailey [restaurant] with Louise.
Dublin Quartet …[30]

---

27. A radio comedy programme on the BBC.
28. This broadcast, apparently from an overseas recording bought in by RÉ, should not be confused with the performance of Bach's B minor Mass given in Dublin on 29 September 1950 by the Culwick Choral Society and the RÉ Choir and Symphony Orchestra conducted by Otto Matzerath as part of the Bach bicentenary celebration organised by the MAI.
29. The fully written-up diary ends with the entry for 2 June. The following entries are limited to brief pencilled notes, with only selected dates being noted here. The final entry is for Monday 19 June.
30. On the founding of the Dublin String Quartet by Wolfram Hentschel, see 22 January 1950 (above).

4 June 1950. Sunday
Working most of the day – preparing script for this evening.
Discussing pupils with Louise.
Dublin airport – seeing off Louise.
Broadcast 'Music of the Week'.
Boyne [fishing] with Herbert Downes. Lovely warm evening …

14 June 1950. Wednesday
Rehearsal with R[adio] É[ireann] L[ight] O[rchestra] all morning.
Recording session in afternoon. Inefficient delays.
Broadcast 5.30
DOP concert. Enthusiastic audience. Encore of Bach gavottes. Carol Little excellent leader.
Argument between Wolfram and Vaneček about technique v. musicianship.

15 June 1950. Thursday
Work scripts in morning.
Recording session with RÉLO in afternoon – worse inefficiency – idiot engineer turning up an hour late.
Academy orchestra rehearsal …

19 June 1950. Monday
Feeling awful. Collecting material for next script.
Slept two hours in afternoon.
Teaching Academy.
Academy orchestra concert and string items.
Charles and Carol back to hear recording of Vivaldi.

Louise Trenton, Dorothy Stokes and Mary Boydell, May/June 1950.

Select Bibliography

Acton, Charles, 'Music Makers Portrait Gallery', *The Irish Times*, 2 July 1960

_____, 'Interview with Brian Boydell', *Éire-Ireland*, vol. 5, no. 4 (1970), pp. 97–111

_____, 'Brian Patrick Boydell', *Irish Arts Review*, vol. 4, no. 4 (1987), pp. 66–7

Arnold, Bruce, *Maine Jellett and the Modern Movement in Ireland* (London: Yale UP, 1991)

Bodley, Seóirse, 'Boydell, Brian', in S. Sadie (ed.), *The New Grove Dictionary of Music and Musicians*, 20 vols (London: Macmillan, 1980), vol. iii, p. 144

Boydell, Brian, 'Music in Ireland', *The Bell*, vol. 14, no. 1 (1947), pp. 16–20

_____, 'Culture and Chauvinism', *Envoy*, vol. 2, no. 6 (May 1950), pp. 75–9

_____, 'The Future of Music in Ireland', *The Bell*, vol. 16, no. 4 (1951), pp. 1–9

_____, 'Orchestral and Chamber Music in Dublin', in A. Fleischmann (ed.), *Music in Ireland: a symposium* (Cork: Cork University Press and Oxford: Blackwell, 1952), pp. 222–31

_____, *A Dublin Musical Calendar, 1700–1760* (Dublin: Irish Academic Press, 1988)

_____, *Rotunda Music in Eighteenth-Century Dublin* (Dublin: Irish Academic Press, 1992)

Cox, Gareth, 'Octatonicism in the String Quartets of Brian Boydell', in P. Devine and H. White (eds), *The Maynooth International Musicological Conference 1995: Selected Proceedings*, Part 1, IMS 4 (Dublin: Four Courts Press, 1996), pp. 263–70

_____, 'Boydell, Brian', in S. Sadie and J. Tyrrell (eds), *The New Grove Dictionary of Music and Musicians*, 29 vols, 2nd edn (London: Macmillan, 2001), vol. iv, pp. 163–4

_____, 'Boydell, Brian', *The Encyclopaedia of Music in Ireland*, ed. H. White and B. Boydell (Dublin: UCD Press, 2013), vol. i, pp. 115–19

Cox, Gareth, Axel Klein and Michael Taylor (eds), *The Life and Music of Brian Boydell* (Dublin: Irish Academic Press, 2004)

Doyle, Niall (ed.), *The Boydell Papers: essays on music and music policy in Ireland* (Dublin: Music Network, 1997)

Dungan, Michael, 'Everything except Team Games and Horse Racing', *New Music News* (February 1997), pp. 9–11

Farrell, Hazel, 'The String Quartets of Brian Boydell', MA thesis, Waterford Institute of Technology, 1996

Fleischmann, Aloys, 'Boydell, Brian', in E. Blom and D. Stevens (eds), *[Grove's] Dictionary of Music and Musicians*, Supplementary volume (London: Macmillan, 1961), pp. 45–6

_____, 'Brian Boydell', *Hibernia*, vol. 32, no. 9 (1968)

_____, 'Boydell, Brian', in B. Morton and P. Collins (eds), *Contemporary Composers* (Chicago and London: St James Press, 1992), pp. 110–13

Graydon, Philip, 'Modernism in Ireland and its Cultural Context in the Music and Writings of Frederick May, Brian Boydell and Aloys Fleischmann', MA thesis, National University of Ireland, Maynooth, 1999

_____, 'Modernism in Ireland and its Cultural Context in the Music and Writings of Frederick May, Brian Boydell and Aloys Fleischmann', in G. Cox and A. Klein (eds), *Irish Music in the Twentieth Century*, IMS 7 (Dublin: Four Courts Press, 2003), pp. 56–79

Kennedy, Brian, *Irish Art and Modernism, 1880–1950* (Belfast: The Institute of Irish Studies, 1991)

Kennedy, S.B., *The White Stag Group* (Dublin: Irish Museum of Modern Art, 2005)

Klein, Axel, 'Brian Boydell', in H.W. Heister and W.W. Sparrer (eds), *Komponisten der Gegenwart* (Munich: Edition Text und Kritik, 1992–), 6. Nachlieferung, November 1994

_____, *Die Musik Irlands im 20. Jahrhundert* (Hildesheim: Olms, 1996)

_____, 'Irish Composers and Foreign Education: a study of influences', in P. Devine and H. White (eds), *The Maynooth International Musicological Conference, 1995: Selected Proceedings, Part 1*, IMS 4 (Dublin: Four Courts Press, 1996), pp. 271–84

_____, 'The Composer in the Academy (2) 1940–1990', in R. Pine and C. Acton (eds), *To Talent Alone: the Royal Irish Academy of Music, 1848–1998* (Dublin: Gill & Macmillan, 1998), pp. 423–4

_____, 'Boydell, Brian (Patrick)', in L. Finscher (ed.), *Die Musik in Geschichte und Gegenwart*, new edn, Biographical Section (Kassel: Bärenreiter and Stuttgart: Metzler, 2000), vol. iii, pp. 600–2

Lee, David, 'Boydell, Brian', in F. Blume (ed.), *Die Musik in Geschichte und Gegenwart*, 1st supplement volume (Kassel: Bärenreiter, 1973), pp. 1031–2

Murphy, Daniel and Joyce Andrews (eds), 'Brian Boydell', *Education and the Arts* (Dublin: University of Dublin, 1987), pp. 219–29

Murray, Peter, *The Language of Dreams: dreams and the unconscious in 20th century Irish art*, Exhibition Catalogue, 2 October 2015–16 February 2016 (Cork: Crawford Art Gallery, 2015)

O'Kelly, Pat, *The National Symphony Orchestra of Ireland, 1948–1998: a selected history* (Dublin: RTÉ, 1998)

Pine, Richard, *Music and Broadcasting in Ireland* (Dublin: Four Courts Press, 2005)

_____, *Charles: the life and world of Charles Acton, 1914–1999* (Dublin: The Lilliput Press, 2010)

Pine, Richard and Charles Acton (eds), *To Talent Alone: the Royal Irish Academy of Music, 1848–1998* (Dublin: Gill & Macmillan, 1998)

White, Harry, '"Our Musical State Became Refined": the musicology of Brian Boydell', *The Progress of Music in Ireland* (Dublin: Four Courts Press, 2005), pp. 151–66

White, Harry and Barra Boydell (eds), *The Encyclopaedia of Music in Ireland*, 2 vols (Dublin: UCD Press, 2013)

Index